# BENCHED
## PASSION
### *for* LAW REFORM

# BENCHED

## PASSION
## *for* LAW REFORM

✺

# NANCY MORRISON

*For Ron —*

*A true car*
*enthusiast.*

*Very best wishes,*

*Nancy M*

**DV** **DURVILE**
**PUBLICATIONS**

## Durvile Publications Ltd.

Calgary, Alberta, Canada
www.durvile.com
Copyright © 2018 Nancy Morrison


NATIONAL LIBRARY OF CANADA
CATALOGUING IN PUBLICATIONS DATA
Morrison, Nancy

BENCHED: *Passion for Law Reform*
Issued in print and electronic formats
ISBN: 978-1-988824-13-0 (print pbk) ISBN: 978-1-988824-18-5 (epub)
ISBN: 978-1-988824-25-3 (audiobook)


1. Biography, Judges
2. Law and Gender


I. Morrison, Nancy


*Book Four in the Reflections Series.*

*Alberta*

*We would like to acknowledge the support of the
Alberta Government through the Alberta Book Fund.*


First edition, first printing. 2018 | Printed in Canada
Photos within the book, unless indicated otherwise, are from Nancy Morrison's collection.

Photo on page 199 republished with the permission of: *Vancouver Sun*, a division of Postmedia Network Inc..
Photo on page 269 used with permission of Niagara Falls Public Library Local History Collection.
Excerpts on pages 290-291 from *Bruno and the Beach* used with permission of Harbour Publishing.

❧

The statements, views, and opinions contained in this publication are
solely those of the author and not of the publisher and the editors.

*To the Memory of my Parents*

*Jessie and William Morrison*

# Contents

# Foreword

## *Stevie Cameron*

THERE ARE far too many ways to describe my friend Nancy Morrison, the distinguished, much-admired lawyer and former BC Supreme Court judge in Vancouver who has written this marvellous memoir of an extraordinary life.

But first I must begin with her kindness to me over the years I spent in Vancouver writing a book on Robert Pickton, the pig farmer who murdered at least twenty-six women, almost all of them working as prostitutes. Nancy's home, her support and her wisdom, gave me the push to continue the Pickton story and for that I am beyond grateful. Not only is Nancy my wise and thoughtful friend — as she is for so many people — she also happens to be a brilliant raconteur and excellent cook. No one goes away hungry from Nancy's table.

Nancy grew up in Saskatchewan. She graduated from Osgoode Hall Law School. After being called to the bar in Ontario in 1963, she immediately — after a raucous graduation celebration — took over the legal practice of Judy LaMarsh in Niagara Falls.

Nancy's description of Judy LaMarsh's abrupt move to Ottawa and Nancy's first day as a lawyer was fraught with fear and amusement but, as she tells it in the book, she quickly took on the client files — her "rocket launch" into the practice of law.

It would be a shame to tell you much more about her days as a smart, funny and sparkling young lawyer, but suffice to say she eventually moved to Vancouver despite her love for Saskatchewan and became one of the city's brightest lawyers. That was a time when female lawyers found it hard slugging. My guess is her sense of humour, her compassion and her experience brought her a fine reputation not long after her arrival. As I read her manuscript, it filled in the stories that I hadn't known, particularly her life with Bruno Gerussi, one of Canada's foremost actors and radio broadcasters.

Nancy Morrison is one of a kind — a steadfast friend with a wonderful sense of humour, a woman who made her life in law, and the best friend one could ever have. I speak for many who have been given a push forward with Nancy's encouragement, kindness and common sense. Brava!

*— Stevie Cameron*
*Investigative journalist*

# Preface

SOME PEOPLE ARE BORN LUCKY. I was, mainly because of the country my ancestors chose and the parents I chose. Dad, a lawyer, was wise, gentle and funny. A Cape Bretoner, he did a mean step dance. He thought he was a most fortunate man to have two daughters, once saying, "Any fool can have sons, it takes special luck to have daughters." My sister Moira was the smart one.

Mom, a teacher before marriage, was the raconteur, mimic and fixer around the house. She could sew, cook, chop wood, paint, upholster and fix the toilet. Dad, who adored her, was wowed. We teased he could barely hang a picture. Mom beat him at badminton but he was dangerous at poker and bridge. My Mother rejected the label 'housewife'. She was 'self-employed'. Mom was appalled when Ken Mayhew, editor of our award–winning newspaper, *The Yorkton Enterprise*, referred to his wife in his weekly editorials always as "LHM" — Little Help Mate.

I didn't have to voyage far to discover my feminist leanings. It was a longer voyage to discover politics and the law. There was much misogyny along the way. It was not difficult to get into law school in1958, especially if your family could afford it. Less than three percent of law students were female; many males would have preferred zero percent.

On being called to the Ontario bar in 1963, the only person who would hire me, other than my Dad in Saskatchewan, was another female, Judy LaMarsh, a young Member of Parliament from Niagara Falls.

There were a lot of divorces in the 'honeymoon capital' and even more crime. After three years in Niagara, I returned to Saskatchewan to practice law with Dad, and for a disastrous attempt to become a Member of Parliament. A later second attempt in British Columbia fared no better.

In 1972, LaMarsh introduced me to her friend, actor Bruno Gerussi, saying, "You always said you would give your left arm to meet Gerussi." It was love, and would last twenty-four years until Bruno's death in 1995.

I spent fifty-plus years in the law profession, twenty-four as a judge. The laws and the profession itself were often hostile to females and minorities. In those first years of practice in the early 1960s, many of my clients, especially women with crushing stories to tell, had few legal rights, fewer resources, no legal aid, no money, no voice, no lobby.

This book is partly my obligation to them, to witness what occurred in the past and question how much is still ongoing. My interest in law reform began in those early years, the recognition for change to some of our laws, the need for public awareness of existing inequalities. It was law reform that motivated giving speeches too numerous to count on women's rights and other minority rights, on problems in family and criminal law. It is partly what caused my reluctance to go on the bench, as that meant forgoing politics.

I loved my time as a lawyer and as a judge. I have always been fascinated with people, their lives, their stories, and with the legal, political and social issues I encountered: capital punishment, abortion, education, domestic violence, women's rights, aboriginal concerns, drugs, prostitution, the right to die.

And for those who have griped, "If God had wanted women to be lawyers or judges...," well, of course She did.

— *Nancy Morrison*

# CHAPTER 1

# *Rocket Launched*

*With Judy LaMarsh at her home.*

---

T HE Queen Elizabeth Highway between Toronto and Niagara Falls, busy and mean, was always ready to welcome another accident. I had a noon appointment in Niagara Falls and was navigating the highway with a crushing hangover. A headache pierced my eyeballs; the urge to be sick persisted. I wanted to pull over into a quiet spot and just lie down on the front seat. There were no quiet spots.

It was Sunday, April 22, 1963, and I was en route to Niagara Falls to meet with my new employer, Judy LaMarsh, a Liberal backbencher and lawyer, just re-elected as the Member of Parliament for Niagara Falls.

That Friday, in Toronto, I had been called to the bar of Ontario, a newly minted lawyer. My parents had driven from Saskatchewan to Toronto for the occasion. My sister Moira, working then in Toronto, was also there. Monday, April 23 would be my first day as a practising barrister and solicitor. The weekend partying with classmates had been enthusiastic. We had survived three years of law school, twelve months of articling and the six-month Bar Admission Course. Now our jobs were scattering us.

Judy had given directions to her home on Corwin Avenue, near Lundy's Lane. At noon, I rang her doorbell. Judy, a large woman, impressive in every way, whipped open the door, towering over me.

*Good. I'm so glad you are on time,* she said. *Come in. I have something I have to tell you — but you can't say anything about it to anyone. The Prime Minister, Mr. Pearson, has informed me I am to be appointed the federal Minister of Health and Welfare. I will be sworn in at nine tomorrow morning in Ottawa, with the rest of the new cabinet. That means I will no longer be able to practice law, so you will be running my office. I have to leave for Toronto, for Malton Airport around three this afternoon.*

Standing in front of this exhilarated woman whom I had met briefly only once before, I recall thinking, *Dear Lord, this has to be one of my worst nightmares — let me wake up, now.*

These might not have been her exact words, but Judy rushed on ... *I have asked my banker to come over and bring the documents that will give you the sole signing authority over the two bank accounts at the office. Just remember, the pink cheques are the trust cheques, and that money belongs to our clients, not us. I'll take you down and show you where the office is, not far from here.*

She went on, *There are two secretaries who work at the office. Lois, who has worked for me for a long time. I forget her last name. She is very good. You will like her. She's married, has six kids and red hair. The other secretary is Chris. I never did know her last name. You will have to let her go when you go into the office tomorrow morning. She primarily did my political work.*

As I was grappling with all that, she continued, *Oh and I brought a file home for you to go over. It is a negligence case, set for trial in three weeks time in Welland in the Supreme Court (of*

*Ontario). It has been dragging on for a few years. It is a difficult case, so even if you just recover a small percentage and some costs, that would be good. Go over it and give me a call in Ottawa after you have read it.*

I thought, *Some costs? What costs?*

Judy continued, *You may as well stay here at my house for a time. It will be good to have someone here. That will give you time to look around. And I won't be back here that much.*

In three brief hours, Judy handed over her office, law practice and home to me, a virtual stranger, and then left for Ottawa. She never set foot in her law office again in the three-and-a-half years that I ran her law practice.

That Sunday evening, before my parents drove back to Yorkton, I was to have dinner with them at the home of my cousins, Daphne and Norman Williams in Burlington, halfway between Niagara Falls and Toronto. I don't remember the dinner or driving to and from Burlington. But I know I told my parents about Judy's new job, and mine.

Settling down for the night in Judy's large bungalow home felt strange. I was exhausted, and sleep took over — until 2:00 a.m., when I woke suddenly to the smell of gas. It was all through the house. I leaped out of bed and raced out the side door of the house onto the cement of the carport. In horror, I realized that the gas smell was all over the neighborhood. Everyone was in danger.

The door clicked shut behind me. I stood there in the cold, barefoot, in a brief nightie, heart pounding.

Where was everyone? Were they crazy? Sleeping when gas was about to blow us all to smithereens? I waited. No lights came on in the houses on the street. No one dashed out of their homes. The gas smell was pervasive; then I noticed it had funny 'other chemical' odor to it. Was this an industrial smell? It must be. Then I looked back at the door that had clicked shut so efficiently on its own.

*Oh no!* If I am locked out, and have to go and wake up some strangers — that will be the last straw. I tried the door. It opened.

The next morning, I went to the office and introduced myself to the secretaries, Lois and Chris. I let Chris go. She seemed to be anticipating it. The office could not have been a less inviting place. Near the corner of a nondescript small business area in Niagara Falls, with more gas stations than retail stores, it was a second floor walk up. The street-level door announced "LaMarsh and LaMarsh Law Office." That would have been Judy and her late father. The stairs were just stairs. Not light, or bright or promising anything once you climbed them.

There was a counter, chest high, separating clients from the secretary at her desk. A few chairs for clients, metal filing cabinets with the cozy clang of a prison door. If there was any art on the walls, it was not memorable.

The inner sanctum overwhelmed me, a small room filled with a large solid oak desk. Judy's father had been a big man; Judy was a big woman. This was their desk. The chair was huge and deep, to match the desk, and when I sat in it, I disappeared. There were two chairs for clients on the other side of the desk. No rug impeded the chairs being scraped forward as the client tried to lessen distance from the lawyer.

There was no art or soft tones, no cartoons to brighten the mood. Probably some diplomas were on the wall. It was not my office to decorate. It was Judy's.

There was a back door and fire escape stairs to the street which the previous junior lawyer had used frequently to disappear from incensed clients wondering where their lawyer was and why their work was not done. Judy, a gifted speaker, had been crossing the country, election campaigning for the last eight weeks.

Small wonder there was a lineup of excitable, primarily Italian male clients waiting for their lawyer. My love affair with Italians began long ago, and has never abated, but those first Italian clients, crazed by neglect, roared into the office that first week, full of anger, passion, injustice. Gesturing, yelling, pounding the sturdy desk. Outraged their case was on hold, demanding action. Gino, Ciso, Alberto, Luigi, Roberto. They were special, and they needed a lawyer who would not disappear on the political campaign trail, or flee down the back stairs.

The Italians were not all that endearing on my first day of practice. I explained to each that this was my first day in this office — not daring to say — *my first day as a lawyer.* That I would read their file that evening, and we could discuss their legal problems the next day. A follow-up appointment was made, and in strode the next Italian.

Earlier, before 9:00 a.m., Lois had announced that people from some of the local law offices would be arriving to take all the red colour-coded files from our office. These were the Central Mortgage and Housing Corporation (CMHC) mortgage files Judy had been doing. This was patronage work, divided at that time amongst the Liberal lawyers in town, thanks to a federal Liberal minority government in Ottawa.

As a federal cabinet minister, Judy could no longer do any other job, in her case, practice law. First thing that Monday morning she had called Lois with instructions that all CMHC files would immediately be sent out of her office to other lawyers. I later learned this was easy, lucrative work, which we now could not touch. Judy was scrupulous.

Good for her. Not that good for me. I was about to learn how a law office had to operate in 1963 with a $12,000 bank overdraft in its general account. About $100,000 today. A law office with an overdraft? Unheard of in those days.

A momentary break in that hectic morning came when I shut my office door at about 11:00 a.m. I had seen maybe eight clients and made appointments for each in the following days. I was overcome by the volume, chaos and scope of Judy's practice and the unbelievable situation I was in. She had a large general practice, which served clients in criminal and civil litigation, family law, real estate, wills and estates, small business corporation law, contracts, collections and everything else except tax and admiralty law. I had come to Niagara hoping to get some general experience, and maybe an occasional chance to appear in court if Judy was busy in Ottawa. I had not come to replace her. This was unbelievable.

I put my head down on that huge desk and began to cry.

The break ended when Lois buzzed to say that my Mother was on the other line, calling from Toronto. I picked up the phone to hear Jessie, ever cheerful, say, "Hello, dear. We're just calling to say goodbye. We are all packed and ready to hit the road."

"Put Dad on the phone." On came Dad. I said, "You've got to come down here. You will not believe this mess." And down they came. We had a quick lunch, then Dad came back to the office with me. He took the big file for the trial that was to begin in three weeks, and retired to a small back office where files were stored. I continued dealing with one client after the other, taking notes, assuring each I would read his file, making appointments for later in the week.

By mid-afternoon calm reigned, both in the office, to some degree, and in my mind. At five o'clock I closed the office, thanked Lois, and Dad and I went back to Judy's house, where Mom was making dinner. Dad said, "Well, I read the file, and it seems to be in good order. I don't think you'll have any trouble with the trial." I agreed, "Neither do I."

Mom and Dad left early the next morning to drive back to Saskatchewan, and I was rocket launched into the practice of law.

Not much has frightened me since that day.

# CHAPTER 2

# Canada at War

W E WERE FORTUNATE to be living in Canada when World War II broke out. Born in 1937, I was eight when the war ended, but memories of the war remain. Remote and safe from the conflict, our prairie city of Yorkton, Saskatchewan was nevertheless engaged.

Canada had declared war against Germany on September 10, 1939. The government established facilities in airports across the country to train aviators from the Commonwealth countries. Yorkton was one of those airfields, Number 11 Service Flying Training School. Young men from Australia, New Zealand, England and other Commonwealth countries came to join Canadian recruits to train at our airport, just north of the city.

Large green hangars sprang up at our airfield, as at other airfields on the prairies, which provided similar training with safer flying conditions than mountain terrains. Our prairie winters had more snow than many Commonwealth boys could fathom. Home movies in the early forties show my best friend Jacquie Vaughan and me playing on snow banks piled higher than telephone poles near the entrance to the airport.

The recruits practiced their take-offs and landings, day and night. The planes would climb, glide, achieve different speeds and noise levels. They sometimes flew low, and often in formation. The planes all seemed to be yellow. I didn't know a Tiger Moth from a Cessna Crane (still don't), but I do know that in the last years of the war, I became frightened that I would wake up to find the insignia of the Japanese rising sun on the planes overhead. I scanned the planes with childhood fears that I kept to myself. The night flying was the worst. I was in bed and in the dark could not see their insignia.

The future pilots were still kids, and homesick. Residents in Yorkton welcomed them and our Sunday dinners always seemed to include some of the young fliers. One who came to

*I was a happy kid. Mostly.*

our home had a sister my age. This young man wrote me my first letter. I was six, and I remember the excitement of receiving a letter from overseas, England. It came on the tissue thin, single-page airmail paper of the day, the text of the letter printed for me to read, complete with a drawing of a plane and a stick man, captioned, "This is me and this is my plane."

This was the first of several letters, then they stopped coming. The young pilot had been killed in action.

No television existed in those years, to bring the war into our living rooms. We saw the war in our movie theatres, the Roxy and the Princess. Before a movie began, the newsreel would be shown. It was jerky black and white footage of the war — in Europe and in Asia — with voiceover by renowned war correspondents, whose gravel tones conveyed the fear, horror and tragedy of the battles. Then *Bambi* would be shown.

I don't have fond memories of *Bambi* either. That roaring forest fire, and if that was not enough, they killed off Bambi's mother. The Disney sugar-coating never erased those images.

During the war there were victory gardens, and Vico chocolate milk every day at school for every child. There were Canada Savings Bonds. As children, we were encouraged to save nickels and dimes and donate to buy bonds. It would help our troops, help our country and all the other countries who were fighting with us. The women knit socks for the boys overseas, and warm scarves. Boxes of cookies and gifts were sent to the troops, and many letters.

War brought rationing. For gas, coffee, tea, butter, sugar, meat and liquor, you needed coupons to purchase them. I remember Mom trading butter coupons so she could make a birthday cake in May. And the trade would go the other way in the next month when another mother needed to make a cake for her child. Mom, who drank little, had to trot down to the liquor store with her monthly ration of coupons to get a bottle of rye or scotch or rum.

My grandparents had all died before I was born, but my friend Jacquie shared her grandpa, Mumpa. Jacquie and I, born thirteen days apart, were inseparable from the time I can remember. We had a piercing catcall that could summon the other from over a block away. We often picked whose home to eat dinner at, depending on the menu, chocolate pudding often the winning factor. Mother loved it when Jacquie, after one of our sleepovers, would call out as she was dashing home, "Don't change my sheets, Mrs. Morrison, I'll be back."

Mumpa used his gas rations to drive his rumble-seat coupe all over the frozen prairie fields in the winter snow, towing screaming youngsters behind on toboggans roped end-to-end. We'd be terrified but begging to be on the last toboggan so we'd be the ones dumped into the snow when Mumpa made those deliberate sharp turns.

On Christmas morning, Moira and I would wake and find our stockings at the foot of our beds, with small gifts in each: some prized chocolate, always a book (to keep us quiet for as long as possible) and sometimes the rarest treat of all, a Japanese mandarin orange.

An Indian rubber ball could bounce as high as the sky. Moira's and mine was the size of a baseball, dark grey, battered and treasured. Rubber was needed for the war effort; for tires for tanks and trucks and planes, in those far away theatres of the war. Moira and I knew that if we lost that ball, there would not be another.

November 11 was observed at the Cenotaph, a block and a half from our home. The parade would end there. Many were in uniform, always led by Brigadier General Alexander Ross, revered from his days in the Great War. He was the one who said, after the Battle at Vimy Ridge, "This is the moment that Canada became a nation."

At the end of the war, the grainy newsreels from Europe began showing the death camps and shower rooms where Jewish and other war prisoners were gassed, and the ovens. Always given to nightmares, I had many.

As kids, we never played war games. Maybe the boys did, but not that I recall. Slowly, rationing was over, goods became more available. Veterans came home, some to jobs waiting, some to preferred spots in the universities — post-war affirmative action. Wartime houses sprang up in every community, a nation grateful to its veterans. Women quit their wartime jobs to stay at home as the veterans filled the universities and jobs. And too many who fought never came home.

# CHAPTER 3

# *Prelude to Politics*

I T WAS AUGUST 13, 1947. Six thousand people filled the grandstand bleachers at the Yorkton Fair Grounds to hear a political debate whose main speakers were Premier Tommy Douglas, leader of the CCF Party (Co-operative Commonwealth Federation) versus Walter Tucker, leader of the Saskatchewan Liberal Party. In 1944, Saskatchewan had elected the first socialist government in Canada, the CCF.

My parents had taken Moira and me to the event. In Saskatchewan, there was never any thought of leaving the kids at home for such an outing. In our house, politics was the conversation of the day, over dinner, among friends. Politics was part of everyday life. There was no men-of-the-village-only mentality.

I don't remember much except the excitement and the cheers of the crowd for both men. Douglas was a brilliant and funny speaker, Tucker was tough and bombastic. One was small in stature, but not in substance. The other was imposing in size, but had to make sure the little guy did not beat him up, as Douglas had the superior wit and debating skills.

Everything about that day delighted me. If politics can be likened to malaria, that was the day I became infected. Douglas won the day. In our home, a verboten mixed-marriage would have been CFF and Liberal. No love for the CCF or Douglas, but admiration for his skills and political savvy.

There was always deference for those who went into public service, especially political life, regardless of party affiliation. Politics was the highest calling, according to Dad, second only to the clergy. We attended public schools where lessons in civics were absorbed through daily interactions. Moira, also addicted to politics, campaigned, worked for candidates wherever she lived, and knew her politics.

The CCF was a predecessor to the New Democratic Party (NDP), which was formed in 1961 when the CCF merged with the Canadian Labour Congress. Like all political parties, then and now, the CCF were fierce in their patronage. When Tommy Douglas and the CCF were in power, suspicions were confirmed: Whose farms were electrified first? Whose roads were paved first?

In later years, Dad was critical of some of those around Douglas, like Clarence M. Fines, the long-time Finance Minister in the CCF Government. Fines made the leap from modest prairie schoolteacher first elected in 1944 to millionaire retired in the Bahamas when he and the CCF government were defeated in 1961.

By age sixteen I had helped organize a Young Liberal club in Yorkton and attended a Young Liberal convention in Moose Jaw, where I fended off my first creepy convention delegate. One of those early skills you don't tell your parents about.

# CHAPTER 4

## *Books and Mickey Spillane*

R EADING HAS ALWAYS been a passion. Mom read to Moira and me every night as she tucked us into bed. We three sobbed in unison to *Black Beauty* and *Flicka*. Books with heroines multiplied by my bed. Nellie McClung's children's books were there, notably *Sowing Seeds In Danny*.

Our house was filled with books. Mom was catholic in her tastes. She read everything, including banned books like Henry Miller's *Tropic of Cancer, Kitty*, and *Lady Chatterley's Lover*, thanks to her elderly English widow book mate, Hettie Hukins, who lived one street over. Hettie's relatives in England kept her supplied with the latest books. When one of the shocking banned books crossed the Atlantic, she would bring it over to our house, saying, in her soft English accent, "I think you will find this an interesting book, Jessie. It is a bit naughty ... but it is beautifully written."

Dad veered to history, Scottish writers and the latest thrillers. When I was a child, Rotary ran the local library. Dad, a Rotarian, was on the library committee. He had a mission. Children were not allowed in the library. The librarian was a dignified older woman, grey hair pulled back in a bun. She had never acquired a husband or children. When Dad approached her to open the library to children, she was adamant. The library was a place of quiet and study. There would be no noisy little children running around.

Dad could be persuasive. He suggested a six-month trial, and he gave his word: if she wanted to return the library to 'adults only' after six months of children using it, that would occur. She knew he would keep his word, so reluctantly she agreed to the trial run. After six months of watching children troop in, helping them find an age-appropriate volume, seeing them sink down on the nearest floor space to read, our wonderful librarian was ready to throw out the adults.

From an early age, my asthma attacks meant complete bed rest for a week, sometimes two, interspersed with wheezing trips to the bathroom. My favourite volumes from the *Books of Knowledge* were stacked beside my bed, along with the Nancy Drew series, *Anne of Green Gables, The Scarlett Pimpernel.* My favourite book was *The Secret Garden.*

At eleven or twelve, someone gave me a Mickey Spillane thriller. It seemed well-advised to conceal the paperback and read it after bedtime under the bed covers with a flashlight. But some light escaped from under the covers one evening. My upstairs bedroom window looked down on the snowy, low roof of an adjacent bungalow. Mother was in the dining room directly below my bedroom writing letters. Catching those intermittent flashes of light, she came to investigate. I was relieved of the book and flashlight, and Mom said Dad would talk to me the next day.

At noon the next day Dad asked if I thought Mom was a good cook. Yes, I did. He looked thoughtful. "So you would never go out in the alley and eat garbage from a trash can, knowing your Mother's good food was here on the table?"

Dad then pointed to our bookshelves with the works of Charles Dickens, Shakespeare, Balzac, Sir Walter Scott and other notables and suggested that by the same token, it didn't make much sense to read garbage either.

I read one or two more Spillanes to satisfy my curiosity. No one said I couldn't.

It was fortunate I loved to read and was content being still for long periods, as an unwelcome visitor came calling in my early teens — polio.

# CHAPTER 5

# *Polio*

IN 1951, the summer I turned fourteen, I was diagnosed with polio. When Moira and I were growing up, everyone was terrified of this killer disease, where children were particularly vulnerable. It was occurring in epidemics, especially in the summer months. No one knew the cause, or how it spread. There was no preventive vaccine, no cure.

Polio left victims disabled, some paralyzed, some able to breathe only with the assistance of huge iron lungs, some dead. When a polio epidemic occurred, public swimming pools were closed. Children who contracted polio were isolated, everyone terrified of contagion.

Polio, short for *poliomyelitis*, is also referred to as infantile paralysis. We now know it is a viral disease, very infectious, spread orally, often through fecal matter in food or water. As populations moved, this disease hitch-hiked along. Bill Gates, a champion of worldwide preventive vaccinations for polio, has referred to it as "an ancient, crippling disease."

Polio was different from other diseases. For one thing, you seldom mentioned the word if you had polio. The very word struck fear, like AIDS when that first began. It was before Canada had universal health care. It was cruel to the poor. It hit the rich too, and adults.

In August 1921, Franklin D. Roosevelt fell suddenly ill, and within a day or two, he had lost control of the movement of his legs. He was diagnosed with *poliomyelitis*. That did not stop him from being elected president of the United States eleven years later, in 1932, but the public never knew that because of polio, Roosevelt could not walk. He was never seen in public in his specially fitted wheelchair.

It was not until April 1955 that the polio vaccine developed by Dr. Jonas Salk of the University of Pittsburgh became available. That was four years too late for me.

In Grade 8, a curvature began developing in my spine. I was active in many sports, and taking ballet and tap dancing lessons. Concerned, our family doctors, close friends, Doctors Sigga Houston and Clarence (CJ) Houston, referred us to an orthopedic specialist in Winnipeg, Dr. Jamison, in June.

Dr. Jamison told my parents the scoliosis, the curvature of the spine was simply due to bad posture and I should be fitted with a steel brace to be worn continuously until the curvature was corrected.

It was a disquieting diagnosis. Rather than be fitted for the brace in Winnipeg, as recommended, we returned to Yorkton. Doctors Sigga and C.J. Houston did not agree with the diagnosis. Sigga told Mom and Dad to let me enjoy the summer, after which they would send me to another specialist in Winnipeg.

Dr. Sigridur (Sigga) Christianson Houston was a remarkable pioneer female doctor of Icelandic stock, who, beginning as a teenager, put herself through school and university. She was renowned, particularly for her skills with sick babies. She was also a mother, seamstress, cook, hostess and gardener. A diminutive powerhouse, she and her beloved 6'4" husband, C.J., were like godparents to me. Sigga was a lifelong role model for many of us, and confirmed the message from my home that women can do anything.

We drove to Winnipeg the end of August. Dr. Deacon was a burly man, with a pronounced limp from his own encounter with polio. He examined me carefully, gently touching the muscles in my arms, legs, shoulders and back. Each touch hurt. He said, "You have been tired for a long time, haven't you, Nancy?" I burst into tears.

"This child has had polio", he announced to my parents.

"Does that mean she will have to wear a steel brace?" Mom asked. Deacon was astounded.

"Lord no. You do that to this child, she will be in a wheelchair by the time she is sixteen. Where on earth did you get that idea?" Mom pointed across the hall to the office of Dr. Jamison.

That began my belief in second opinions. In any field.

And that began my year in bed. Not the beginning of high

school I had been anticipating. Dr. Deacon said I was fortunate, that I had a lesser case of the destructive bulbar polio. It must have infected me the previous summer, and the weakened muscles were becoming progressively worse. No longer contagious, I did not have to be isolated.

Polio had affected the muscles in my legs, arms, back, shoulders and neck, but not the muscles that controlled my breathing. Common with polio, the effect on my muscles was asymmetric, causing stronger muscles to develop on one side of my spine and body, weaker on the other.

In 1951, the heroine of polio treatment was an Australian, Sister Elizabeth Kenny. She lacked formal training as a nurse, but had considerable practical training. She clashed with the medical profession in Australia, and later in North America, when her recommended treatment for polio patients ran counter to the medical profession's insistence on immobilizing muscles that had been affected by polio. By the 1930s, Sister Kenny had set up her own polio treatment facility in Australia. She refused to immobilize her young patients' muscles and limbs in splints, plaster casts or braces. Rather, she treated with hot compresses, or hot foments, exercises, and fresh air; no confinement in closed rooms.

Sister Kenny was not feeling the love from an Australian government Royal Commission that published a report in 1938 that opined, "the abandonment of immobilization is a grievous error and fraught with grave danger...."

Sister Kenny spent eleven years at the Mayo Clinic in Rochester, from 1940 to 1951. Dr. Deacon was insistent that I immediately begin the Sister Kenny therapy and remain in the Children's Hospital in Winnipeg for a year of treatments. Hearing what was involved, my mother believed she could handle the treatments as well or better at home, and looking back, Sister Kenny would have approved.

Before going back to Yorkton, I saw my physiotherapist, Mrs. Bell, at the Winnipeg Children's Hospital, a noisy, full-of-life place. On my initial visit, I was in a curtained cubicle, undressed except for panties, when the curtains exploded open as a handsome six-year-old boy in a wheelchair roared in. "Hi, Mrs. Bell!"

"Hi Terry" she smiled.

"What are you?" he demanded, looking at me. I had no idea what he meant.

"She's a polio, Terry," said Mrs. Bell.

"Me too!" he yelled with delight, and out he zoomed with a cheerful "Bye now."


I spent my first year of high school in bed, except for attending school daily. The hot foments began at 4:00 p.m. and were changed every hour, the last one taken off at 10:00 p.m. On weekends and holidays they began at nine and went until ten at night. I had one day off that year with no foments, Christmas Day.

The foments were on my legs, arms, back, shoulders and the back of my neck. This meant lying on my stomach for the entire time, from which position I ate my meals and read. The blankets initially used for the foments caused a rash all over my body. My doctor, Sigga Houston, was a constant visitor, and she and Mom resolved the problem by digging out all their soft cotton and wool garments not in use.

The cloths were in a huge pot boiling on top of the stove downstairs, a witches' cauldron of ugly grey water. Mother would haul the heavy pot up the stairs every hour, unless Dad was at home. The water was pressed out of the compresses through a small portable hand ringer in the hall outside my room.

On the advice of Mrs. Bell, my physiotherapist, large mirrors were installed in my bedroom, to remind me to do my exercises, twenty minutes each morning and evening to keep the muscles flexible. To this day, I am not big on mirrors.

My Mother parked her life for a year, her days circumscribed by the demands of those foments. With the heavy hauling, she claimed she was in the best shape she had ever been. She was inventive with tempting meals. I drank all liquids out of a little antique teapot through the curved spout. (Try drinking out of a glass, lying flat on your stomach.) I laughed at my Mother's small and big tricks.

Homework was never a problem. I had the time. I devoured books. Friends came to visit and sit on the other twin bed. Moira's boyfriends were sweet, coming up to my bedroom for a visit before taking my lively sister out.

On school days, lunch hours ruled. Lunch would be ready the minute Dad, Moira and I were home. Then Jessie would remember an errand that had to be run. "I forgot to pick up a cabbage. Can you go and get me one." At the age of fourteen, I was driving our car every day during those lunch hours. Dad and I would head out on these trumped up errands. I would drive, park the car, and Dad would go in and buy the amnesic item. We took the long way home. We went out every day, blizzard or black ice no impediment. Not one Mountie seemed to notice a small fourteen-year-old girl driving a big yellow Buick around town Monday through Friday each noon. I lived for those lunch hours.

By the end of that year, my muscles were almost back to normal. A sizable tender muscle area lingered in my back, so for the next couple of years, I would go to bed with a large sheet of cotton batting soaked with hot paraffin wax on my back, that kept the heat in for hours as I slept. Today I call that now diminished patch of sore muscle "Horace." He only acts up if I have been acting up.

Until age twenty-one, I did forty minutes of exercises each morning and each evening which included twenty minutes of stretching my spine by hanging by my hands from a bar suspended from the ceiling, letting the weight of my body pull the spine straight.

By Grade 10, I could do after-school activities for the first time in high school; except curling, deemed too hard on my back. Tough, because everyone curls in Saskatchewan.

I had missed out on learning how to dance in Grade 9. Dad had shown me how to waltz and do the Charleston. But he used to embarrass me by doing this strange dancing-on-the-spot when Don Messer and the Islanders came on television. Dad died before Riverdance stormed North America, when I realized that Celtic step dancing was cool.

School dances were about to start, I had never been to a dance, and needed dance lessons. So I turned to television — Dick Clark and *American Bandstand*. They were jiving, jitter-bugging. I loved it. After school when no one was home, I tied one end of a long dish towel to a closed door handle, and learned to jive with my mythical partner, watching and mimicking the television dancers. I found it easy to dance with all sorts of partners after that, even those less talented than the dish towel.

Grade 10 held another trauma. In Home Economics sewing class, I chose a pattern for a skirt with an inverted pleat in the front. When the skirt was ready to hem, I put it on for the teacher, Mrs. Stein. Because my body was so out of kilter thanks to the crooked back, and one hip convex, sticking out, and the other hip concave in, the inverted pleat swayed off to one side. "Girls, girls!" cried Mrs. Stein. "Gather round please. I want to show you something." And she told me to hop up onto the long sewing table. Which I did, as the girls gathered around.

Mrs. Stein explained to all the girls in Grades 10A and 10C what was wrong with my body, which caused the pleat to hang incorrectly, and that the skirt would have to be altered at the waist to correct for this. I apparently went home after class, up to my room in tears where Mother discovered me. She said I would not be returning to Home Ec class. This was a shock, coming from Mom, a former teacher, who instilled respect for all teachers in Moira and me.

Home Ec was a compulsory course for all girls Grades 9 to 11. I stood in the top few in my classes. I had to keep attending. But Jessie had fire in her eye, and said, "You will not be returning. Don't worry about your grades."

Sure enough, I was out of Home Ec, never to return. But I blocked the entire incident from my mind for many years, until I began woodworking in my forties. I expressed surprise to my mother that I was actually good with my hands, and enjoying every aspect of woodworking. How come I was so lousy at sewing? Jessie reminded me of the incident. It all came back. I still hate sewing.

In later years, Bruno used to hem my slacks or skirts. Knowing my discomfort in the fashion world, he made shopping fun. But I still have as my mantra Gilda Radner's wisdom, "I base most of my fashion sense on what does not itch," from a card my friends Fanny Kiefer and Darlene Haber gave me long ago.

Something else came out of the polio that I did not realize until years later. I learned to cook. Jessie was a splendid and organized cook, a wizard who would haul a summer rhubarb pie out of the freezer and into the oven in the middle of a January blizzard.

During those years of exercises and "hanging around" on the bar set high in the corner of the kitchen, I was spending a lot of time with Mom. She was great company. I would do my twenty minutes on the bar twice a day, invariably in the kitchen as Mom prepared meals.

Polio is a disease we have demonized through fear and lack of knowledge. I had been so successful in the past in never mentioning polio that Jacquie, at our fiftieth high school reunion, assured another classmate that I had never had polio — it was just scoliosis. That word polio was just not spoken.

Now I read with kinship that former Prime Minister Paul Martin, one of my heroes, had polio as a child. The list of fellow travellers also includes Neil Young, Joni Mitchell, Donald Sutherland and Alan Alda.

Polio was just something that happened to me. It was a lesser case of it, a roll of the dice. I knew from an early age what the inside of a children's hospital looked like. I have felt an unearned kinship with those who are physically disabled. During that year of hot foments, Mom said, "You know, you are so lucky. The two health problems you have, asthma and polio, cause no pain." Where I was truly lucky was to live in a country with excellent health care, to have a family with the financial means, time and ability to care for me, and not to have to face the dangers and deprivations of poverty and lack of facilities so many polio victims have in the past, and still today, worldwide.

Polio should be gone, but it is not. There is still no cure, but with easy vaccinations, it is preventable. Once the vaccines were available, the developed countries wasted little time. In Yorkton, on March 1961, the front page of *The Yorkton Enterprise* headlined "Polio Clinic — Be wise — Immunize."

The Kinsmen Foundation has raised money for decades to fight the effects of polio worldwide. They recognized polio was paralyzing millions, that iron lungs and other aids were needed for the victims. Rotary International and the Bill and Melinda Gates Foundation continue their crusade to eradicate polio.

Polio remained endemic in a few countries. It is also making a comeback in countries where outlier politicians and some religious leaders claim the polio vaccine is a Western plot to sterilize, or a campaign to cover for spying. Health workers have been killed as they sought to distribute the vaccines.

Equally disturbing is the trend of many educated people in Western countries to deny the validity of all vaccinations. They need to hear this again — there is no cure for polio; it can be eradicated with vaccines.

On October 24, 2011, World Polio Day, Paul Martin wrote a piece in *The Globe and Mail* urging the continuation of international aid against polio. His own struggle with the disease sounded familiar — "I was one of the fortunate ones and fully recovered after a long spell in the polio ward at the Hotel-Dieu Hospital in Windsor."

# CHAPTER 6

# Ancestors and Prairie Roots

*William and Ted Hopkins.*

WITH no grandparents alive when I was born, and few family members around, late in life I began the ancestry search. My maternal ancestors came from England to the prairies of the North West Territories in 1882 — to what is now Yorkton, Saskatchewan — and experienced the reality of the prairie seasons. The first four white settlers in the area in the winter of 1882 included two of my great uncles, William Patrick Hopkins and Edward (Ted) Hopkins, twenty-one and nineteen years of age, pictured above before they left London for Canada.

Their first winter was one of survival. William and Ted and two other young men lived crammed into a log and sod shelter, 'the wintering place'. Their clothing, adequate for the English climate, left them ill-prepared for the harsh winter conditions. Their food supplies, basic and meager — flour, oatmeal, tea, syrup, dried apples, dry salted pork — were running low. Without help from the local native Indians, they might not have survived, according to my Mother and her older brother, Bob Christopherson.

The young government of Canada was seeking settlers for its West. Treaty 4 had been signed in 1874 between the Crown and the Indigenous nations of the area covering part of what became Saskatchewan, ceding 74,000 acres over to the Crown.

Under Canada's homestead legislation, *the Dominion Lands Act,* a settler would receive 160 acres of land. It became deeded to his name after three years if at least ten acres a year had been cultivated, the settler had lived on the land for no less than six months of each year, and he swore allegiance to the Queen of England.

The last condition of swearing allegiance to Queen Victoria was a deal breaker for many Russian Doukhobors who came to the area north of Yorkton around 1899 and 1900 under the sponsorship of Leo Tolstoy. Rather than swear allegiance to anyone other than God, and face possible military conscription in the future, the pacifist Doukhobors walked away from their partially cultivated homesteads, sparking a greedy land grab in Yorkton in 1907.


Because Mother was a talker, unlike Dad, I know some ancestry on her side of the family. She referred to her three uncles, William, Ted and Rowland Hopkins as "Remittance Men." This meant they received some financial assistance from England, from their grandfather, but were expected to establish their independence in Canada.

The promise of homestead land would have been significant for the Hopkins brothers, with little hope of ever owning their own homes in Great Britain. Single women, like my grandmother, Jessie Ellen Hopkins, their sister, would not have been eligible for a homestead grant, unless she was a widowed head of her household.

Originally from Glamorgan, Wales, part of the Hopkins family had moved to London. My great grandparents were William Hopkins, a "piano forte tuner", and Bridget Byrne of Ireland, whispered to be "a lady of the stage." They had five children, one of whom died at eighteen months, of consumption, known now as tuberculosis. In the same week, William Hopkins, the young father, died of the same disease at age thirty, leaving his twenty-seven year old widow, Bridget, and four small children; William Patrick, age six; Ted, age four; Jessie Ellen, age three; and Rowland Arthur, age one.

William's father, also named William Hopkins, raised the four children in his home in London, but where was the young widow? She was not on any of the subsequent census records with her children.

We all wonder, what kind of people were our ancestors? What drove mine to cross a huge and dangerous ocean in small, punishing vessels, to live as pioneers in a new country unknown to them?

William and Ted crossed the Atlantic in January 1882, something I would not hazard at that time of year even today on a caviar-drenched Queen Mary 2. They made their way to Winnipeg — Canada' version of the Wild West — taverns, hotels and boarding houses overflowing with men and booze. Prohibition and the Bronfmans would come later, particularly to Yorkton.

All four Hopkins siblings eventually came to the Yorkton area, with Jessie Ellen being the last to immigrate, in 1889, travelling on her own. I began to understand one of my Mother's mantras: "When you are eighteen, you leave the nest."

With the help of researchers Judy Thompson and Terri Lefevre Prince, we uncovered part of the mystery of Bridget Byrne. Nine years before her death in 1903, Bridget Byrne had immigrated to Canada under the name of Emma Hopkins, to live in Yorkton with her eldest child, William Patrick Hopkins. Her life after her husband's death? Still a puzzle. What circumstances led her to leave her four small children with her husband's father? Her secrets lie with her, buried in the Yorkton cemetery, far from her Emerald Isle.

IN 1890, my grandmother, Jessie Hopkins, married Henry Christopherson, a young man from England who had ended up in Yorkton in 1888 at age twenty-three. Our search of the Christopherson family background shocked me out of the warm ancestral thoughts I had while exploring the Hopkins/Byrne lineage.

Henry Christopherson was the only child of Jane Preston and Captain John Christopherson. John, born 1825, became a master mariner who purportedly ran a sandalwood trading ship from East Africa to Sumatra. Except his cargo was not sandalwood. It was slaves, long after England had outlawed slave trading (1807) and slavery was abolished anywhere in the British Empire (1833).

We surmise the English caught him. In any event, John Christopherson, one of my maternal great-grandfathers, purportedly spent fifteen years in a Singapore prison for illegal slave trading. His name does not appear in the English census records of 1841, 1851 or 1861. His only child, Henry was born in 1866. John appears in the 1871 census as a 'master mariner.' That long absence from England would seem to confirm his appalling activity and imprisonment.

His father, also named John Christopherson, was a lighthouse keeper near Liverpool, known for his integrity and bravery. These Christophersons were from the York region of England for a number of centuries, Vikings doubtless roaming in their past.

Thanks to Mother, the history of Yorkton was part of my upbringing. Dad was not helpful at all on ancestors. I knew his small slice of the Morrison Clan came to Cape Breton from the Isle of Lewis in the Outer Hebrides of Scotland, and that Gaelic was the language. After reading John Prebble's *The Highland Clearances*, I asked Dad if that was why our family left the Isle of Lewis. He said he didn't know. I asked, "What did your father ever say?" Dad's reply, "We didn't talk much." The best was when I asked what our family did in Scotland before coming to Canada. "They ate porridge and stole sheep from the English."

Dad's grandparents had immigrated to Canada around 1840. They were farming. His father, born in Canada, was a stonemason.

There was a sense that neither my Mother nor Father's family looked back, but rather, embraced their newly adopted country, hardships and all, raising large families. There was an attitude of optimism and independence about these ancestors, and certainly in my own parents.

# CHAPTER 7

# My Parents and Moira

*The young William and Jessie*

Iᴎ ᴛʜᴇ mid 1920s, when William Harold Morrison first saw Jessie Christopherson at a dance in Yorkton, he had a feeling this was the woman he would marry. He was a young lawyer from Nova Scotia, on the quiet side. She was a young teacher, vivacious dark-eyed. Dad was the second youngest of eleven children, living on their small farm on Boularderie Island on the Bras D'Or Lake in Cape Breton, looking across to Baddeck, the picturesque town made famous by Alexander Graham Bell.

Until age six, Dad spoke only Gaelic. He went to school in North Sidney, finishing Grade 12 at the age of fourteen. He never talked about school, but did tell of being given five cents each day to buy a lobster for lunch from a beach vendor. Lobster then was the food of the poor.

Six feet tall, slender but underage when World War I broke out, Dad enlisted by lying about his age, and was on a troop ship in Halifax harbour in 1914 or 1915 when his father, learning of it, rushed to Halifax to tell the commanding officers to get his young son off the ship. After he reached eighteen, Dad tried to enlist in the fledgling Canadian Air Force, but was rejected due to his colour blindness.

He enlisted in April 1918 in the Army, the Canadian Overseas Expeditionary Force, and was sent to England in June 1918, where he was assigned to the headquarters of the newly formed 1st Tank Battalion in London; he remained there for his thirteen months overseas. His Attestation papers listed his occupation as 'clerk.' He was a wizard with numbers, so perhaps those skills were useful to the Army. He also spent fifteen days in a London hospital with the flu, deadly in 1918. I learned this by accessing Dad's war records. He never spoke of it.

He avoided the fate of one of his older brothers, Murdock Rory Morrison. Murdock, a miner, was drafted and fought in France. He was wounded, shot in the abdomen, recovered, and was sent back to the front. He had survived the carnage in Passchendaele, but Murdock was one of the many Canadian soldiers gassed by the Germans, and never recovered his health, dying at age fifty-three.

Dad was the only one of his family to attend university. When he left home, his mother told him all she had to give him was a US $5 gold coin, which Dad held safe and close all those years, and that I now wear on a chain around my neck. After the war, he enrolled in the School of Medicine at Dalhousie University in Halifax; however, six months into the course, they gave each student their own cadaver. The world lost a squeamish doctor. He transferred into law and graduated silver medalist in the Class of 1923, with a scholarship to Harvard to continue his studies and obtain an LL.M. He lacked the funds to take advantage of the scholarship. Instead, he moved out west, to Saskatchewan. Those were the years, as so many years have been, where Maritimers went west to find work.

Before moving west, Dad wrote a letter to his closest sister, Annie, who lived in Plymouth, Massachusetts. The letter concerned their youngest brother, Daniel, and was given to me years after both Annie and Dad had died, by Annie's daughter, Peggy McLean. Daniel, at the age of nineteen or twenty, had become desperately ill.

> Dear Annie,
>
> Poor Danie I am sorry to say is much worse the last few days and the doctor fears he hasn't many days left. He may pass into the great beyond any day and if you intend coming to see him, you can't come any too soon or you may be too late.
>
> May the Good God bless his dear soul and take him where pain is never known, the wish of everyone who ever knew or saw him, and I am sure that is all we ask since it seems his time is nearly up.
>
> Goodbye dear sister. I only wish I could give my life for his and I would gladly and willingly.
>
> With love, Bill

So Dad must have come west with a heavy heart; also with an empty wallet. Before articling and being admitted to the bar in Saskatchewan, he joined a farm threshing crew, 'stooking'; stacking sheaves of wheat on the fields for the threshing machine during the grain harvest. Grueling work. Earning money not only to live but also to buy his court attire.

From 1924 to 1928 Dad practiced law in Yorkton and then moved to Estevan, on the border with the United States. He was a junior counsel in one of the infamous Bronfman trials during those prohibition days. But it was Jessie who had tales of the Bronfmans from their years in Yorkton, where the Bronfmans began their empire. Tales of tunnels under the streets of Yorkton, big touring cars tricked out with unusual compartments, buildings acquired close to the train station for special shipments.

By the time Dad moved to Estevan, he and Mom were engaged, writing one another daily. They were married July 23, 1929 in Regina. The newlyweds left Regina on a month long motor trip to St. Paul, Des Moines, Yellowstone Park, Banff, Lake Louise and Waterton Lakes.

Jessie talked of their honeymoon often, and mentioned Dad's new Buick. In writing this, I had to wonder, *was that really a Buick? Did they even have Buicks in 1929? What kind of roads were they travelling on?* So I looked up Buicks. Well. No wonder Mom mentioned it. The 1929 Buick (called McLaughlin Buick in Canada) was a beautiful big four-door sedan. They were large touring cars favoured by those same Bronfmans.

Three months after their honeymoon, the Great Depression hit, with the crash of the stock market in New York on October 29, 1929. That was followed by the Dirty Thirties, years of severe drought in the Midwest and killer dust storms. Like all prairie kids, Moira and I were raised with acute awareness of the Great Depression, of those droughts and devastating farming conditions.

The Depression confirmed Jessie's views of the inefficacy of housework. You dusted, turned around and an hour later, you could write your name in the dust on the same table. One of her more endearing sayings to Moira and me was, "Remember dear, housework is drudgery. There is really no point in having the shiniest waxed floor in town." Nevertheless, she made sure we knew how to clean the house and did not get out to play on Saturdays until all our chores were done.

Mother, born in Yorkton on October 9, 1903, was the youngest of seven children born to Jessie Ellen Hopkins and Henry Christopherson. In her later years, she lived in mock fear of being hauled up on stage at the Yorkton Fair along with the rest of the old pioneers.

Henry Christopherson may not have been the most beloved man in Yorkton. After an unsuccessful attempt at ranching, he became a businessman, and then the first sheriff of Yorkton. He also served as a Justice of the Peace, a magistrate, with no legal training, where he appeared to lean heavily in favour of the Northwest Mounted Police at all times, and was rather tough on some of the local citizens. After one well-publicized dust-up, the owner of the local paper swore Henry's name would never appear in the paper, and it never did. My grandfather's $50 fine to one of the Bronfman brothers for a violation of the liquor laws was significant for the times, and perhaps marked the earliest brush with the law for that entrepreneurial clan. He was too tough a father on his sons, and the two eldest had neither time nor love for him.

Jessie was an accomplished mimic at a young age. At six she began school. Her parents were English and there were a number of other English families in town. One family came from the part of London which boasted strong cockney accents. One of their children, Agnes, was in Grade 1 with Jessie.

Shortly after school had begun, Jessie came home and informed her mother that she was feeling quite ill. "What seems to be the trouble, Jessie?" "Well, I'm just feeling a bit faint and I'm just not sure," said Jessie. My grandmother pressed a little, "Well, what do you think it might be?" To which Jessie replied, in her perfect new accent, "It's me *noiyves*."

The mimic had picked up a splendid new accent, along with a brand-new ailment, although she never lived down suffering from "her nerves" as a six year old.

For Jessie, school was something to be skipped, particularly if the sun was shining. She was sometimes discovered sitting under the big front steps leading up to the school. So at age eleven, she was sent off to the private school in Winnipeg, St. Mary's. She hated it.

On December 31,1919, Jessie's life changed. Her father died suddenly of heart failure. Private school hell in Winnipeg was over. Jessie needed to find employment. If jobs for young women were few when I went looking, my mother's options were really scant in 1919. Just sixteen, she had not completed high school.

A minor problem. Jessie applied for the six-month normal teacher training course in Regina, assuring them she was twenty-one. She was accepted and completed the course. By the fall of 1920, before her seventeenth birthday, she was teaching Grades 1 to 12 in a one-room school, out in the middle of the prairie. She was only five feet tall, a slight, dark-haired young woman, completely on her own. Buchanan, Saskatchewan was the nearest small town.

She had room and board with a farm family who lived three miles from her school. They provided a horse for her to ride to and from the school. As the teacher was the first to arrive at the school, she was the one to care for the horse, shovel the snow and light the fire in the stove that provided the only heat for the school. Jessie was teaching farm children older than her. She soon had some of the senior boys organized shovelling snow and stacking firewood.

Jessie taught for about three years at that one-room school, and then moved into Yorkton to teach at Burke Elementary School. She loved her students, and that seemed to be reciprocated. All my life, older men would come shyly up to my mother at community events and say, "Are you Jessie Christopherson? You taught me." They would be beaming. Jessie, who could never remember a name, but always a face and a person, would beam back, "Of course! I remember you."

She may have lacked math and spelling skills, but her love of literature, art, history and people and her incredibly positive outlook on life more than compensated.

After she married, Mom never taught again, or worked outside the home, which was unfortunate, because she was restless as Moira and I grew older.

She once said to me, "I should have been a political cartoonist." I think she was right. She grew up with politics. Jessie knew the issues of the day. More important, she knew the politicians, by sight, sound and foible. She could draw, and being a deadly accurate mimic, she noticed traits and mannerisms the rest of us did not.

Every now and then I benefited from my Mother's relaxed view of attending school. I loved going to school, and did well, and did not share my Mother and sister's penchant for skipping out. On one of my teenage birthdays, Jessie suggested we play golf that day. It was a sunny midweek school day toward the end of May. We threw our clubs in the car. En route to the golf course,

Mom stopped on Main Street to run an errand. As I was sitting in the car, who should appear but Russ Baldwin, our law and order school principal. This was the man who would yank the boys out of the pool rooms during the day when they were supposed to be in school. The boys did not dare smoke even off school grounds, if Mr. Baldwin was around.

Here I was, sitting in a car when I should have been in class. Out from the store came Jessie. She threw a cheery greeting to Mr. Tough Guy. "Russ! How are you?" He seemed delighted to see her. She said, "Nancy and I are off to play golf today. It's her birthday." He just gave the biggest grin and said he hoped we had a good game, and off he went.

That would have killed those bad boys in the poolroom.

I don't think I went through any difficult teenage mother and daughter years. I always thought my parents were fun and enjoyed their company. But I do recall the summer after my first year at university. I had come home for the summer, and obviously brought some attitude with me. I don't remember what led up to this conversation, but will never forget Jessie saying to me, "You know, dear, we are not sending you to university so you can learn how to become obnoxious." I have this image of me graduating in Obnoxious 101.

Jessie was the real progressive in our family, a feminist. Moira and I grew up knowing Nellie McClung was a woman to be admired, that we could do anything we might choose to do, that we should always have our own bank account, and it was fine to beat the boys at school or sports.

Mother and Moira had a touch of the con artist in them. They shared that mischievous side, and loved people. Born saleswomen, they could work a room better than any politician.

The pejorative side of Jessie's con artist ways surfaced when it came to cross-border shopping. Having lived for eight years in Estevan, smack on our border with the US, shopping in nearby Minot, North Dakota was a regular pastime, an annual pre-school event when we moved north to Yorkton.

With Dad, smuggling was illegal and not done. This presented a dilemma for Jessie. There were those dollar limits on

*In later years, Dad on an office coffee break and Mom at Gibson's.*

how much could be brought across the border after a weekend in the States. Easily solved. If it was an expensive item, Jessie and the helpful saleswoman, in Dad's absence, would decide that an alternate bill showing a much lower dollar amount was more suitable for customs purposes.

Jessie's larcenous border ways continued into her final year. After she moved to Vancouver in 1984, five years after Dad had died, she and I would drive to nearby LaConnor, Washington, to see the fields of tulips, the soaring bald eagles. On our last trip, she invited two friends from Crofton Manor, the elegant retirement home where Mother spent her last six years.

These three women scouted the shops of LaConnor like the experts they were. Gifts for grandchildren, some clothes, jewellery, lovely scarves. We had lunch overlooking the water. The sun was out; it was a good outing. We headed north for the border and home.

I have never dodged paying duty at the border, and knew some money would be required, especially for Jessie's purchases.

"Anything to declare?" the Canadian border guard asked.

Before I could say a word, the three white-haired angels in my car chimed, in unison, "No. Not a thing ." The guard was trying not to smile as he waved us on into Canada.

DAD WAS THE steadying thread that has run throughout my life. His Maritime sense of humour was gentle, self-deprecating, never mean. As a kid, I would have done circus tricks if I knew how, and thought they would get a laugh. Instead, I made up stories. Funny things said and done at school. I was not the only one trolling for laughs at the dinner table. Dad was our best audience.

But Dad had that Scottish quirk that decreed it was not becoming to brag about one's own clever deeds or words. So if it was something I had said or done, I attributed it to Merv Kuryluk, one of my favourite classmates, known for his quick wit, brains and cheeky ways. Merv said and did many amusing things on his own, so it was easy for me to fraudulently piggyback onto his reputation.

On winter weekends during high school, my friends and I would sometimes gather around our dining room table to play poker with Dad's poker set. Our dining room light pulled down, like a 1920s gambling dive; we lacked only armbands and a honky-tonk piano to complete the mood.

One Sunday afternoon, Mom and Dad came home to find the teenage poker game in full swing. Merv challenged Dad to join in. My father was a very skilled poker and bridge player. "Now William, don't take on the children." This caution from Mother. Cheeky Merv said, "No, let William play."

So Dad smiled and sat down. He cleaned out the boys faster than a badger goes over a fence.

Although Dad was a lawyer, my being a lawyer was not Plan A. I wanted to be a journalist. But I also talked about a career in law. Dad was not encouraging. He would tease me by calling me "A. Friend Morrison." This was after an older unmarried woman real estate lawyer in town whose name was A. Friend Milligan. At other times he would say, "Whatever you do, don't become a lawyer." I was sixteen the last time I remember him saying that to me. I asked, "Why? Wouldn't I be a good lawyer?"

"No, you would be a wonderful lawyer. No matter what you do, you will be wonderful. It's just that I do not want you having to work that hard." He was encouraging a career in journalism. My journalist friends will be charmed to learn their profession apparently does not entail hard work.

Dad was not one to lavish big hugs on his daughters. His hugs were more verbal. As when, as a small child, preschool, pigtails, missing front teeth and all, I came into the living room to meet someone and was introduced by my father, "John, I want you to meet one of the great people of all time." Sometimes he added, "We think we'll keep her." Dad loved having daughters. Although later, his definition of a father was suspect — a pedestrian with one car and two daughters.

## Moira

Moira was my big sister, four years older, my only sibling. From the beginning, she took it as her job to protect me; fiercely, when required. I never felt the need to be protected, but Moira took a dim view of my political and street smarts.

Moira was arguably the smartest one in the family. She had Mother's quick wit and total charm. Her mind moved fast. But she hated school, never graduating Grade 12. Her aversion to school began early.

With no kindergarten or preschool in our day, we went straight into Grade 1 at age six. Moira decided she had had enough of school after two weeks. So she quit. She sensed Mom and Dad might not be on side with this, but her scheme did not need them anyway.

She would leave home at 8:45 a.m. for the two-block walk to Victoria School. Instead of going to school, en route, she would pick up Warren Boucher, her neighborhood pal and six-year-old classmate, and off they would go and play. Well out of sight of parents. When she saw the kids streaming home from school at noon for lunch, Moira and Warren joined them. Then supposedly back to school at 1:15 for the afternoon, from 1:30 to 4. That gave them two and a half more hours to play.

*With big sister Moira in 1937.*

She got away with it for two weeks. Until Essie Johnson, her treasure of a Grade 1 teacher, ran into Mom and asked how Moira was doing, was she feeling better? In those days, truancy was not allowed, but as Mom was a former teacher, it did not occur to anyone to phone and check up on Moira being absent.

If anyone could bust Moira, it was Jessie. Mom set up her own scheme. At dinner time that night, the phone rang. Mom answered it. "Yes, she's here. Moira, it's for you." A wide-eyed Moira went to take her first ever phone call. It was the truant officer! The wicked Jessie had persuaded a deep voiced male friend to impersonate a truant officer on the phone. Moira returned to school, but she never enjoyed the classroom. It was not until Moira was in her thirties that I learned why.

It was also that first year at school that Moira's problem with her name arose. Mom had carefully picked the name 'Moira' for that first daughter. But when Dad went to register the birth, his love for his wife and his Scottish heritage took over. For a Scot, one's name often reflects ancestry, and Moira's mother and grandmother were named Jessie. So he registered her as Jessie Moira Morrison, to the dismay of Mom, who had never liked the name Jessie.

Moira came home in tears one day. Her full name had become known to the other classmates. On the prairies, cows were often called Molly, Dolly, Ellie, Bessie, Jessie. One of her classmates had taken to calling Moira " Jessie the cow." Mother asked who was calling her that. It was Hugh Anderson. Mother said, "All right. You go back to school this afternoon. And if Hugh calls you that again, you call him "Pew-ee Hughie."

Moira came home from school in triumph to report that Pew-ee Hughie had not enjoyed his new name and the teasing had ended. But the seed was planted. She wanted her name changed to Moira Margaret Morrison. Dad obliged by changing it legally a few years later.

By Grade 8, it was apparent school was not Moira's forté. It drove Dad crazy that Moira did so poorly in school, because he knew how bright she was. In those days, there was no testing, assessing or understanding of children with learning disabilities. So Moira's dismissal of school remained a frustration.

What was apparent was that Moira was a gifted natural athlete, with wonderful coordination, low heart rate, great stamina and ability in any sport she chose. She swam expertly at a young age.

Raised on prairie winters, she was skating by three. By thirteen, she had surpassed the local figure skating instructors. She was also racing on her figure skates, outpacing competitors on speed skates. Her skating skills were such that the coach of the junior boys hockey team had Moira demonstrate skating backwards for his players. The long-time janitor at our public school told Mom and Dad that in thirty-five years of watching kids skate, he had never seen anyone with the skating ability that Moira possessed.

Mom and Dad believed that Moira's best chance of a career lay in sports and recreation, so they enrolled her in a private girls' school in Winnipeg, Rupert's Land, later to become Balmoral Hall, beginning in her Grade 9 year. This was an opportunity for her to take skating lessons from Rosemarie Henderson, one of Canada's outstanding figure skaters at the time. Moira hated being sent to private school. She skipped classes, and skipped so many skating classes they were eventually terminated.

For Moira, school could not end soon enough. She was a rebel who danced to her own tune.

## Submarine Parents

Our parents were not our best friends. On occasion they ganged up on Moira and me. They were always a united pair, and any attempt to divide and conquer them ended badly.

"Dad says I can go to the movie."

"Really? Let me just check with your father."

We never saw that coming. We should have, based on past defeats.

There was little democracy in our home. Majority rule? Let's all talk it over and take a vote? You're kidding. It's a wonder Moira and I ended up with such a high regard for democracy. Jessie had a saying: "My house, my rules. When you have your own home, then you get to decide."

In this age of helicopter parents, mine would best be described as submarine parents. When I left home at eighteen for UBC, my parents put me on the train for Vancouver. I went home for Christmas and summer holidays, but at university, I was on my own. In my three years at UBC, they surfaced in Vancouver only once, on graduation day.

At the end of my three years in Toronto attending Osgoode Hall Law School, my submarine parents surfaced again, at graduation time. At least they knew how to throw a party when they did show up.

# CHAPTER 8

# *How to Choose a University*

IT WAS ALWAYS A GIVEN I would go to university. Which one? Mom helped me decide as I was in my final year of high school. "Dear, we can afford to send you to university, but if you plan to attend the University of Saskatchewan, you will have to pay your own way." Moira and I had been given stocks as gifts over the years, and I knew I had about $3,000 worth, enough in those years for two or three years of university.

"Why do I have to pay my own way if I go to the University of Saskatchewan?"

> This is your one chance to go someplace different, meet new people, have new experiences, on someone else's money. If you go to Saskatoon, where most of your friends are going, it will be like a continuation of high school. You will miss out on that chance to be somewhere new. You will never lose your friends. Close friends always remain friends. In any event dear, it's your choice.

Having been dazzled by Vancouver, the ocean and mountains on a family visit when I was fourteen, the University of British Columbia was an easy choice. And Mother was right. You never lose good friends.

She was just booting me out of home and my comfort zone. Jessie was tough. "If you go on to university, we will pay; but if you fail, you are on your own, working."

As I grew older and learned more of both Mom and Dad's backgrounds, I understood why Moira and I were expected to be independent. I sent for the University British Columbia calendar and remember lying on the rug in the living room one evening, trying to decide on one or two elective courses. This was before school career counsellors existed. I was trying to understand the difference between psychology and philosophy as they were explained, briefly and badly, in the calendar.

As Dad had gone to university, I asked him which one I should take. "You decide. It's your choice." he said. I didn't really know which one to take, and I wanted his advice. Dad demurred.

"William, help the child out," said Mom.

"No, it's her choice. She should decide."

I ended up with psychology, interesting but not a favourite.

When I left for university, I was looking forward to the social and political aspects of political involvement and a career in journalism. But UBC was an overwhelming experience

At eighteen, my first time away from home, I moved into one of the three girls' dormitories on campus. I had a single room, with a rod installed as a bar from which to continue my hanging exercises. Dad had arranged for that with his friend and former classmate from Dalhousie, Larry MacKenzie, then president of UBC.

The President was the only person I knew at the University. There were 8,000 students at UBC in 1955. Yorkton's population then was 8,000. In the first week, the annual campus club day was held in the armories on campus, where the clubs had their booths. I had three clubs in mind, the student Liberal Club, the campus newspaper, called *The Ubyssey*, and the Debating Club.

Knowing no one on campus, I wandered through the huge armories on my own. There were crowds of students, screams of recognition everywhere. It was one huge reunion of students from all the local high schools in the Lower Mainland.

I sought out the campus newspaper, *The Ubyssey*, but it was clear they were not recruiting. Those present were having a glorious September meet and greet with all their old friends. It was a large and boisterous group. I hung around the edges, too shy to engage.

My next booth was the Liberal Club. The small group of mostly male students were scanning the crowd for colleagues. There were reunions going on there too, but not noisy and joyous like the ones going on at *The Ubyssey*. They were looking for old friends, not new recruits. I strolled on. Next came the Debating

Club. Here were a few tall haughty males. Recruiting? Hardly. This was not going well.

Then I almost became a Tory. I wandered by the Conservative booth; there was only one person there, and he was looking for new Conservatives. A tall good-looking man, slightly older than most of the students, with a warm smile. In politics, you always keep your eye on the opposition, whether they be CCF or Conservative.

The charming recruiter was Phil Govan. With a big smile he invited me to stop and chat, and asked if I would be interested in joining the Conservative club on campus. It was tempting. Somebody nice was talking to me. Political conversion seemed a possibility. But I smiled back and told him that I was a Liberal. He expressed his sympathy, and I moved on.

For the next three years, every time I saw Phil on campus, I smiled broadly at him; little did he know he was the first friendly face I had encountered on campus. Many years later, we became friends when we were both Provincial Court judges in Vancouver.

On graduating from UBC on my twenty-first birthday with a Bachelor of Arts in political science, I found there were no jobs; certainly not for females. In the eyes of one aunt, I was "one of those unfortunate B.A.s." The only job I could find was in Prince Albert, Saskatchewan as a social welfare worker. I had never been to Prince Albert, and knew no one there. Nor was I trained as a social worker. My job pertained to the welfare and financial assistance side of social work, not with child apprehension or family counselling. I boarded with a welcoming family, had the use of a Department of Welfare car, and settled in to enjoy a summer in northern Saskatchewan.

One of my tasks was to check and ensure people on welfare due to medical conditions were really ill, and not faking it. The local doctors would scream as you phoned to check up on the recipient: "Is that all you Goddamn people have to do with your time?! Phone doctors seven times asking the same Goddamn questions?!"

Wow. I had never been sworn at like that. Who knew my predecessors had called the same doctor so many times? At home in Yorkton, the doctors were family friends and very unlike this rude bunch.

Many of the cases that came into our office were disturbing, especially the number of single mothers on welfare. One distraught woman had been deserted by her husband, leaving her alone with five young children. He had sold their farm out from under her, kept all the money and taken off for Alberta with his trollop of a girlfriend, where he bought another farm and settled down. He refused to send any money for his wife or children. So they were all on welfare, destitute.

On one of my weekend visits to Yorkton, I told Dad how awful it was that we could do nothing to get this man to pay any maintenance for the wife and children, because he had skipped over to Alberta, beyond our control and jurisdiction.

"That's nonsense," said Dad. "He can be made to pay. They should bring an action against him and have it enforced in Alberta under the Reciprocal Enforcement of Maintenance Act."

When I went back and told my supervisor this, I was told that yes, that remedy did exist, but the Department did not do that. The woman could hardly keep her family fed, let alone begin and finance her own court action.

Then the fair came to town. My instructions were to give all welfare recipients a one-time modest extra sum so families could take their children to the fair. That beat being yelled at by crabby doctors.

I was on intake one afternoon, as the fair began. As I was called down to interview a couple who were seeking the small supplement, a large beige file was placed on my desk. It was obviously the wrong file. The welfare recipient files were not beige. I left it on my desk and went to meet the couple.

The husband, a tall, good-looking Indigenous man, spoke with eloquence. His wife remained quiet, nodding on occasion.

He realized I was new to the area and the job, and after some pleasant introductory conversation, he asked me if I knew anything about the Indian treaties between his people and Queen

Victoria. I didn't. He smiled and began to give me my first lesson on Indigenous rights in Canada.

He spoke about the trust relationship between the Queen and the Indians in Canada, and the inherent rights that had been guaranteed by Queen Victoria, in perpetuity. That these rights would exist "for as long as the sun would shine, the grass grow and the rivers flow...."

I was entranced, delighted to meet this quiet, educated and well-spoken man and his wife. I authorized the cheque for the supplement, bade them goodbye and returned to my office with a warm glow.

It was a bit annoying to see this big fat beige file still on my desk. It was a child apprehension file. Obviously the wrong one, but the names of that husband-and-wife were on the file.

I opened it and began to read, with horror. It contained reports and transcripts of apprehensions of their two little daughters, whom this father had raped before they were six years of age. The file indicated that while the children had been apprehended on more than one occasion, they had later been returned to their home. There was no evidence in the file that any criminal charges of rape or incest were brought against this father, although the allegations were clearly there. The girls were twelve and fourteen by this time, and had been prostituted on the streets of Prince Albert by their father throughout their young lives. They were still active teenage prostitutes.

Then came the rumours into our office of a ring of teenage prostitutes — local high school girls earning money by servicing local johns, men from all walks of life. The ring was supposedly discovered when a businessman opened his motel room door to find his own teenage daughter was his date.

My few months as a social welfare worker made it obvious that I had no relevant education, skills or training to help people. It was also my introduction to the crushing demands and impossible caseloads we put on professional social workers; the people whom we expect to take care of all those vulnerable adults and children left at the side of the road, the flotsam and jetsam we would like others to fix, to clean up, and keep out of our sight.

It was time to go back to school. Summer was ending, fall semesters would begin soon, and another prairie winter was coming. I wrote three letters. The first letter was to Carleton University in Ottawa to enroll in their Bachelor of Journalism course. Carleton was the only university in Canada then offering such a degree. This was my first choice.

The second letter was to Dean Leal of Osgoode Hall Law School in Toronto and the letter was a bit flippant. I sought enrollment in the law school, but added that my father, a Dalhousie Law graduate, was unaware of this application. The rivalry between Dalhousie and Osgoode was legendary. Dalhousie had always offered a legal degree, the LL.B., whereas Osgoode did not offer the degree until the late 1950s; rather, you read law for four years under mentorship with a firm, a type of continuing articles or clerkship. Dalhousie grads had been known to refer to Osgoode as a school for plumbers and carpenters. Dean Allan (Buck) Leal from Tweed, Ontario, understood. He wrote back immediately welcoming me to the law school that fall, and promising never to tell my father that I was there.

The third letter went to the University of Toronto inquiring about a Master of Arts degree in history. The Dean of Arts replied with sniff about my lackluster marks from UBC, letting me know there was no room at their inn for someone who had clearly played her way through a three-year Arts degree.

I never did hear back from Carleton.

So Osgoode it was. It would be nice to write that entering law school fulfilled a lifelong dream, but I had in mind only one year of law. If I liked it, I might stay on. If not, I would leave. I still had those stocks, so I could afford a year of curiosity.

After receiving that letter from Dean Leal, I telephoned home to tell my parents that I was going to law school. "You haven't quit your job, have you?" worried the Scot in the family. I told Dad I had not, but I was about to give my notice. I assured him that I would pay for this year of law school, that I was not expecting them to pay for more university.

This was one of the many times I knew I had won the parent lottery. Dad said, no, they would pay, and never once murmured about my choice of law school. That luck again. I was able to go on in school with the support of parents who encouraged higher education. They did not believe that higher education was only for boys, and wasted on girls.

I packed up, said goodbye to the lovely family I was boarding with in Prince Albert, stopped in Yorkton to visit my parents, and drove across the country to Toronto, a city where the only person I knew was an engineer whom I had dated casually during my first year at UBC. While I looked for a place to live, I sheltered at the YWCA residence.

# CHAPTER 9

## *Calgary's Gain*

WHILE I WAS at university, Moira had moved to Calgary in her early twenties to work as a secretary for Sun Oil. In Regina earlier, in her spare time, she had been certifying Red Cross swimming instructors for their accreditations as well as volunteering as an instructor, working particularly with handicapped children and adults. Moira had been at home part of the year I was in bed with polio treatments, and she was a believer in the therapeutic benefits of exercise and warm water activities for compromised muscles.

On arriving in Calgary in 1959, Moira contacted the Red Cross to teach swimming to the disabled. She was told there was no such program in Calgary. Moira found that unbelievable. So, new to the city, knowing no one, she began to organize.

She talked the Calgary YMCA into opening their pool for the first time on Sundays, and heating the pool to 85 degrees, a temperature suitable for those challenged. The classes were for children and adults in all stages of disability. The program Moira organized became one of the largest swimming programs for the handicapped in Canada. She had fifty qualified instructors by 1960, and dozens of swimmers with individual coaching throughout each half-hour lesson.

Volunteers did babysitting services for children of instructors and participants. Kiwanis Club members acted as chauffeurs, Girl Guides helped the girls in the dressing rooms, served hot chocolate and helped babysit. Calgary General Hospital Alumni Association provided Registered Nurses to stand by at the pools. The Red Cross donated a hundred blanket towels. The Western Canada Epilepsy League did laundering. Lumber companies donated lumber for necessary benches, and a local dairy donated five gallons of chocolate milk each week.

Moira conscripted the young geologists from her office to build the benches and provide lifting from vehicles to

*My sister Moira.*

wheelchairs, from wheelchairs to benches to pool. Every Sunday, approximately a thousand people would be involved, directly or indirectly with the handicapped swim program. Moira organized and supervised the program for four years. In her first full year in Calgary, she was nominated for citizen of the year. She did not win the award, but the nomination spoke for itself.

My sister was petite, attractive, funny and smart. People of all ages were drawn to her. She had wonderful sex appeal, which men certainly recognized, and she adored being around children. It was mutual. It would be hard to find a kinder person than Moira, or one more generous. I used to tease that if she had two dollars in her pocket, she would spend four, but on others, not herself. Money management was not her strong suit.

She was not above playing practical jokes. When I was attending UBC, I was dating Garry Fletcher, a young druggist in

Yorkton who, at age twenty-four was the youngest president of a Kinsmen Club in Canada. Garry had a younger brother, Gil, whose rascally side matched that of my sister. Gil was a radio announcer in Yorkton, a local celebrity. He and Moira had been with a group of people at one of the Yorkton beer parlors one summer evening. They conspired over a few beers and Gil suggested they should check out the evangelical revival tent that had been set up at the local fairgrounds west of town. The Rev. Theodore Rudd was saving souls.

They attended, and those two Anglicans watched with interest as people were being saved. When the call came for all those who had been saved to stand, everyone stood except Gil and Moira. They were urged to come up front and be saved. Which they did.

They cheerfully gave their full names and addresses so the congregation could pray for them and Rev. Rudd could not only do the laying on of hands, but also send them mail for the next five or ten years. Their names? "Garry Fletcher" and "Nancy Morrison." Rev. Theodore Rudd wrote to both Garry and me for a number of years, earnestly soliciting funds. Moira and Gil were delighted with themselves. Initially, Garry was not amused, but we both came to see it as the price we paid for having such interesting siblings.

This most liberated of young women never had much time for my feminism. She viewed my feminist leanings and speeches with patient indulgence, referring to it as "Nancy and thatwomenslibshitstuff."

## CHAPTER 10

# *Welcome to Law School*

IT WAS SEPTEMBER, 1958. I was twenty-one. Osgoode Hall Law School, one of the oldest law schools in the country, was then set in the heart of Toronto, in the building that housed the Supreme Court of Ontario and Court of Appeal, behind iron gates designed over a century ago to keep cows out.

Unfamiliar with the city and knowing no one, I found a miserable room in a dive off Davenport Road, with a hotplate, no phone and a bathroom down the hall. The landlady's greasy twenty-year-old son took to lurking near my door.

On my first day at law school, overwhelmed, I was wondering what had prompted me to take this leap.

When you are in a strange place, where everybody seemed to know one another, and you know no one, the urge to find a corner of comfort is strong. So I went looking for the library. As I approached, a young man exiting the library came over to me. He was tall, thin and serious, apparently a law student. I was so grateful someone was actually coming to talk to me that his words did not sink in for a minute.

"You must be one of the new girls." Out of a class of 265 first-year law students, with only seven female students, we were not hard to spot. (Two to three percent of law students were female at that time.) Yes, I smiled. He did not introduce himself, although I later learned his name and that he was a third-year law student. He fixed me with a humourless look and said, in a chilling tone, "Well, I hope you realize what you have done."

"No, what?"

"By the very act of enrolling in law school, you have lost your femininity. And now, no matter what you may do in the future, you can never recapture that." He carried on by saying, "Even if you don't complete law school, and it's doubtful you will, you can never regain your femininity. You have no business being here anyway, taking the place of a man, a breadwinner.

It's a waste and you won't make it anyway." He continued, "Do you see Annette over there?" He pointed to a beautiful blonde girl in a pink angora sweater and matching pink skirt, a double for Marilyn Monroe. He advised me she was a student who was having to repeat her first year.

"You may not think it, but she has lost her femininity too. By doing the same that you have just done." I stood looking at this lovely creature, and the point was made. If she had lost her femininity, there was no hope for me.

With that welcoming speech, the mean little bastard walked back into the library. I retreated back down the stairs. Even after I made friends with other classmates, I never told anyone about that welcome. But his words stayed in my head.

I began to think maybe I should change my style of clothes, less tailored, more frills. My Chanel No. 5 was amped up. Those were the days nylons had seams running down the back of the leg. Daily checks for straight seams increased, higher heels were contemplated. I never went near the library that entire first year. I had no appetite for confrontations.

Years later, when I was checking the dictionary for a word, I happened to glance at one of the meanings of masculinity. It said, "pertaining to the male genitalia". I started to smile, and checked the dictionary for the meaning of femininity. Sure enough, one of its meanings referred to the female genitalia. I began to laugh. I had not lost my femininity after all.

The meanness of that welcome was echoed over my three years in law school in other ways, sometimes by other students, on occasion by a professor. There was a resentment by many that female students were there. It was a place for breadwinners, not housewives. I was even seriously lectured by a classmate for being a female from Saskatchewan, taking the place and tax dollars that should have gone to a male from Ontario. My introduction to provincial transfer payments.

When I was told that I did not belong, I tried to defuse with humour. I sought to assure that I was no threat. Indeed, it was not uppermost in my mind that I would ever work as lawyer. I was not thinking that far ahead. I was approaching law more as a postgraduate degree than a means to earn a living, and it prolonged my fondness for school.

It was not until November of second-year law that I finally entered the law library. During first year, I had studied at home with my casebooks, texts and notes from class. I seldom missed a lecture. It is strange to write that now, recall my timidity. The late fifties were a very different time for females.

I was never late for class. That first year I probably would have skipped class rather than walk in late. I never wanted to draw attention to myself. Annette sometimes came in just before class started, and I watched the male reactions as she walked up to her seat. The only way to enter the classroom was at the lower level, the students fanned out above you. I was braver by second year.

I liked law school. Reading was my forté. The other women, few in number, were terrific. Many of my male classmates became lifelong friends. With the exception of tax law, most subjects intrigued me. There was an extraordinary mixture of town and gown in our professors, full time practising lawyers, plus the academics.

G. Arthur Martin, whose doppelganger was Alfred Hitchcock, was the dean of criminal lawyers in Canada. He was not just an occasional lecturer. He was our professor of criminal law in our first year, a role he filled for years, leaving a legacy of lawyers who gained an early understanding of the importance of legal history, ethics, civil liberties, the rule of law and the rules of natural justice.

Most of the leading cases cited by Martin were his, but you learned that only if you read the actual cases after class. Martin was a defence counsel in practice, but he inspired a legion of ethical prosecutors, defence counsel and future judges. In his later years on the Ontario Court of Appeal, Martin's concise judgments exemplified his lifelong commitment to all that is superb in the English common law. We were fortunate students.

No professors or visiting special lecturers were women. The handful of women judges in Canada were associated mostly with Family Court, where they were generally deemed to belong. There were few female role models and no female mentors. The female law students were not allowed into the student lounge. That was the boys' lounge. The school gave us our own small lounge. That reminded me of elementary school where we had to line up to go into school, the boys through one door and the girls through their separate door. Was that so we wouldn't fight? Or hold hands?

When I inquired why there was not simply one student lounge, someone murmured that they had the separate lounge for the girls so we could lie down at that special time of the month when we are 'indisposed.' And there it was, our little room complete with a fainting couch.

Some of the sexual politics and pranks at Osgoode were good-natured, some were not. Generally, you went along to get along. Like the time in the first month at school, in public in the cafeteria where, to much laughter, I was encouraged to embark on exercises, demonstrated for me, to enlarge my breasts. The student of today might snap back about penis enhancement.

One of the great litigation lawyers in Toronto was Walter Williston. He taught civil procedure to first-year students at Osgoode. Early in the year at a social gathering, Williston, aware I was a first year student, heard me say, " I would give anything to see the Montréal Canadiens play the Toronto Maple Leafs." Williston turned to me and said, " Anything?" He was tall and imposing, with a voice that rasped. I said, " Sure, anything."

All right, he said, he had two of his law firm's tickets he would give me, "in the reds." In spite of growing up listening to NHL hockey games by Foster Hewitt on the radio, I had no idea what the reds meant, but it sounded promising. He would give me the tickets on one condition: that he could deliver them to me in class. I agreed. He asked where I sat in the large class-room. I told him.

We law students had an exaggerated view of the sexual prowess of some of our professors, and Williston was in that exalted category. So when he glowered his way into the amphitheater classroom that next Monday, paused long and dramatically at the podium, and then scanned up to where I was sitting near the back, I knew it was my turn in the barrel. Without a word, he left the lectern, something he had never done, and walked slowly all the way up to my seat. The class was silent. He put his hand in his jacket, drew out a sealed envelope, slapped it before me on my desk, and in his deep tones, for all to hear, said, "For services rendered." And then walked back to the lectern.

As this was near the beginning of first year, I knew few students. And no one ever asked me what that was all about. But the hockey game was great and seats in the reds were swell. I got to see the magnificent Rocket Richard play in his final year of hockey.

Throughout those three years at Osgoode, the calibre of law professors made most hours in the classroom a pleasure. We had our favourites. The rascals like Desmond Morton won our hearts. He was Irish, a drinker, and dedicated to drilling the Law of Evidence into our skulls. On St. Patrick's Day, our first-year class presented Morton with a case of twelve bottles of Irish whiskey. He was delighted.

The following day, what was left of him walked cautiously into our large classroom, up to the podium, where he leaned on his arms and gazed out at us. "I wish to thank you for your generous gift. I enjoyed each and every one of them."

A couple of weeks into law school, two classmates decided my prairie education had left some gaps. I had never been to a strip show. Osgoode was bordered on the south side by Queen Street, and on the opposite side of Queen Street was a seedy strip joint called The Casino.

One afternoon, my two classmates and I crossed the street into the grubby theatre. Down the long dim aisle before the show began, they marched me into a seat dead centre in the second row. I tried not to ponder what might be breeding below the seats or on the floor. The entire front row was filled, a row of baldheaded men. On came the greasy, slicked-back master of ceremonies. The va-va-boom-boom music was pounding out. To my horror, his first remarks were to me.

"Well well! Hello there! I've never seen a little lady sitting up this close before!" as he gazed down lasciviously. Then on came the women. I was mesmerized. Great dancers, athletic, some with humour, all were sexy. The boys were right; my education was expanding.

In law school, it was usually easy to stay out of the way of the swines. Unless he was a professor. I have wondered if one of the professors in first year flunked me in Contracts deliberately. I liked Contracts, and had studied hard for the exam. I believed I had written a good paper; I knew when I wrote a good exam. That first year in final exams I had six B's in other subjects, and his mark in Contracts, a failure, was a shock. That summer, between first and second year, I worked in Yorkton, in Dad's law office. I was preparing to write the supplemental exam in Contracts later that summer in Regina. As I studied, Dad would wander in to my office and chat with me about contracts. He told me I knew my subject.

Toward the end of the summer, I drove into Regina and wrote the supplemental exam. I thought I had written a good exam and had few worries. However, my mark came back a D, barely a pass. I could not believe it.

My father, normally a quiet man, was furious. "They are trying to pluck you." he said. It would not have occurred to me that a professor would try to fail a student. The professor in question was a large and fairly young man, who had few dealings with other students that I knew, and none with me. I later wondered whether my feminine handwriting would have given me away, that the exams were not as anonymous as advertised. Was he one who resented women in the profession?

Dad said I must write to the school and demand a reread. What was a reread? He explained that when a student demands a reread, two or three other professors read the paper and either confirm the mark or give a more appropriate mark.

There was no way I wanted to draw that kind of attention to myself, and I shrugged it off, I'm sure to the disappointment of Dad. The only thing he said was that I knew contracts before I even began to study for my supp, and I knew it even better when I went to write the exam. I thought so too. But I also knew that professor was going to be teaching me in the next couple of years in other subjects. I let it go. I had passed the supp, which meant that I could continue my studies in law school.

Some of my deepest friendships were formed in those years of law school. We were often too ready to party and parked our brains at times, until before exams, and then studied long and hard. One of our favourite classmates who took partying to new levels, beloved by everyone, was Ron Ianni. He disappeared to Europe for a couple of years after law school, came back with an extra degree or two, became Dean of the Law School at Windsor and ultimately President of the university. ALS took him from us way too early. Then there was the erudite and endearing Jack Kenney, a year ahead of us, on his way to become god of the Ontario Jockey Club. He also left us too early.

Those of us who took the route to a law practice found you really learn the law once you begin practising it. Your clients and the lessons of the real world continue your education, and so do the judges.

# CHAPTER 11

## *The Yellow Morris Minor*

FOR MY LAST YEAR at the University of British Columbia and my years at law school and articling in Toronto, I drove a 1958 pale yellow Morris Minor with red leather seats. A beauty. I won it on a bet, made when I was eleven.

My parents had put a wager on the table for Moira and me — if you do not smoke or drink until you are twenty-one, we will give you each $1,000. Mom was a smoker; Dad had been; both drank moderately. Mom theorized that twenty-one was the age of reason; I would be finished university by then and earning my own money. Then it would be my choice whether I wished to begin smoking or drinking. They should not have to pay for such on top of university.

It sounded like a good bet. I was on my honour to keep my side of the bargain, and the subject never came up again. I went through three years at UBC, everyone's designated driver, and drank gallons of tomato juice at the Georgia Hotel Pub.

Instead of the cash, I got the Morris Minor before my twenty-first birthday. It cost $1,200. The bet had fended off years of peer pressure. I never did start smoking.

There were adventures with that car. I drove across the country numerous times, to and from university and on various side trips. A young female alone on the highway in those years sometimes drew unwanted interest. Curious cops who pulled you over to check licence and chat. More unsettling would be a car persistently following with one or more males in it. I would drive into the next town, following the signs to the local police station, and pull up in front. The car following would speed ahead and vanish. Five minutes later, I would continue on.

The Morris Minor gave me freedom and independence, the ability to roam and vacation on my own; to see Canada from a protective cocoon. It was my personal tank. I had loved cars from an early age, learning to steer and feed the gas pedal sitting beside Dad on flat prairie fields and roads. As a kid, I would sit in our car in the driveway on a rainy day, reading and taking imaginary trips. Now I could take those trips on my own.

One evening in Toronto the yellow Morris Minor had a nasty excursion without me. The car had Saskatchewan licence plates, so I had ignored all traffic tickets for parking violations in Toronto. Flagrantly, I adopted the yellow fire hydrant at the back door of Osgoode Hall as my personal parking meter. For over two and a half years at law school, I received dozens of yellow parking tickets. I joked I was going to use them as wallpaper.

This evening, toward the end of my third year at law school, I was leaving the law library and exited the school via the back door. My car was gone. It was ten at night. A classmate, Ross Butters, had followed me out. "You have been towed." He directed me to the City of Toronto Police station nearby and wished me luck. By the time I was shown to the desk of the Staff Sgt. on duty, it was 11:00 p.m. He looked up at me and said, "We have found twenty-six of your latest tickets. There are a lot more, I know. You've been parking there for a long time, haven't you?" I nodded.

"I told the boys to quit looking and wasting valuable time." The cost of each ticket was two dollars, $56 in total. It sounds trivial today, but my monthly allowance for everything then was $200.

The Staff Sgt. was an older officer, world weary. He looked at me in disgust, "So that's the kind of lawyer you're going to be, is it."

I was ashamed beyond words.

# CHAPTER 12

# *External Affairs*

A S LAW SCHOOL was ending in 1961, a career in Canada's foreign service had entered my mind. A minor in International Studies at UBC, a great course by the modest Dean Fred Soward, was maybe where the seed was planted. Then later, an elective course at Osgoode in International Law.

My paper for that course advocated Red China be admitted to the United Nations. Research had introduced me to the Institute of Foreign Affairs, housed then in a small heritage building in downtown Toronto, a goldmine of information on international politics, history and news.

To apply then for a position in Canada's foreign service, you wrote a six-hour exam, three hours in the morning, general knowledge, then three hours in the afternoon writing an essay from a number of topics not revealed until you sat down to write. That had worried me. My friend, Norman Gish, who had written the exams a few years before, and was then successfully serving Canada in Trade and Commerce in Hong Kong, had told me to read *The Globe and Mail* daily, cover to cover, as a good way to bone up on possible topics.

Visions of trying to write for three hours on the policy of the French in Indochina in the years before and after the fall of *Dien Bien Phu* gave me nightmares.

At the beginning of the essay part of the exam, about fifteen topics were presented to us. Many would have been difficult for me. But there, in their midst, my topic: You are posted to a foreign country, and asked, by someone about to visit Canada for the first time, to recommend three books to read, to get a feel for Canada; which three books would you recommend and why.

Can Lit was difficult to find in those years. But three of my favourite books were: W.O. Mitchell's *Who Has Seen The Wind,* and two by Hugh MacLennan, *Two Solitudes* and *Barometer Rising.*

With a father from Cape Breton, who was alive when the

terrible Halifax harbour explosion happened in 1917, I knew the lore before I read *Barometer Rising*. Here was the Maritime connection, history, drama, and knowledge of the people in that special part of Canada.

*Two Solitudes* was a must. The struggles between the French and the English in Canada, the language issues, politics, history, religion, all there.

My love of the prairies and books on the land had been seeded long ago. All of us find beauty in the land where we are born. I wrote my heart out on Mitchell's classic probably more than the other two books. Three hours disappeared in a wink.

Later I worried. They wanted serious students of foreign affairs, I kept thinking, not people who wallow in books. I was surprised when I made it to the final stage, a personal interview before a five-man panel. It was to take a half hour. I was there for an hour and a quarter.

I was dressed in my finest. The black wool suit Mom had bought for me in the late summer of 1955, as I readied to leave home for the first time, to go to university. Over the suit, a pale blue cashmere coat.

No one had warned me that I would be finger-printed just before the interview. I didn't mind any invasion of civil liberties; I knew there had been security checks. I did mind black ink that would not come off, under my finger nails, distracting me as I tried to present my meticulous best. I stuffed my white kid gloves into my coat pocket before heading in to the interview room.

**The Interview**

From an early age, I knew that when you entered a room, you shook hands, with everyone. So I did. Five serious, middle-aged, white men were standing up to greet. I recognized one of them, a law professor of note, Ronald St. John MacDonald, introduced, I believe, as a history professor from Queen's. That surprised me. If that were true, no lawyers on the panel. But it wasn't true. He had been at Osgoode for at least a year when I attended, although I never took one of his classes. He was a glamorous, semi mysterious prof — to our student eyes.

When he ultimately asked me a question, I said that I knew him from Osgoode. The others looked mildly amused at his outing. He did not seem perturbed in the least.

The interview was long and friendly. Curious, all five asked many questions and it was obvious they had read my essay. There were questions about my background, and finally, why would I want to do such a job. Surely, "a pretty young girl like you will be getting married and having children." No, I tried to assure them. That was not on my mind. I wanted this kind of work. I had been joking to friends that I had the steamer trunk ordered and the trench coat hanging in the closet, ready to travel. I didn't share that with the interviewers.

That interview was one of the most pleasant I have ever had. But at the end they told me that Foreign Affairs hired only twelve applicants a year, and an equal number for Trade and Commerce, and never women. They said there had been one exception, but that had been under special circumstances. Never explained. They were direct in telling me — we don't hire women.

When I left the room, I knew I was not getting the job. Official confirmation came later. I remember thinking, why waste all that time?

# CHAPTER 13

## *Finding Articles*

ONE OF THE JOYS of law school was becoming politically active. We had a Liberal club at Osgoode, and I attended a couple of Young Liberal conventions, including one in Ottawa where I was deemed the only representative from Saskatchewan. That put me next to the soon-to-be Prime Minister Lester Pearson at a banquet, where I was tongue-tied.

The high point of our Osgoode Club was inviting the Right Honourable Louis St. Laurent to speak to our club, shortly after he retired as Prime Minister. This was thanks to Burke Doran's initiative.

Burke was a classmate and natural politician. He and Pat LeSage became my closest friends at law school, and remain so to this day. Looking back at some of our partying, it is a wonder any of us graduated. Burke managed to squeeze out a living as a top litigator and managing partner of the prestigious Lang Michener law firm in Toronto, while raising prize-winning sheep as a hobby. Pat had to settle for being Chief Justice of the Superior Court of Ontario and the fireman who is called in to stamp out legal conflagrations around the country.

But that was all to come. With graduation over, articling was next. Except I could not find anyone to hire me. I had the wrong appearance and equipment: female.

After three years of law school, law students were required to article, to intern to a senior lawyer for twelve months, then take a six-month Bar Admission Course. My search for articles in Toronto was one long list of rejections. Phone calls and no interviews, or no luck after a very short interview. Female law students were rare and unwelcome.

Labour law had been a chosen elective for me, and a chance to article with one of the few small firms specializing in this area was with Norman Matthews. A friend, Jim Kennedy, offered to introduce me to Matthews. Jim, a year ahead of me at Osgoode, had articled for the Matthews firm. They wanted Jim to stay, but he had accepted an offer from the Osler firm.

Jim took me to the firm and introduced me to Matthews. Matthews, speaking politely, told me they could never hire a girl, as the clients would never accept that. They would not be free to speak their language. He was talking about swearing. Little did he know that the young law student in front of him could and did talk the talk. I was too nonplussed to assure him that I could more than keep up with the men.

Girls and women were not supposed to swear. That had been the message, loud and clear, all my life. I just never bought it. In our home, there was no real profanity. For unknown reasons, my swearing began when I was three. I was jumping up and down on the couch, looking out the window at Stewart Dewar, my little pal from across the street. I was waiting for my snowsuit to be put on, yelling, "You big ship! You big ship!" My father said, "We know what she is trying to say. Just ignore it, and it will pass."

It never did. I liked the shock value when I swore. My mother wondered where I had learned to swear like a sailor on leave. I wondered how Mother had learned about these sailors.

Something happened when I was seventeen. A friend, one year older and more worldly, was having a discussion with me about my swearing. Girls were not supposed to swear he told me. I should stop it. No, I argued. Boys did it, so could girls. No. He was emphatic. There was a big difference, he said. Girls were never supposed to swear; and, above all, there was one word no girl could ever, ever say.

We both knew what that word was. This was 1953 — even I had never dared to utter that word. But the gauntlet was down. He could say it, but I could not, simply because I was a girl. So we argued. My friend became more exercised, even angry, and commanded me, "Don't you dare ever say that word."

"Fuck, fuck, fuck!" I could not believe I was actually saying That Word.

In the next second he swung his right hand and slapped me hard on the face. I instantly kicked him back so hard on his leg that I thought I had cracked his shin bone. We stood in mutual shock.

It was a telling lesson, but one I did not analyze until years later. Women were not supposed to invade a male domain; some men get very angry when their territory is invaded. I would never tolerate personal physical violence; swearing was very powerful.

Part of my university experience at UBC involved participation in a sorority. My discomfort with certain elements of sororities increased with the annual anonymous letters sent to each sorority sister. They were sent to help us correct our faults. With me, it was my language. Receiving the letters immediately revived my kinship with those sailors on leave. I'm sure none of the fraternity brothers got letters about their language. That was guy talk.

After law school, I was chagrined at being told that I could not be hired in a labour law firm because the clients would not feel comfortable swearing in the presence of a female.

(Years later, when I was a Vice Chair and the only female member of the BC Labour Relations Board, there was an interesting twist to this language dilemma. My swearing made my fellow Board members uncomfortable, especially the union ones! So I tried never to swear in their presence.)

My problem finding articles was finally solved when Smith, Rae Greer, a distinguished small law firm of six excellent but (sadly) Tory lawyers, took me in. It was an act of charity.

Soon-to-be Senator Harry Willis was Treasurer of the national Progressive Conservative Party. He was also the father of Mary Lou Willis, my Osgoode classmate and dear pal. She was articling with her father's two-man firm. I know she persuaded Harry to intercede for me. I was a frequent guest at their home in the Caledon Hills north of Toronto. Harry was never offended by his cheeky daughter and her friend, and I never missed a chance to remind him of Liberal glories and Tory foibles.

Harry called his old friend, the well known criminal lawyer, Joe Sedgwick, a senior partner at Smith, Rae Greer, and my articles began there the summer of 1961. Six lovely men who tolerated this Liberal in their midst.

# CHAPTER 14

# *Jails*

FOR THOSE who mock 'country club jails', my assumption is they have never been in a jail. Jails are not nice places. My introduction to jails was Toronto's infamous Don Jail, which opened in 1864. The Don, named after the nearby Don River, has been described as a hell hole. It was.

Near the beginning of my articling, Joe Sedgwick sent me there to interview a client. I made it through the huge oak and iron main entrance door, which clanged shut with such ferocity you knew you would never be allowed to leave the place. Before I could make it through another set of doors I was ejected, back onto the street. They scoffed at the thought that this young female was an articling lawyer.

Mr. Sedgwick was amused when I reported back. He called in his faithful secretary, Lillian, and had her type up a letter on his elegant embossed stationary, introducing me to the keepers of the jail, assuring them of my *bona fides*, and beseeching them to grant me the same courtesies they extended to all members of the bar.

Back I went. The letter worked. That colossal front door detonated behind me again; I was shown through a series of steel doors, each clanging behind me as I passed through. For someone with claustrophobia, scary verging on panic.

I was shown into the round central rotunda, and looked up to see the circular tiers of cells off the metal balconies that ran around the open rotunda. Prisoners and guards could look down from those tiers. Twin benches were separated by a wooden barrier over which one would speak. The barrier ensured that nothing could be passed back or forth. I was ready to interview my inmate. I never looked up to the tiers again. The noise was metal and menacing.

The prisoner was brought to his side of the bench. I could hardly see over the wooden partition to interview him. He seemed surprised but pleased to see me, and the interview went well.

Then the relief in walking out into the fresh air again.


After that, as a defence counsel, interviewing clients and witnesses, I was in many jails, in Welland, in various towns in Saskatchewan, often cells in police detachments, and in BC, federal and provincial jails. I never got used to the sound, or of being locked in.

My sister Moira also had some time in jails, and mused later about writing an article, "Eastern Jails versus Western Jails." I suggested she wait until Mom and Dad had passed on.

Her Eastern jail time came in Toronto in the early sixties, when I was articling, and she had moved to Toronto to be in advertising. A large lease-breaking party was taking place one evening. Our friend, Hugh Lyons, was going through the time-honoured activity of students: breaking the twelve-month lease at the end of nine months of school. Big noisy party, neighbours finally at wit's end, police arrive, party disperses, and the lease is terminated by the annoyed landlord.

During the 'police arrive' part of the scenario, Moira, local football hero Chris Novakowski and Hugh Lyons were outside, drinking beer. Moira had put a case of beer on top of a nearby car — hers. The police told her to take the beer down and that drinking was not allowed on the street. Moira contested that, having generously sampled the beer, and then assumed my persona; she told the police that she knew the law, she was a lawyer.

The police, weary of the quarrel, took Moira and Chris down to the police station. While Chris was talking himself out the cells, Moira was still talking herself into one. It was the standard put–them–in-to–sober-up policy. But first they removed her shoes and the pins in her hair, to her annoyance.

The night wore on; Moira was still feisty. Around 4:00 a.m., the police opened her cell door, returned her things to her and told her she was free to go. "Go where?" she demanded. "Home," they replied. The unrepentant then said they would have to drive her home. She was not going out in that neighborhood at that hour with no car and no money. They offered bus fare. No way. "You brought me here, you can take me home." She was advised that was not the way it worked.

You had to know Moira. She was in sales. The police drove her to her front door.

The Western jail experience was not as pleasant. Moira had moved back to Calgary and was selling real estate. She had a disregard for 'No Parking' zones, and a dangerous disregard for court notices that warned of dire consequences on long-overdue tickets and ignored court Notices to Appear.

Early one morning, she was awakened by pounding on her door. Two large City of Calgary police officers confirmed her identity and told her she was under arrest. They allowed her to put on slacks and a sweater, and off she went to jail. Same routine — hair pins and shoes gone. She was placed in a cell with three other female occupants.

As Moira described them, they were big women, looked like they had been in jail before, frequently, and they were very curious about their new cell mate. Moira was slight, weighing maybe 110 pounds, and by now, frightened. She sized up her new roommates and decided this was not the time or place to talk about traffic tickets.

"What are you in for?" One of the women asked.
"Embezzlement."
"What's that?"
"I stole money from my employer — a *LOT* of money..."

That received slow nods of approval. Not trusting this new friendship, Moira lay on her stomach on the bunk they indicated was hers, and stayed awake the rest of the long night. At 9 a.m. she was paraded up from the cells into the courtroom, where her employer, a close friend, was trying to keep a straight face as he bailed her out.

# CHAPTER 15

# *The Death Penalty*

I WAS A terrible articling student. I enjoyed studying law, but school and articling had not sparked a desire to practice. Articling, I was more intrigued with the old-fashioned phone switchboard, like the one Lily Tomlin's Ernestine sits before. I learned how to run that, playing tricks on the occasional caller I knew, while voluntarily relieving the receptionist during a lunch hour.

On one such occasion, a middle-aged rather nondescript man came into Smith Rae Greer, stayed briefly in one of the offices, then left. Paul Greer, my principal, confided that the man was Igor Gouzenko, who, in 1945, as a young Russian clerk in the Soviet Embassy in Ottawa, famously defected to the West. He brought valuable documents with him, and Canada was stunned to learn the extent of a Soviet spy network in Canada and beyond.

Gouzenko was routinely collecting payments from our government, some through the law firm. Even after all those years, he was still a man in need of secrecy and protection, afraid of Soviet retaliation.

I found the solicitor side of the practice at Smith, Rae Greer uninteresting, and that was what I was mostly doing. Then I began dropping in on two back-to-back murder trials.

These were the trials of Arthur Lucas and Ronald Turpin, now infamous as the last two persons hanged in Canada.


Courtroom 33 in Toronto's old City Hall, was an English style courtroom with heavy wood panelling and massive furniture. The word had gone out; defence counsel Ross MacKay, a twenty-nine-year-old doing his first murder trial, was defending Arthur Lucas, a black pimp and hitman from Detroit.

MacKay had been chosen by the great G. Arthur Martin to article with him five or six years earlier. That was the coveted articling job for any law graduate in Ontario. MacKay was on his own now, defending a very tough case. MacKay, Hollywood handsome, had the reputation of a natural in the courtroom.

On November 17, 1961, Thurland Carter and his girlfriend Carol Ann Newman, a prostitute, were found murdered. Arthur Lucas, an alleged hitman from Detroit, was charged with their murders. His preliminary hearing took place in late March, 1962, and on April 30, 1962 his trial for the murder of Thurland Carter began in Courtroom 33. The formidable Chief Prosecutor for Toronto, Henry Bull, was prosecuting. MacKay was defending and the presiding judge was Chief Justice James McRuer. It was a jury trial and it went from April 30 to May 10, 1962. Lucas was found guilty and sentenced to hang.

Ronald Turpin was the accused in the second trial, a small dark-haired man, often likened disparagingly in the press to a ferret or a weasel. He was charged with the murder of Toronto City police officer Frederick John Nash on February 11, 1962.

MacKay was representing Turpin as well, and Turpin's trial began May 28, 1962, eighteen days after Lucas had been found guilty and sentenced to be hanged. A later trial date had been sought by MacKay, but Mr. Justice George Gale, the trial judge in the Turpin case, ruled it would go ahead in May. That trial took approximately three weeks. On June 13, 1962 Turpin was found guilty by the jury and sentenced to hang.

I attended both those trials almost daily while articling. Sometimes for maybe only half an hour, sometimes much longer. I would try and organize my work, brown bag my lunch and work through the lunch hours (the start of a lifetime habit), and then take time to attend the court whenever I could.

"Are you studying to be a lawyer or a murderer?" This was Paul Greer, my principal, a warm man with a gentle sense of humour. Paul would quote A.A. Milne to me on occasion when I rushed in with a crisis. "Nancy Nancy Morrison Morrison DuPree, who was so good to her mother, even though she was only three...."

It was the early days of legal aid in Canada. MacKay had few funds at his disposal, and received a minimal amount for his legal services.

Our criminal courtrooms are set up for the benefit of the judge and jury, never the accused. The judge has the best seat in the house, on high, with the vantage point of an eagle in a tree. Off to the side, well-positioned to view all, sits the jury.

Tables facing the judge are for the lawyers. Behind them is the prisoner's dock where the accused must sit, isolated, under guard, unable to catch the eye of his lawyer, and under the constant watch of the judge and jury. Especially the jury.

During the Lucas and Turpin trials, Ross MacKay was intuitive, kind and respectful to each client, relieving the isolation of the client on the regular breaks each day. He would go and stand by the accused, quietly conferring, head courteously inclined, talking, listening.

When the jury walked back into the courtroom, often they would see MacKay beside the accused, clearly his advocate, signaling there was still some decency in the accused, regardless of the charge against him.

MacKay's entire demeanor was one of respect, for the judge and everyone else in the court. He was smart and quick, and moved with the physical grace of an athlete. In both trials he was frequently hammered by the judges, McRuer and Gale, two of the toughest on the bench. MacKay never lost this courtesy or respect, or his temper that I saw. He stood his ground, and seemed fearless.

Ross MacKay sat quietly at the counsel table as he watched each witness testify. His back was partially to those of us sitting in the near empty courtroom. He sat slightly slouched back in his chair, his eyes rarely leaving the witness. Occasionally, he would reach for his pen on the table and jot a few words on the paper before him, before returning that concentrated gaze on the witness.

When he got up to cross-examine, there was no drama, no theatrical or unnecessary movements or wandering. His questions were easy, deceptively simple, never wasted or rambling. Few bring such economy of words and movement in examining and cross–examining. Few lawyers achieve greatness in cross-examination. MacKay did.

I never met Ross MacKay, even though I was almost daily in courtroom 33 during those two trials. It would not have occurred to me to intrude, to go and speak to him. He appeared oblivious to anything or anyone outside the trial. He was in two life-and-death struggles. Which he lost.

I was spellbound by those trials. Within the first few days, I knew that was where I wanted to be, in the courtroom. The unquestioned view was that females did not belong in the courtroom. That no longer occurred to me. It never entered my mind again.

My eternal gratitude goes to Paul Greer, my principal and friend. He never discouraged those daily court attendances, he never begrudged that time away from the firm. He allowed a lifelong passion for litigation and the law to begin.

By the end of the Lucas trial, I did not believe that Arthur Lucas was guilty of murdering Thurland Carter or his girlfriend. To this day I believe he was wrongly convicted and hanged.

It was not just the issue of capital punishment that drew me into those two trials. It was the people. With each witness, and especially MacKay would draw out some evidence adding knowledge or insight into the background, the life, the tragedies that made both Lucas, and later, Turpin, individuals who were more complex, multi-dimensional, more human, less heinous.

By putting Lucas in the witness stand to testify on his own behalf, Ross MacKay not only had to deal with the history of crime that Lucas had lived, but he also knew that his client would be subject to devastating cross-examination by Henry Bull. The most significant fact for me was that MacKay was indicating that he believed his client, that Lucas was not present and did not kill Carter and his girlfriend. The cardinal rule for all defence counsel, all trial lawyers, is that you never put a witness on the stand knowing that that witness will commit perjury. You are first and foremost an officer of the court, and to knowingly allow perjury violates a most basic principle of our profession.

Turpin also testified at his trial. His evidence was that he shot Constable Nash in self-defence. Turpin had just robbed the

Red Rooster Restaurant when he was pulled over by Constable Nash. Nash was shot in the chest by Turpin, while Turpin was shot in both arms by Nash. Constable Nash left a wife and four young children. The public was outraged by his death. MacKay's attempts to have a change of venue were not successful before Justice Gale. That both Lucas and Turpin came from incredibly disadvantaged backgrounds as children comes as no surprise to anyone who has been involved in the criminal courts.

Arthur Lucas and Donald Turpin were hanged together at the Don Jail in Toronto on December 11, 1962. Throughout their time in prison as they awaited death, they were befriended by Brigadier Cyril Everitt, the steadfast chaplain of the Salvation Army. Everitt accompanied them to the execution chamber. He was present when they were hanged. Everitt believed that Arthur Lucas was innocent of the murders of Thurland Carter and Carol Ann Newman.

## Capital Punishment

Capital punishment remains a live issue in North America. Thirty-one of the fifty states in the United States still have the death penalty.

> *January 10, 2003 – 3:30 PM.*
> *CNN*
> *Gov. George Ryan of Illinois is making an announcement that in his final 48 hours as Governor, he is commuting all death sentences in his state. He recounts the sleepless nights for him and his staff over the years. He says he will sleep tonight.*

Gov. Ryan acknowledged that the machinery of the state with regard to the death penalty was flawed, broken. He had just commuted the death sentence for 157 doomed men. He was talking about giving victims' families more than just revenge.

"I have always found mercy bears richer fruits than most

other... "He is quoting Lincoln. And he referred to Nelson Mandela's encouragement of this position, setting an example. Earlier, when Ryan had been considering his position on those on death row in Illinois, he had received a telephone call from Nelson Mandela and later, Ryan met with Mandela at Mandela's home in South Africa. He referred to Mandela as "a towering figure of courage and tenacity and forgiveness."

I have always believed that it is wrong for anyone to kill, even — or especially — the state. That any level of risk is unacceptable in the event of a wrongful conviction and the death penalty. That even those who commit the most heinous acts are capable of redemption.

At the University of British Columbia, one of my courses was Russian Literature, favoured as an easy course. The professor at the beginning of the year told us to read, and at the end of the year, write a paper on our author of choice. Most wrote on Dostoyevsky. I chose Tolstoy, whose adherence to social reforms and non-violence against force I admired. He profoundly influenced Ghandi who called Tolstoy "the greatest apostle of non-violence..."

I don't recall religious discussions on capital punishment, even during those student years when I tortured my Protestant parents with boyfriends of the Roman Catholic persuasion and a UBC course on Thomas Aquinas.

There were certainly discussions of the death penalty at law school. Those are debates for every law student, I hope, world wide.

It was near the end of law school when I read *Attorney For The Damned*, which featured excerpts of many of the legendary American lawyer, Clarence Darrow's submissions to the courts on legal, political and social issues of the day. The first chapter of that book deals with his defence of Leopold and Loeb, the two young Illinois students who coldly planned and killed a fourteen-year-old to see what killing someone felt like.

Their wealthy families were able to hire the famous defence

counsel, sixty-seven-year-old Clarence Darrow. The three-week trial of Leopold and Loeb began in Chicago with a guilty plea, which meant no jury, just a judge alone; and for three weeks, Darrow spoke to sentence, arguing against the set–in–stone death penalty which existed in Illinois at that time, 1924.

Richard Loeb, eighteen, called Dickie, was the son of the wealthy vice-president of Sears, Roebuck and Company in Chicago. He was the youngest graduate of the University of Michigan, a brilliant student who was fascinated, obsessed, with crime and crime literature.

His best friend was nineteen-year-old Nathan Leopold Jr., nicknamed Babe, the son of a Chicago millionaire businessman. Also a brilliant student, he was the youngest graduate of the University of Chicago, deeply interested in ornithology, philosophy, and Nietzsche. He was fascinated and in love with Richard Loeb. Loeb wanted to commit the perfect crime, and Leopold had no trouble going along with the plan.

On May 21, 1924, the two young men kidnapped and murdered fourteen-year-old Bobby Franks. They sent notes to the family demanding ransom. Bobby was already dead. It was far from the perfect crime and the two students were caught quickly by the police, and confessed.

The crime achieved worldwide notoriety. As did the three-week sentencing trial. The prosecution and defence called many witnesses, including alienists, professionals we now know as psychiatrists. At the conclusion of the trial Darrow, in a twelve-hour submission to the judge, urged life imprisonment for both boys, rather than the death penalty.

On September 10, 1924, the Chief Justice of the Criminal Court of Cook County sentenced both young men to life in prison for the murder, and ninety-nine years for the kidnapping of Bobby Franks. They were both sent to Joliet penitentiary. Twelve years later, Loeb was killed in a prison razor fight. As Loeb lay dying in the prison hospital, Leopold was at his side.

Darrow had called the relationship between Leopold and Loeb "weird and almost impossible." Leopold was intimately and sexually drawn to Loeb, whom he wanted to please.

Accounts later suggest that Loeb did the actual killing of Bobby Franks, but he refused to acknowledge it publicly, in spite of pleas from Leopold.

Leopold became a model prisoner. He volunteered for medical experiments that were often performed on willing convicts hoping for earlier parole, and during his thirty-four years in prison, he continued his education. He taught others within the prison, learned foreign languages, was an x-ray technician in the prison hospital, and worked in the prison library.

On his release from prison in 1958, Leopold, by then fifty-three, moved to Puerto Rico. He continued his university education there, taught mathematics and worked in hospitals and some missionary outposts. He pursued his interests in ornithology and wrote *The Birds of Puerto Rico*. He became ill and died in 1971. According to some, Leopold felt continuing remorse, that he could never atone for the terrible wrong that he had done.

For me, their history confirmed the possibility of rehabilitation, the senseless barbarism of a death for a death. While Loeb appeared to take to prison life, Leopold began to better his world both within the prison and once he got out. Killing him would have served no point but revenge. The same with Loeb.

The ironic circle Gov. George Ryan set in motion that January day in 2003 in Illinois was completed in 2011 when the State of Illinois abolished the death penalty.

The death penalty is still present in a number of states in the United States, and the issue is still raised from time to time in Canada. No persons were hanged in Canada after Lucas and Turpin, although Parliament did not pass a bill to ban capital punishment until November 30, 1967. Those who were condemned to death in the meantime had their death sentences commuted.

I do not believe that monsters are born as such, but that they become that way through circumstances. Some persons we, as a society, destroy when they are small children; there are some who cannot ever be allowed to live free in our society again, such as Olson, Pickton, Bernardo. Killing them would be cheaper, easier, and satisfy the human urge for revenge. It would also mark us as a different society, where revenge ruled over our belief in our basic goodness and the rule of law.

Revenge is much overrated.

When the weary and dedicated Israeli Prime Minister Yitzhak Rabin was assassinated November 4, 1995 by the fanatic young Jewish law student, Rabin's wife Leah was asked what her thoughts were about the killer; in effect, what fate should there be for him?

She replied she gave him no thought. He did not matter. What did matter was the life work of her husband, his goals. He had fought for peace in the Middle East.

I would not have been able to serve as a Supreme Court judge if the death penalty still existed in Canada, where I might have had the duty to sentence a person to be hanged. That Canada abolished the death penalty marks it as a truly civilized country.


In some ways, Ross MacKay may have been a victim of the death penalty. Jack Batten, the lawyer turned journalist who knew MacKay from early school days, has written about his friend. Batten set out the brilliance and the tragedy that was Ross MacKay. MacKay was an alcoholic, beginning at an early age. His drinking had been a serious problem for two or three years after he was called to the bar, but by the early sixties, he was establishing his own criminal practice. And that is when he was referred by one of his friends to act for Arthur Lucas. At twenty-nine, he was young, but skilled.

MacKay was apparently deeply affected by those two trials, by those two verdicts, those two hangings. His life spiraled again, until several years later, when he joined Alcoholics Anonymous. Robert Hoshowsky, a journalist, wrote *The Last To Die*, published in 2007 by Dundurn Press. It is an account of the Lucas and Turpin trials, fascinating and well researched, a book to which I am indebted. It brought back memories and filled in gaps of the two trials.

One of my favourite lines in Hoshowsky's book comes from MacKay's daughter, Alison MacKay, who followed her father into law and is now a judge of the Ontario Court of Justice. She is quoted as saying, "A lot of the older fellows have this phrase: 'Who are the two best criminal lawyers in the country? Ross MacKay drunk and Ross MacKay sober.'"

I had been practising in Niagara Falls for about three years when I saw Ross MacKay one last time. It was in Provincial Court in Niagara Falls. He came into court with two well-dressed thugs, to fix a date for trial. His clients were known mobsters, and their verbal abuse toward MacKay was appalling. I hardly recognized MacKay. Unaware of his personal history, I was shocked to see the dissipation so evident on his face. He addressed the court briefly, with the same respect and courtesy, but the man in the Niagara courtroom that day was so different from the lawyer I had watched three years previously. Capital punishment leaves many victims in its wake.

MacKay in the courtroom was clearly a role model for me. His preparation was evident. He did not have to refer to notes when he examined or cross-examined. He had done the work, it was in his head. His courtroom manner was impeccable. He was praised at the end of each trial by both those tough judges. Also by Henry Bull, the hard-nosed prosecutor. More than anything, his treatment of his clients was exemplary, two men who were despised by everyone. MacKay brought passion and compassion and a sense of justice to each case and the importance of the issues before the court.

Those trials changed the course of my career. I was going to be a trial lawyer.

# CHAPTER 16

## *My First Court Case*

**M**Y FIRST COURT CASE was early in my articles. Your law firm trots you out as cheap labour in a small claims case for a valued client. They know you will prepare as if for the Supreme Court of Canada. They forget to tell you that you will be so busy nervously visiting the bathroom in the courthouse that your client may not be able to find you.

The scene was the small grubby Small Claims Court in Toronto. It was a landlord and tenant dispute, with our client, the landlord, claiming $75, one month's rent, from a middle-aged tenant. The judge was an older man, close to retirement.

Our case was called just before the lunch break, at ten to one. My client and I had watched the parade of cases being sped through the court all morning. The judge seemed ready for some bran or prunes.

As plaintiff, we went first and I called my only witness, our quiet client from Kitchener. He began to tell the court of the landlord/tenant relationship, and the failure of the defendant to pay the one month's rent.

Suddenly, the defendant, representing himself, leapt to his feet, jabbed his finger at my client in the witness box and yelled, "You're lying!"

"Siddown, Mr. Rose. You'll have your chance to tell me your story." The judge was weary.

My client continued. Another interruption.

"That's not true, you're lying!!" The defendant was up, screaming and pointing for the second time.

"Mr. Rose! Siddown! Be quiet. Your turn will come. Don't let me have to warn you again." The judge nodded for my client to continue.

The landlord was losing his courage. No one had told him court was going to be like this. Hah. No one had told me either. All my preparation, burrowing into the law books, preparing my client for testifying — had not conditioned us for this. My client continued, speaking carefully.

The horror show on my right leaped up for a third time and shouted, his right arm and fingers jabbing toward my client like a prize fighter. "I don't have to listen to this! He's a liar!!"

"Mr. Rose! I will not tell you this again! Siddown!! You hear me? If there is one more interruption from you I will have the bailiffs jail you for contempt of court. Do you understand? Siddown."

"Continue," the judge commanded me. My heart was pounding. My client took up the tale again. But before he could finish, Mr. Rose leaped up and bellowed out one more time.

The judge snapped.

"Bailiffs!" he screamed. "Arrest this man. Put him in the cells!" Then, glaring at me, the judge yelled, "Case dismissed. Court is adjourned." He swept from his chair and left the courtroom.

Mr. Rose was being dragged backwards out of the courtroom by two large uniformed bailiffs. Others left the courtroom, and I was left staring at my client who was still standing in the witness box.

"What happened?" he asked.

"I don't know. How can he dismiss our case?" I said.

It was time to get help. The men of my law firm lunched at their favourite restaurant and I knew I would find most of them there. Arranging to meet my client later, I sought out my lawyers.

They were having lunch at the Savarin, and were expecting the report of my first trial. I rushed in and told them of the scene in the courtroom. They exploded with laughter.

Phil Isbister, a tall, urbane litigator with a great sense of humour, said, "Nancy, you are too tough. You're not supposed to put the opposition in jail in a civil case." More laughter.

Then Phil got up and said that he had better call old Fred, musing, amidst the laughter, that Fred must be having a bad day.

Phil came back to report that the judge would resume hearing my case at 2:30. I declined lunch and my lawyers wished me well as they chuckled their way into dessert.

A subdued Mr. Rose was brought up from the cells, and sat perfectly still while my client finished telling his side. The judge then invited Mr. Rose to come into the witness stand and tell his side of it, which he did, politely. I have no recollection of cross-examining him.

The judge found in our favour. I had won my first case.

# CHAPTER 17

# *My Job Hunt*

S OME IN MY GENERATION have been heard to say, "Jobs were so easy to get when we left university. There were lots of jobs." One classmate recently said, "Having a law degree was like having a licence to print money." Those were not women talking, believe me.

"Lots of jobs" was true in 1963 — provided you were a white male. For the rest of us, it was a very different picture in the sixties and seventies.

After twelve months articling, and nearing the completion of the six-month Bar Admission Course, I began looking in Toronto for a job. My aim was a firm that did litigation. The rejections were piling up.

The head of the Bar Admission Course advised me to seek out the (few) women lawyers, who were doing real estate law mainly, to see if one of them would hire me. He meant well. He also suggested that I use only my initials rather than my first name in my future practice and letterhead, so firms and individuals would not know they were dealing with a female lawyer. He didn't advise what to do when the appalling truth would be revealed.

## Charles Dubin

Set on a career in litigation now, I applied for a job with Charles Dubin. I knew Dubin did some interesting labour work as well as general litigation. I also knew his wife, Anne, a bright lawyer, worked in his office.

Charles Dubin in his later years became one of the most respected jurists in our country, a Chief Justice of Ontario, and before that, one of the pre-eminent counsel in Canada. He showed that promise early in his career, and had already earned an excellent reputation by the time I was job hunting in 1963.

Mr. Dubin received me courteously, but when he realized

that I wanted a job there as a lawyer and not a secretary, he immediately shook his head, and said he would never hire me. His clients would not accept a girl. I don't recall all his words, with the exception of the following: when I told him one of the reasons I had come to him was litigation, and also that I knew his wife was a lawyer and worked there, and that I thought he might feel differently, Dubin looked at me and said, slowly and deliberately, with a look that conveyed how little I really understood the world, "She-just-does-research."

### Barrie

Charles Dubin was a prince compared to the boys in Barrie. With Toronto law firms not inclined to hire me, I began responding to ads in smaller cities in Ontario. One advertisement in *The Ontario Reports*, which went to all members of the Ontario bar, was from a small firm in Barrie, just north of Toronto, for a recent graduate lawyer interested in doing general law, with an emphasis on litigation.

That ad looked promising, and as few of my classmates wanted to leave the big cities, I thought my chances were good. As a bonus, Barrie was close to ski country. I called one of the two partners, Charlie Seagram, and offered to drive up for an interview. Seagram said he would be in Toronto that Saturday and arranged to interview me at ten o'clock that Saturday morning in Toronto. He said he would call when he arrived in the city, to tell me where to meet him.

There was no call. I waited all day for his phone call, not daring to step out for even a moment. I tried calling his office in Barrie later in the day when I had not heard from him, but the office was closed.

Maybe I'd made a mistake. Had he meant Sunday? So I waited in all day Sunday, and tried calling the office in Barrie again, with the same negative results. My friends had gone skiing at Collingwood for the weekend, but I had stayed in the city for this important job interview.

On Monday morning, I phoned Mr. Seagram at his office in Barrie. Had I misunderstood about the interview? No, he replied.

He had been in Toronto on Saturday, but he and his partner had talked it over, and they did not feel a female would be suitable. No, he had not tried to call and tell me that.

The following month, in the next edition of *The Ontario Reports,* the same ad from the Barrie law firm appeared, with two additional words, in parentheses : ("Male Only") I felt sick.

It wasn't just the lack of opportunity for women in the law profession, it was the pervasive lack of respect for females, bordering on contempt. The message: you don't belong. The echo from my first day in law school. You won't make it anyway.

# CHAPTER 18

# *Judy and a Job*

T HE JOB HUNT was beginning to get a little frantic. I could always go back and practice with Dad in Yorkton, but that would mean articling again. Going back home would also mean defeat, that I could not get a law firm willing to hire me, only my Dad. And who knew which foot Mom would use to boot me out of town again.

My male classmates were all talking about their new jobs; I dreaded every time anyone asked me where I was going to be working. I was too embarrassed to tell anyone about all the offices where I had been shown the door, the interviews I had been refused; the phone calls, letters and resumes that went unanswered. I would murmur about a couple of irons in the fire. In fact, I did not have a marshmallow at the end of a willow stick.

Carol Mahood, (now retired Justice Carol Huddart) a law student a year behind me, mentioned that a lawyer named Judy LaMarsh was looking for a junior associate for her law office in Niagara Falls. Judy was a Liberal backbencher, the Member of Parliament for Niagara Falls in the opposition at that time in Ottawa. More important, she enjoyed a rare and excellent reputation as a trial lawyer, particularly in criminal cases. Perhaps she might need someone to cover for her in court the occasional time. It was worth a phone call.

My call from the law school payphone reached her secretary in Niagara Falls. When the secretary heard I was interested in possibly coming to practice in Niagara Falls, she gave me a number in Welland where I could reach Judy. I dialed the number, asked for Judy, and waited for a time until she came on the line.

I told her I heard she might be looking for a junior lawyer, and I was about to be called to the bar.

"You got me out of the middle of a rape trial to ask me for a job?" yelled the soon-to-be-famous voice. Yes, I quavered back, having had no idea she was in the middle of a trial.

Her temper cooled, and we arranged a one-hour early morning meeting a couple of weeks later in a hotel north of Toronto. Judy was still campaigning tirelessly across the country prior to the April 1963 federal election. After that one-hour interview, I had the job. Two things had cinched it. I was the only applicant, and Judy was desperate for help in her office. She had also done a background check on me and found that my Dad was then head of the Saskatchewan Law Society. She later said she felt we came from similar backgrounds, which added to her trust in me.

She also could not believe that anyone would get up at six in the morning to get to an eight a.m. breakfast meeting north of Toronto. She was a nighthawk. I am a morning person.

That was late February 1963. Around that time, Judy was involved in the Truth Squad, where she, journalist, Jack McBeth, and an economist, Fred Belair, were assigned by the Rainmaker of Liberal party politics, Keith Davey, to follow John Diefenbaker around to his speeches and point out the error of his sometimes stretch-the-truth ways.

Few were better than Prime Minister Diefenbaker when it came to handling hecklers, and he turned the tables on the Truth Squad more than once. Judy did not have wide national recognition at this time, but thanks to the Truth Squad, that was remedied. I remember one awful picture of Judy on the front page of *The Globe and Mail* shortly before I was to join her in Niagara. It was an upfront and in-your-face shot of Judy yelling her way out of an auditorium in Halifax. Good grief. This was my new boss?

# CHAPTER 19

# *Reality*

REALITY SET IN quickly after that first day in Judy's office. With no warning or preparation I had a busy law office to run, trials to prepare, solicitor work to do, solo. The comprehensive six-month Bar Admission Course we took after articling proved invaluable.

I also had help from many unexpected sources: from Lois Booth, the calm and experienced secretary; from Charlotte Penny, who ran her own business as a conveyancing researcher, knowledgable and popular with all of the law offices in the area who used her services; the other lawyers in town who never failed to make time for a call from me; and patient court staff, all earning my undying gratitude.

One darling older man, a veteran of the war, who was a court officer in Welland, came up to me during an early break in the first Supreme Court trial I did in Welland, to say," You are doing a very good job. Now you must keep your voice up so everyone in the courtroom can hear you clearly." May every new lawyer have such kind and wise advice.

Judy's office overdraft of $12,000 posed an unforeseen problem for me. In that turbulent first week, Lois had shared her worries of the bank cutting off credit for the office; that she feared each week her pay cheque would bounce.

She joked I should practice what she did when she was entering the bank — pretend to be just leaving, so the manager would know it was too late to stop cashing our pay cheques.

Her worries became mine. It was obvious I could never add to that debt. The office had to carry itself. And it eventually did. In just over a year, the overdraft was paid off. The bank manager was impressed; Judy seemed to take it for granted. We never talked about the office finances. No doubt because it was painful for Judy.

Judy was not very good when it came to her own finances.

She was a prodigious worker, but also a spender, usually in debt, and impatient when faced with financial realities.

I had bargained hard with Judy that first Sunday over my own salary.

Judy: "How much should I pay you?"

Nancy: "I don't know."

Judy: "I think Charlie was getting around $100 a week."

Nancy: "That sounds fine."

(Every street kiosk vendor in the Middle East and Asia dreams of me as a customer.)

That was $5,200 a year. That beat my articling wage of $35 a week.

My self-interest bargaining skills were deficient, but not my awareness of money and frugality. I had been a saver since grade school. If Moira or I put any money we received as a gift from an uncle or godmother at Christmas or birthday into our bank account, Dad would match that amount in the bank. I liked that, and banked most of the money that I received. Our Scottish father giving us an early awareness of banks and saving.

Judy had a lively and varied clientele. There was money in trust for future civil and criminal cases, with significantly more money in trust for estates that were ongoing, and real estate transactions. Once these files were completed, we did the bill and received payment either from the trust account or directly from the client.

It was more than gratifying to see a bill go out and the money come in. But I soon realized I was deceiving myself by looking at the gross amount of the bill. Only the net amount, our actual legal fees, what was left after payment of all expenses, would count to pay the overhead, Lois, me and that overdraft.

There was no joy for me in mathematics or accounting. But my Dick and Jane versions were quick and made sense. I began writing four columns in the back pages of my office diary after a bill was sent out: the name of the client, the amount of our actual fees, the disbursements, and the total of the bill.

Then I knew how much I needed to bring in to the office each month to pay expenses and salaries; not just bill out, but actually collect. As the end of the month would near, I would do a quick calculation on the 'fees' column. Was it time to work hard on that estate right now, and send out a bill where we had money in trust, or will we be okay for this month, and that estate could be worked on next month?

When I was working in Yorkton with Dad in later years, he asked what I was noting in my diary one day. He, who kept his eye and hand on everything, and was a born numbers man, thought my rudimentary accounting was great. He chuckled his way out of my office, murmuring that he wished some of the other young lawyers who had been practising with him previously had adopted a similar procedure.

# CHAPTER 20

# *LaMarsh and the Canada Pension Plan*

A T THE AGE OF THIRTY-EIGHT, as Minister of Health and Welfare with the huge portfolio that included the Canada Pension Plan, Judy was making history. She was Canada's second only female federal cabinet minister. The first had been Ellen Fairclough, appointed by John Diefenbaker's prior Conservative government in 1957 as Secretary of State and later as Minister of Citizenship and Immigration. In 1963, Judy's first portfolio was all-encompassing, complex and life changing for Canadians. She was quickly mastering the proposed Canada Pension Plan, actuaries, life expectancies, and funding.

I seldom discussed any office or client problems or issues with Judy. It was clear she had moved on to a much more demanding stage of her career. But she was always open to calls from me and there were occasions, especially in the first six months of practice, when I did call Judy to seek advice.

One time in the first few weeks was when a slight young man came in wanting to lay assault charges against a police officer. The client was a novice realtor, who had just joined a local real estate firm. He was in his new office in the evening, keen to go over files. A senior sergeant of the Niagara City Police force, Don Harris, driving by, noticed lights on in an office usually dark that time of day. Going up into the office, Harris demanded to know what the young man was doing there. My client, somewhat cocky, did not give a satisfactory answer to Harris. The young man found himself quickly grabbed and thrown up against a metal filing cabinet and held there while Harris coaxed a more appropriate answer from him.

From my client's telling, I believed it was a common assault, an offence under the *Criminal Code of Canada*. All first year law students knew that it was an assault to apply force intentionally to another without that person's consent. The young realtor was incensed and wanted the officer charged. This sergeant, as I soon found out, was well-known and respected. Also very tough.

I was not quite sure what route to take, as I suspected the police would probably not lay a criminal charge of common assault against one of their own. Judy's advice was to initiate a complaint under the *Police Act*, which I did.

My client and I appeared before the police commission, where Sergeant Harris, a tall, imposing officer, gave evidence, as did my client. The commission decided in favour of Sgt. Harris, dismissing our complaint. At the end of the hearing, Sgt. Harris came and spoke to me. "You will be doing a lot of criminal cases, I assume." I nodded. He looked down at me for a long moment and said, "You might find you have trouble getting particulars from the police from time to time." Another long look at me. "If that ever happens, give me a call."

Judy frequently came back to her riding of Niagara Falls. Most of her time was taken with constituency matters, but we usually managed a dinner. Clarkson House in Lewiston, New York, just over the bridge into the United States, was her favourite restaurant, and soon mine. Steak and lobster at their finest. One or two double martinis for Judy would begin the dinner. I was the designated driver.

During her visits, Judy was consumed with the upcoming CPP legislation, which she eventually shepherded through the House of Commons. It is said to be the most complex piece of legislation ever passed in Canada. Judy talked of endless meetings with actuaries, contribution levels, cost of living complications, longevity predictions, etc. I grew to dread the topic, the very mention of the CPP. Today I think, how ungrateful could I be, as I cash my CPP cheque.

We never discussed clients' problems in the practice. Judy never asked. And it would have taken more courage than I had to interrupt that flow of Ottawa/CPP/government dissemination.

This is not to suggest Judy was not good company. She was amazing. Funny, smart, generous to a fault, always interesting. She drew people to her like a magnet, especially small children. Dinners with Judy remain vivid for me, whether in Ottawa, Hull,

Niagara Falls, or Lewiston, New York. She loved the staff, they loved her. The martinis flowed, as did the rum and coke. Or the wine. At Lewiston, always the double lobster feast. "While you are eating your first, we are preparing your second."

You could not invent a better dinner companion. She teased you, laughed at your jokes, assumed you were as interested in every subject, domestic or international, as she was. Her interests and knowledge were encyclopedic. But there were also times when you felt protective towards Judy. She did not have a thick skin. There were many times when her emotions were raw and she was being kicked around in Ottawa. Her book *Memoir of A Bird In a Gilded Cage*, written after she left politics, said it all. It was not easy being a woman in Ottawa in those times.

# CHAPTER 21

# *The Clients*

IN HINDSIGHT, that first day as a lawyer dealing with panicked and angry clients provided insight into what a client needs and expects from his or her lawyer, in addition to skill and knowledge of the law — honesty and availability.

Dad was always available to clients. He took calls at home regularly with equanimity and grace.

In dealing with clients I found myself thinking of Mother's oft-cited Golden Rule, "Do unto others as you would have them do unto you." I figured if I were the client, I would want to be able to contact my lawyer if some urgency arose, to know that my file duplicated her office file, and to be kept up to date. Throughout my years of practice, my clients always had my home phone number, and knew where I could be reached on vacation. Clients seldom contacted me at home, but they knew they could.

I liked my clients, some more than others. That was a bonus.

## The Women

Wedged between the criminal and civil trials was constant real estate and estate work. The solicitor work could not have been done without Lois, an experienced paralegal secretary, and Charlotte Penny, my instant new friend, the entrepreneurial title researcher who helped guide me through the intricacies of the archaic land titles system in southern Ontario. We became roommates, until she married Bob Lewis, her lifelong partner.

Into that mix came the women clients and family law. During law school, I had made two resolves. I would never be in the courtroom (not a place for women) and I would never practice family law. It was apparent in law school that family law was the lowest form of life in the legal world, fit only for social workers. It was not real law. Nor was it lucrative. That last point had a lot to do with what was considered real law.

Watching those two murder trials during my articling had changed my attitude on women in court. Those first months of practice in Niagara, women clients in family law cases, changed my view of family law and the focus of my politics. Family law and the need for reform became, and has remained, a cause, verging on crusade.

They came alone, almost always, often in secrecy, some clutching money earned covertly over months and years. They knew you had to pay to see a lawyer. Their life stories were like never-ending punches. It soon became apparent they were coming to a lawyer who was female. I had no idea women were being treated in such ways, no idea our society and laws were so rigged against females, especially married women.

I did not discuss these clients with anyone. My classmates were in other cities and not in a practice like mine. One of my classmates who did family law in a large big city firm said recently, "I never saw those women." Solicitor client privilege meant you did not discuss your clients with others. Dad never spoke of his clients or cases at home.

These women clients were my responsibility. Decades later, they still are. They are part of the reason I have written this book.

Their lives told me how wrong and unfair our laws were for so many women, what few resources and rights married women had at that time. How unprepared so many women were if disaster struck their lives, should their husbands become ill, unemployed, or die suddenly, or desert them and the children, or beat her and/or the children, or leave them with no assets or maintenance and nowhere to turn. Legal Aid was new and did not exist for family law clients; there were no transition houses for battered women and children.

Men were raised to know it was important to have an education, and to keep their employment options open. That was not a mindset for girls and women in the early 1960s.

### Forty-five and Out of Luck

They had been high school sweethearts. She was now forty-five, he forty-eight. They had been married for twenty-five years, and had four fine children, two still in high school, the other two in university.

It had been a wonderful marriage and life. Or so she thought. He had done well at university and then in business. She was a stay-at-home mom, devoted to her husband and children. Then the roof fell in. He announced he wanted a divorce. He was in love with his twenty-five-year-old secretary, whom he intended to marry.

"What did I do wrong? It must be my fault. I thought we were happy; but he wasn't. What do I do now?"

My new client was slender, attractive, well-dressed, well spoken and devastated. She was still in shock over her husband's bombshell. What I viewed as his betrayal, she viewed as her own shortcomings.

She had been looking forward to more time at their Muskoka cottage with her husband once all four children were independent, and to the joys of eventual grandchildren.

He was planning a new life with a beautiful young wife.

Again, she asked, "Where have I gone wrong?"

Our course in family law at Osgoode had not prepared me for this. The gentle Professor Baxter had laid out family law with precision. But his course was not dispensed with any indication or indignation over gender inequality.

This was 1963 and the law was clear. To obtain a divorce in Canada, you had to prove your spouse had committed adultery. There were no other grounds. (Except in Nova Scotia, where cruelty was also grounds for divorce.) If a husband beat his wife for years, she had no way to obtain a divorce, and in those years, nowhere to go.

If a woman was to live "separate and apart" from her husband, she could be entitled to maintenance, but only if she remained 'chaste.' If the husband could show that the wife had committed adultery, even just one act of sexual intercourse with someone other than him, she could be disentitled to maintenance for herself, unless the parties had a separation agreement that stated otherwise. But those agreements were never negotiated from positions of equal strength and bargaining power.

This client had done nothing wrong, except lose a race she did not know she was in, to a younger trophy filly. It was not a case of physical cruelty either. The emotional smack-down by her husband was nothing compared to the beating the law was about to give her. She was entitled to no assets because nothing was in her name.

The asset picture was devastating for women in those years. Here is where the dry facts in cases cited in law school met the reality of the sobbing woman across the desk.

This couple had a lot of assets. No. That is incorrect. The husband had a lot of assets; the wife had none. Everything was in his name: the house, the lovely property and boats at Lake Muskoka, the two cars, the stocks, bonds and bank accounts. He had always looked after the finances. She took care of him, his business entertaining, the four children and both homes.

For two years after high school and before marriage, she had worked as a sales clerk, but after marriage, had never worked outside the home. Or, as it was put in those years, "She had never worked."

She was the first of so many women around the same age to come to the office with the same story. The husband was always around the age of fifty. It became predictable. The male menopause manifesting itself, and the woman blaming herself for failure to maintain the marriage.

Regardless of where the blame might lie for the failure of the marriage — and it was never black and white — what so appalled me was the unfairness to the wife, the total lack of justice that saw the woman dumped with few, if any, assets and tenuous rights to maintenance. She had no education, training or job possibilities to take her to the next stages of her life, to ensure her financial security. She had spent her life embracing and enhancing her husband's career. Her career as a housewife did not count at law or in any future workplace. Her résumé read, 'No experience.'

In trying to obtain a separation agreement, you scored a victory for your female client if you could get the husband and his lawyer to agree to let her stay in the home for a period of time and to reasonable terms of maintenance for herself and the children; and to agree to the *femme sole* clause. That meant the husband gave his wife the permission to live as if she were a single woman, and not his wife. Transferring assets to the wife was his to give, not hers to demand. They were his assets.

It was not a win for a wife if the *dum casta* clause was in the separation agreement. *Dum casta* was short for *dum sola et casta vixerit* — while she remains single and chaste. That meant she had to be and remain celibate, or lose her maintenance, and possibly more, including custody of and maintenance for the children. There were no such restrictions on the husband's behaviour.

The separation agreements we drew up often turned out to be worthless if the husband took off, or simply refused to pay the agreed monthly maintenance. For each month of a missed payment, the wife, alone or aided by her frustrated lawyer, would have to sue for that one month's amount in Small Claims Court, and then try and collect with a court order. It was costly in time and trauma for the client, chilling for me to realize how few women could even afford a lawyer to help in the process.

If maintenance was to be paid to the wife before the divorce was granted at trial, it was (and still is) referred to as interim maintenance. The law had a miserable regard for any woman on maintenance after a separation but before a divorce. Well into the 1970s, the courts confirmed the view, held for years, that the wife, living separate and apart from her husband, must not only be 'chaste', but also "live in modesty and retirement until the trial, bearing in mind her station in life and her husband's ability to pay."

The criteria was never the lifestyle enjoyed by the couple before separation, or her so-called station in life, or even the husband's income. The emphasis was on the sexual purity of the woman's behaviour, and the insistence that she live modestly "and in retirement."

In 1974, the Ontario Court of Appeal reaffirmed again in *Hayward v. Hayward* (1974) that the amount of such interim maintenance should be enough to enable a wife to live in comfort, but not in luxury. There was never any yardstick on the husband's lifestyle. This approach was still being taken in 2000 in a Yukon decision dealing with interim spousal support.

Family law formed only a part of the law practice. I, who had sworn never to do family law, could not say no to these clients.

As if some of these husbands and the law weren't giving women enough grief, into my office one day came this swine of a father. He wanted his will drawn up. His estate would be sizable.

He was land rich and cash rich, educated and a leader in the community. He had four sons and three daughters. His instructions were simple. All his estate upon his death was to be divided equally among the four sons. Period.

"What about your daughters?"

"What about them?"

"Well, shouldn't they sharing in your estate as well?"

"No. They will get married and their husbands will look after them. Not me. My estate goes to my sons."

"What if the girls do not marry? What if their marriages fail? What if something happens to one of them and they need help? Are you being fair to your daughters?"

He went to another lawyer.

I became a feminist in those first few months of practising law in 1963. There was no popularized term of feminist or women's lib then. When the terms became widely used later, I could not deny the label.

# CHAPTER 22

# *A Fawn*

HER MEMORIES were half-filled with dreams of bright lights, strangers, and never being able to grasp what was reality. She was on a bed, immobilized, but she was unsure where she really was. Her splintered images of sex with unknown men were too depraved for her to detail, to even say out loud, too unreal to believe. Her husband ridiculed her fears, denied everything, and told her she was crazy, mentally ill. He could have her committed.

She was twenty-one, blonde, gentle and very beautiful. She was like a frightened fawn. Married very young, with no children and no family to fall back on, she was terrified of her husband and his friends. Without a job or money, she was trying to find a way to get out of her situation. She did not know what rights she had under the law.

"I think my husband is drugging me. And then filming me. On our bed, on other beds. Having sex — with strangers."

This was 1963, nine years before *Deep Throat*; porn movies existed, but in their own secretive and vicious subculture.

She had travelled from a town north of Toronto to Niagara Falls to see a female lawyer — a lawyer far enough from where she lived so no one would know.

I believed her. She had come a long way to seek legal advice, to tell a stranger such things. She had thought of reporting her husband to the police, but she was terrified of his reprisals and his friends, and his power over her. She also knew he had friends who were police. She feared she would be killed.

She wanted legal advice. Divorce? Only if she could prove he had committed adultery. Property? There was nothing in her name. Maintenance? Only if she could prove that he had deserted her or caused her to leave for compelling reasons that she would have to prove. Without proof, her chances were slim. As for criminal assault charges, there was no proof, only her word, and she was too terrified of him and what he would do to her. Who would believe her?

I tried to encourage her to go to the Niagara Police, who would be obliged to investigate and could offer her some protection. But she believed her husband was too well connected, especially with the police. He had too many friends in the right and wrong places.

Her despair deepened. I knew she would never be able to report her husband to the police. She left my office feeling hopeless, I know, and I was feeling helpless. She never returned. I have no idea what happened to her. She haunts me.

# CHAPTER 23

# *Domestic Violence*

DOMESTIC VIOLENCE takes many forms and has many faces. A woman came into my office and I understood why she sought out a female lawyer. She showed me some of the results of her beatings on her upper body, but could only describe her injuries below her waist.

Her husband was intelligent, educated, controlling and vicious. He used his wife as his punching bag and personal sexual property. She had never called the police because he had spelled out what would happen to her and the children if she "put him in jail." No job, no home, no money, and he would get even. Besides, he assured her, no one would believe her anyway. Her friends and family all believed she had a wonderful marriage; handsome husband with a good job; she was living the comfortable life. Except it was a nightmare of hidden domestic violence.

Finally afraid that his next beating might kill her, she found the courage to tell her family and to separate from him.

My new client was attractive beneath her bruised and swollen face. One eye was blackening and half shut. She wept as she took the scarf from over her head. Her husband had yanked clumps of her hair out by the roots. She had three raw almost bald spots, each the size of a quarter.

I was shocked to tears. Then she undid some buttons on her blouse to show me the black and blue welts on her breasts. Her body was bruised in so many places, she said, old and new bruises. She had not seen a doctor.

She felt such shame being subjected to this abuse for so long; she had told no one. Her husband's threats ensured she would never go to the police, because it would be "her fault" if he ended up in jail. So she refused to bring a charge of assault occasioning bodily harm under the *Criminal Code* against him. But she was prepared to bring a civil assault case against him, and seek monetary damages, in addition to her claim for maintenance for herself and the children. And yes, all their assets were in his name.

The trial in family court to hear the maintenance and assault claims was set. She was afraid to testify. At our pre-trial meetings she had assured me she would not back down at the last minute, as many such abused women do, under intense pressure from many sides. On the day of the trial, she arrived at the courthouse looking rested, attractive, much less apprehensive.

In our previous sessions, I had gone over what questions I would be asking, and what she could reasonably expect her husband's lawyer to ask. She need only tell the truth to the judge.

I began to question her, the easy questions at first, to try and get her comfortable in the witness box: name, address, age, education, date of marriage, children, etc. Then I came to the date of that last beating that caused her to leave her husband. I asked her to tell the court what happened.

She was very relaxed, serene, in fact. She said they'd had a quarrel and he had hit her. I asked her to be more specific. I needed the details of the beating, where he had struck her, with what, with what force, resulting in what injuries. But the rules of evidence prevented me from suggesting any specific answers to her to elicit those details. My questions were circling those details, to which she just kept saying they had a fight and she decided to leave him. I kept coaxing her to provide details, but defence counsel was on his feet objecting.

All my client would do was repeat that there had been a quarrel, and he hit her. In desperation, I was asking the forbidden leading questions, and defence counsel kept leaping up and barking his objections. The judge was frowning his warnings at me.

My client remained serene, but she provided no details of the beating, the force, the resulting injuries. She remained calm through the brief cross-examination. Defence counsel knew the case to establish an assault had not been made. My client had refused to see a doctor, so I had no medical evidence. She had refused to go to the police, so we had no evidence from that source, and I was too inexperienced to ensure the injuries had been documented with photographs.

The judge ruled there was insufficient evidence to establish an assault. The claim for maintenance was more successful. My client smiled in relief as we left the courtroom.

Outside in the hall, I asked her, "What is wrong? Why didn't you tell the judge what you told me, about the terrible beating your husband gave you?"

Out it came. She had finally gone to see a doctor, a week before the trial, she was so terrified of giving evidence against her husband. The doctor had given her a prescription for pills to calm her anxiety. She was to take one pill each morning. If the anxiety was still there in the evening, another pill before going to sleep. She told me the pills had a marvelous effect on her. So she had taken two pills the night before the trial, and two more pills that morning.

She wasn't serene. She was medicated out of her mind, "circling Planet Zylon," as my friend Alison MacLennan would say.

That was an early lesson for me, and her experience helped in preparing many clients and witnesses in the years to come. To caution them about the folly of any drug-induced state. That judges expect witnesses to be nervous, even crying was all right, natural with many people. ( Okay, we love it when the bully of an opposing counsel makes our client cry on the stand...)

The stories of these early female clients turned my comfy middle-class world on its tail. Women who were called a "no good, stupid fucking bitch" every day began to believe it. It was many clients and moons later before I appreciated the deep and terrible false shame that battered women so often feel. And how seldom they tell anyone of their beatings and abuse.

My speeches to women's groups moved far beyond wills and estates. It was impossible not to question the fairness of marriage itself, the lack of opportunity for women to keep their options open, to education and training; the urgent need for establishing safety nets and social programs for battered spouses and children; programs ranging from legal aid, transition houses, education opportunities and universal childcare are still not truly recognized.

"I don't understand why those women who are getting beat

up don't just leave." If only it were that simple. Then, there was no money and nowhere for them to go. Even now, it depends where they live, what facilities are available. There were and are added barriers for women isolated on farms, ranches or reserves. The social isolation imposed by a battering, controlling spouse in a city is just as daunting.

Whether it is domestic violence in an urban or rural setting, some of the questions are: Does the woman have money or assets of her own? Are there children? How old are the children? How many? Are there any disabilities? Who would look after the children? Where would she live? Does she drive a car, let alone have access to one? Does she speak English? Does she have the education or training to find work? Can she afford a lawyer? Or qualify for legal aid? Should she trust the safety of herself and the children to a piece of paper called a Restraining Order?

When I began practising law, there was nowhere for these women to go, unless family help was available. Too often, religious counselling urged obedience to the husband, stressing reconciliation, return to the abusive spouse and acceptance by the wife. Domestic and family violence was a tragedy hiding in full view. It still is.

The 1970 *Report of the Royal Commission on the Status of Women* was the culmination of three and half years of public hearings across Canada, hundreds of private letters and submissions, briefs and studies. In spite of the exhaustive consultations with women and groups, not one hint of domestic violence can be found within the final *Report*. Not one word to suggest women or children were being physically and/or sexually assaulted or subjected to other forms of violence. Incest is never mentioned. This hidden 'shame' and reality of so many women was not on the radar in 1970. The victims were silent. Many still are.

Domestic violence cuts across all social and economic, ethnic and racial lines. It can be violence by men against women, men against men, women against men, women against women, and worst of all, against children. It includes the crimes of rape, incest, sexual and physical assaults, and the battered spouse and battered child syndromes.

No country or society can claim to have conquered or even lessened domestic violence in any appreciable way. It is a global problem. The seeds of domestic violence were sown centuries ago, in most cultures, in the interpretations of some religions and some ethnic populations. It is rooted in the historical subjugation of women and children. Domestic violence is further fueled by many factors — war, alcohol and drug abuse, the cycle within a family where a battered child becomes a battering parent.

In 1972, Mary Van Stolk wrote a slim volume, *The Battered Child in Canada*. It detailed the shocking extent of intentional injury and even killing of children in this country, usually by parents or caregivers. She referred to the Battered Child Syndrome where a child's injuries run from bites, bruises, broken bones, skull and rib fractures, a result of the child being hit, twisted, thrown or deliberately knocked about. Van Stolk asserted that often those who batter children were physically and/or emotionally abused themselves as children.

"Children learn from the behaviour they witness." She writes, "Battered and abused children will be the abusive parents of the future...."

It is a cycle we see in our courts.

*The Battered Wife Syndrome* also became recognized around the 1960s. A controlling, physically abusive husband inflicting injuries on his wife, and again, a range of injuries that shock the conscience.

I see little change in the amount of domestic violence from the beginning days of my practice, decades ago. There have been changes to provide better support for women who speak out, better awareness and help within policing and the justice system, transition houses, minimal legal aid. Many women have more options open to them thanks to broader education and training.

But I do not believe the incidence of violence against the vulnerable, most often women and children, has decreased much at all. Not in Canada, certainly not in the world.

# CHAPTER 24

# The Woman I Never Met

IRETAINED Judy's large desk in her office, and the chair to match. I found some cushions to elevate me. One morning, a man came into the office, accompanied by his mother. He was about six-foot-two, with an overbearing presence. His mother was a stocky woman with a babushka, a scarf, around her head. The mother remained silent during their time in the office, but she nodded her added approval each time her son slammed his fist into the palm of his other hand, as he recounted the injustices that had brought him to seek a legal remedy.

He lived in a town north of Niagara Falls, and worked in a factory, from 7:30 a.m. to 4 p.m. He had been married for a number of years. Each morning his wife made him his breakfast, then his lunch to take to work. He owned his home, where he lived with his wife and their seven-year-old son. His mother did not live with them.

He had come to see me because of what his wife had done to him. He was enraged. A couple of days earlier, his wife made his breakfast, as usual, and gave him his lunch to take to work. He drove to work. Everything was normal.

When he arrived home from work around 4:30, he found that his home had been stripped bare. There was nothing left inside the two-story house except for one bed, some towels, sheets and pillows, cutlery and dishes.

Every stick of furniture, the new television, all appliances, rugs and household goods were gone. As were his wife and son He went to all the neighbours to ask them what had happened to all his belongings. But none of them had seen anything. A puzzle, an urban neighborhood where houses were many and close together.

They had only one vehicle, his, which he drove to and from work. His wife had no means of transportation. How could she have done this? How could he get his furniture and belongings back? His new television! They were his. Like the house. He had paid for everything. He wanted them all returned.

With each burst of anger, his right fist drove into his left palm. And his mother nodded, vehemently. I didn't interrupt him as he described his empty echoing house and the thievery and duplicity of his wife. He had no idea where she was or where she had taken his furniture. He demanded I get his property back for him.

"What about your son?" I asked.

"What about him?"

"Don't you want him back too?"

"Well, yes. But she must return all of my belongings."

He had no clue where she might be. Nor, apparently, did any of the neighbours. He had asked them all. But somehow she had stripped a two-story house full of furniture and appliances, in that short period of time, unseen.

I told him I could not help him. Nor did I charge him a fee. He and his mother left, leaving a vapour trail of anger. I sat and thought about that woman and her seven-year-old son. What had driven her to leave in such secrecy and haste? I could guess. It takes planning and time to strip a two-story house. She must have organized that exit like an army general. And had a lot of help. Was the big moving van idling two streets over, waiting for the signal?

Those neighbours. Sight unseen, I had developed a sudden fondness for those neighbours, who had seen nothing. That woman had fled with her son and taken the only assets she could actually remove. To set up her own place somewhere else? To sell some of those items? She appeared to have concluded she would get little help from the law, no maintenance for herself or her son, as she disappeared into the Niagara mists.

She never knew she had this admirer, sitting behind a big desk in a law office, smiling.

# CHAPTER 25

# *The Dog*

S HE WAS TALL AND PLAIN, with dignified carriage, maybe forty-five. Dressed in a less than Pat Nixon brown/grey cloth coat that remained tightly buttoned. My head hardly reached her chin.

She came to see me in my first month or two of practice. I was twenty-five, and so green a young lawyer. But she was clearly afraid, of seeing a lawyer, and of the humble office and everything else. In her hand she had some money, and the first thing she said to me was, "I can pay you." Her agitation increased.

I smiled and asked her to please have a chair and tell me why she had come. "It's my husband. Do I have to look after his dog? He says I have to."

There was no joke, no unhinged lady. She was in a lawyer's office for the first time in her life, with a clutch of small bills saved over almost three years from secret babysitting, done while her husband was at work; a dollar saved here, fifty cents there, until she had built up the fund to over $300. It was the only money she had ever possessed. Her husband controlled all their finances, and he did not know she had it.

She had no car. It must have taken ingenuity and courage to travel from her town near Niagara Falls to see a lawyer. My new client wanted to know if she could take a holiday without her husband's permission.

She was not asking how she could leave her husband, or get a divorce. But could she take a holiday, without her husband knowing, because she knew he would never allow it. She had never had a vacation. Her only family, a sister, lived in Chicago. Would it be legal for her to take a bus and visit her sister, whom she had not seen for many years? Her husband would be away on one of his holidays.

This is where the dog came in.

Her husband worked in a plant, she was a housewife. They

had no children, but her husband had a large dog. Twice a year, the husband took his holidays. He was a hunter. Sometimes he took his dog. He never took his wife on a vacation. His next holiday was in three weeks, and he was not taking his dog.

Whenever he left without the dog, he would threaten his wife with dire legal consequences if anything should happen to the dog while he was away. He was fond of his dog. Very fond. She had sick feelings about what she had seen her husband and the dog doing in the barn behind their house.

The husband never allowed her to have any money in her possession. She had little formal education, and had never worked outside the home except for her surreptitious babysitting.

"What about the groceries? Or when you need new clothing? Surely he has to give you some money then." She didn't cry when she talked about the dog, or the threats or verbal abuse, or the groceries. But she began to cry when she spoke about having to buy new clothes.

They shopped together for everything — groceries, clothes, everything. She was never allowed to shop alone. He chose everything, including the groceries, and he alone paid. The money was never in her hands. The same applied when she needed new clothing. Only he could choose her clothing.

The tears came faster. "I wait until my bra and panties are almost falling off in shreds before telling him I need something new. Then we go together to the department store." In ready sight of the saleswomen, her husband would finger and rub the fabric of each and every bra and panty, to her utter shame, before making his deliberate selection.

She knew he liked to humiliate her, but she had nowhere to go. No friends, no family, except for her sister, no money, job or training. Friends did not exist with him around. He had isolated her, totally. But she had not come to talk about the groceries or the clothes. And she was worried about spending too much time in my office. It would cost more and she had to be home before her husband returned from work. Her problem was the dog, and her overwhelming need to see her sister and have her first break, time away from her husband.

I, who love dogs, tell her she can leave it with a neighbour, or put it in a kennel or put the dog down, but by all means, go on her holiday. She would not be breaking any law. Her husband could not sic the police on her, as she believes. We both know she would never have the dog killed.

But what had he been doing to her all these years? And where could she go?

What happened to her? She came to see me only that once. It cost her no money, but a lot of her courage. Did she take her holiday and see her sister? If so, how did he punish her for that? He would be good at that.

# CHAPTER 26

# *A Chat in the Corridor*

SHORT AND STOCKY, she spoke no English. She had a scarf knotted under her chin in the manner of many Slavic women. Her grown-up daughter accompanied her and translated. She told of being beaten repeatedly by her husband. They owned a small orchard in the Niagara region, close to the picturesque village of St. David's. She wanted her husband to leave the apartment in which they lived so that she could live alone and be safe from his beatings. She would need money to live, and control of the small farm and income.

She had no grounds for divorce. Adultery was not occurring, just beatings. The property was in the name of the husband. There were funds in one or more bank accounts. The wife did not have sole signing authority for anything.

I advised her to lay an assault charge, and to seek maintenance payable by her husband. That was obviously the route that she intended. I prepared the documents and set the matter down for trial in Welland.

On the day of the trial, as I was waiting in the hall outside the courtroom with my client and her daughter, the lawyer acting for the husband approached me. I did not know all the local lawyers at that early stage of my practice, but I knew this lawyer to be ethical, well-liked and respected by others in the bar. He said he would like to speak to me away from both our clients. We walked to the other end of the hall, and he called over a pleasant-looking young man and said he thought I should hear what this man was going to be saying in court that day.

The young man, tall, nicely-dressed, spoke with ease. He introduced himself and said that when he heard that my client's husband was being charged with assault, he felt that he must come forward. He and his wife had moved into the apartment next to my client and her husband, he explained. Frequently, sometimes nightly, they would hear terrible fights going on.

Because my client and her husband spoke Ukrainian, he could never understand what was being yelled; but he would hear terrible crashing and pounding against the walls, and always the voice of the woman crying and screaming. He kept saying to his wife, "That woman is in trouble, being beaten. I must go and try and help her." But for weeks his wife would urge that they not get involved, so he reluctantly complied.

Finally, one evening, the woman's shouting and crying and the sounds of crashing against the wall became so great, he told his wife he could not stay back any longer. He was going to try and help this poor woman. He went into the hall and knocked on the door of the neighbouring apartment. The woman's screams and the crashing sounds continued. He tried the door. It was unlocked, so he opened it. What he saw shocked him.

My client was picking up her husband, who was about the same height and size as she was, and she was throwing him against the wall, screaming at him the entire time. The husband was saying nothing. He would crumple and slide down the wall onto the floor whereupon she would reach down, grab him and hurl him up against the wall again, continuously screaming and yelling at him.

The young neighbour was astounded to learn that the husband was being charged with the assault of his wife. At the end of this tale, I turned and looked down the hall. My client and her daughter were watching with interest, although they were out of earshot.

I thanked the young man and the lawyer, indicating I would like to talk to my client. I walked to the other end of the hall and told my client and her daughter what I had heard from this neighbour. I asked if he looked familiar. Before my words could be translated, my client looked in his direction, then turned to her daughter and said, in English, "We go now." They left the courthouse. I think that was another unpaid bill.

This is one of the stories that I have often told when giving speeches on domestic violence. Over the years, it has almost always brought laughter from the audience. At which point I would stop and comment on the laughter. Which would make the audience feel uneasy and probably guilty. My goal was not to discomfit the audience, but rather to illustrate our prejudice that goes the other way — the lack of understanding and compassion we have for a male so dominated by a female.

One audience was an exception. It was an international gathering of policewomen, many years ago. When I told this story, not one murmur of laughter. Experienced police officers see all the ugliness in our world. Little surprises them.

# CHAPTER 27

# Three Weeks In

MOST OF MY CLASSMATES had the calming advantage of being junior to senior counsel in their initial court cases. That was not my experience. Some lawyers who practice criminal law feel there may be an advantage to being thrown alone into court right from the start, like a baby tossed into a swimming pool where even the youngest find survival skills. In any event, three weeks into practice, I was in the Supreme Court of Ontario on my first negligence case.

In my teens, I had watched Dad in court on two occasions. Seemingly casual, he was at home in the courtroom, speaking easily. I asked him how he could be so relaxed in such a setting.

He said that when you represent a client, you do ninety-nine percent of your work before you enter the courtroom, the interviews, the preparation, briefing the law. Then, "when you enter the courtroom, you forget about yourself."

My reluctance to poke my head above the foxhole while in law school evaporated once I began practising law. Clients came to see me because they had a problem; my training gave the means to help them in most cases. If the case ended up in court, my imperative was to help the client. And Dad was right. You do forget about yourself. It is not about you.

In spite of that blazing introduction to the practice of law, I don't recall ever being frightened or overcome in court. Full of adrenaline, yes.

I did have a lot of discomfort with the courtroom robes lawyers are required to wear when appearing in the Supreme courts of the provinces or the federal courts. The first time I wore the specially designed white shirt with starched choking collars, white tabs that fasten around the neck, black vest jacket and black gown flowing over it all, was at our call to the bar.

Getting the shirts, collars, vest and gown had been an experience in itself. Harcourts in Toronto, old, established and grand, was tailor to the bench and bar in Ontario. When I went to order my robes, they asked only my sleeve and collar measurements. That was the first hint this might not go well, that they were not too familiar with dressing female barristers. Whatever measurements they took, I ended up with court shirts that necessitated leaving buttons undone for my less than awesome hips and bust.

In most jurisdictions, there were no separate robing chambers for women lawyers. Welland County was one of those jurisdictions. There was one small room with its own toilet, where the men congregated to change and chat. As the only female lawyer in the counties of Lincoln, Welland and Haldiman, my solution was to rush in an hour earlier than anyone, change quickly in the bathroom, and beat it before the men began to arrive. At the end of the day, I was last to change out of my robes, killing time outside the barristers room as I out-waited the war stories and leisurely changing of the men.

The imminent case in the Ontario Supreme Court that Judy had left me involved a young man injured in an explosion that occurred as he filled his car at a gas station. He was smoking at the time. The defendant gas station denied all liability, saying it was his own fault.

Judy had prepared the case and the client well. It was obvious he would have to accept the larger portion of the blame, or negligence, but his injuries were such that even a small percentage of liability against the defendant corporation would make his life a lot easier. His damages were extensive, and so were the legal fees and costs incurred.

The defendant corporation was represented by a gentleman of the old school, John Cromarty, QC, who knew I had only three weeks of experience as a lawyer. He never exploited it. During the two- or three-day trial, he cautioned me a few times not to ask leading questions — these are questions that suggest the answer to the witness. I tried not to. It was a skill I would learn, but I was drowning at that point. Other counsel and judges can and do rap the knuckles of inexperienced counsel, and trust me, you learn. But our profession generally is kind to new lawyers, and there was no finer example of that than Cromarty.

At the end of the trial, my client was assessed seventy-five percent responsible for the accident, but the assessment of twenty-five percent liability against the company gave him considerable relief financially and paid some of our costs. Judy was pleased.

John Cromarty was only one example of the kindness and true professional courtesy and help I received from almost every member of the Niagara and Welland bar in those early months and years of practice in Niagara.

I once said to Dad I didn't know how I could repay them. He said that is how the law profession is, that the assistance over the years he had given to younger lawyers was being repaid now to his daughter. Paying it forward, as we say today.

# CHAPTER 28

# *A Jockey Race*

ONE OF THE BONUSES of living in the Niagara Peninsula was the scenic Fort Erie race track. The racing season was not long; the sun seemed to shine each day. The race track beckoned. *The Globe and Mail* stayed open on my desk at *Appas Tappas*, the racing sheet, which set out the races and handicapping. I understood nothing of such things, but I loved being at the track and betting on the beautiful thoroughbreds. I favoured the dappled grey ones for no reason.

One bright day, when the season at Fort Erie was in swing, a new client walked in. Judy had been known as a first-class criminal lawyer before she entered federal politics so I assumed it was Judy's name and reputation that brought him into the office.

He was small and reminded me of a fox; he quickly got to the point. He had been charged as a bookie.

"No kidding? Are you really a bookie?"

I actually said that, with some delight in my voice. I had only read of bookies, never met one. If he'd had any brains, he would have fled at that point. Mind you, if he had those brains, he would not have been caught with his flash paper unflushed He murmured neither a confirmation or denial, and I quit being stupid. Or so I thought.

I got the particulars of the offence from the police, a copy of the information and a description of the counts against him. My client supplied the details of the ins and outs of being a bookie. He told me what flash paper was, flimsy paper easily flushed or burned when you first hear the shoulder of the law at your door. His flash paper did not quite make it down the toilet. The phone lines and recording of bets were part of the particulars. The police had a lot of evidence against him, and he had a previous record for more of the same.

While he may not have been the smartest client in the world, he was a nice man. He perked up when he saw *Appas Tappas* on my desk that first visit, and asked if I played the horses. I said that I did. I didn't tell him I was a two dollar better. That Scottish blood.

Later, when we talked about my fee, he apologized because he did not have much money. But, he said, I think I can make it up to you. Next Tuesday, go to the races and bet on horse X in the fifth race. And tell no one I told you this.

Well, that did not mean I could not tell Charlotte, my room-mate and pal. With her own business, she was earning triple the income of this young lawyer. She and I would rush out to Fort Erie in her Porsche on those late sunny afternoons during the racing season to catch the last four or five races. It would be mid after-noon, and I'd tell Lois, my secretary, "If anyone calls, tell them I am at the races. I'll call them later." She protested "I shouldn't tell them you are at the races!" "Why not? They'll probably be there too."

Sworn to secrecy, Charlotte and I placed our bets on the fifth race that next Tuesday. It was one and one sixteenth miles on the turf, and our horse was so far ahead for the whole race that I began to wonder if it was going to lap the other horses. We col-lected our winnings, jubilant.

My client came in the next week. Had I placed my bet? I cer-tainly had, and he was right, that horse was a winner. "How did you bet and win?" he asked. Although my practice was only to bet two dollars at a time, this time I had gone wild and placed a two dollar bet to win, two dollars to place, and a two dollar bet to show. Six dollars had been plunked down. My winnings? $26.

Even today, writing this fifty years after the event, I cannot believe my stupidity. Nor could my client, from the look on his face when I revealed the amount of my bet.

The fate of the bookie? Well, he had another conviction to add to his record, but we talked the judge out of giving him jail time. And I learned there were such things as jockey races, a chance for insiders to offset low wages and bad luck on and off the track.

CHAPTER 29

# John Anthony Trial

*The Globe and Mail, July 31, 1963 "Fort Erie — A charge of attempted murder was laid yesterday against a 29-year-old Bertie Township truck driver, John Anthony, after police were held at bay for nearly 8 hours in an early morning gun battle. One police officer was wounded by a shotgun blast."*

That eight-hour siege was big news in the Niagara Peninsula, and across the province. Over thirty police and military officers had been called in, from Bertie Township, Fort Erie, Port Colborne, the Ontario Provincial Police, C Company of the Lincoln and Welland Regiment at Fort Erie, and a crack pistol team from Buffalo, New York.

A day or two day after the shootout, I received a telephone call from Mrs. John Anthony Sr., the mother of John Anthony. The family wanted Judy to represent Anthony on the charge of attempted murder. I explained Judy could no longer practice law as she was a cabinet minister full-time in Ottawa. Mrs. Anthony asked who I was; I told her I was the lawyer running Judy's practice. Mrs. Anthony then asked if I would defend her son.

I was not about to tell her I had only been practising law for three months.

Taken aback by the chance to take such a case this early in my career, I told Mrs. Anthony I would like to think about it and could I call her back. She gave me her number, saying she hoped I would agree to. I immediately telephoned Judy in Ottawa. She had heard about the shootout. By this time, I had been in court a number of times, Provincial Court as well as the Supreme Court of Ontario, mostly on criminal trials. I asked Judy if she thought I should take the case. She said, "Do you want to take it?" I answered that of course I did. Judy then gave me some of the best advice I ever received, "Then take it. No one does a better job than someone who wants to win."

The conversation took only a few minutes. I told Judy I had no idea what to charge. She said $2,500 would be an appropriate amount. That seemed like millions to me, but that is the fee that I quoted to Mrs. Anthony when I telephoned her back. It was accepted without question, and paid, in advance.

The accused was John Anthony Jr. who was living at the isolated farm home of his parents near Fort Erie. The police had been called to a domestic dispute at the farm shortly after 1:00 a.m. on July 30. Two police officers on duty in Bertie Township had answered the call. They found Anthony standing on a road at the farm, with a shotgun in his hands. They had a brief discussion, and Anthony told the police to take off. One officer went down the road to where the other officer was waiting near the cruiser, and as they were standing there, a shot was fired in their direction, landing two feet from them. Neither officer was hit. At that point, they called for assistance.

Other officers arrived and as they were about to enter the farm home, a shot was fired from the barn. Again, no one was hit. The siege began. More and more officers arrived, along with more firepower. Efforts by police officers and John Anthony's mother to talk him down from the hayloft of the barn were not successful. Police reported that Anthony refused to surrender, and was cursing and swearing at them from the barn.

At about three in the morning, the police began to fire teargas shells into the hay-filled barn. After twelve teargas shells had been used, the Buffalo police were called and brought some thirty additional teargas shells, including hand grenade, short range and projectile shells able to pierce walls.

In addition to the teargas shells, there were an estimated 450 gunshots fired into the barn. Anthony, up in his haymow, was returning shots and comments from time to time, but no one was hit. By 7:00 a.m., Sgt. William Webb, who had made several trips into the barn to throw teargas shells up into the hayloft, returned once again from the barn to the outside. Anthony called to him, and told him to pull his stomach back in or he would shoot him. As Webb was peering around the shed, a shotgun blast from Anthony struck him in the side, arm and face. Webb was taken to the Douglas Memorial Hospital at Fort Erie, where the shotgun pellets were removed the following day.

Sten guns and FLN rifles were brought to the siege by the quartermaster of C Company of the Lincoln and Welland Regiment. Other police officers brought deer rifles as well.

The siege ended at 9:00 a.m. There had been a period of about two hours when no shots had been fired from the barn. On rushing into the barn, the police found Anthony asleep up in the loft. A loaded single-shot shotgun was found at his feet and another shotgun with a double barrel was nearby, tucked in between bales of hay.

John Anthony remained in custody until his trial. He had been in trouble with the law before, but never anything of this nature. On that night and early morning in question, he had drunk copious amounts of liquor, and fighting had erupted in the home. His mother, whom he revered, was attacked by him; he had grabbed her by her hair and knuckled her down onto the floor. It was that act that caused the family to call the police, as Anthony's behaviour to his mother was so out of character.

I consulted with an experienced psychiatrist from Hamilton. I felt this was a case where the defence of automatism was applicable. It is a defence seldom used and even more seldom successful, as I would find out.

Roughly explained, it is a person in a state capable of doing a certain act, but who is not conscious of his actions — an action without rational intention, not unlike sleepwalking.

The accused was small in stature, slight, polite, mild-mannered. He could offer no explanation for his actions. He could recall nothing. He was an expert shot, raised on the farm. One obvious avenue of defence was that he could have killed any one of the officers at any given time from his vantage point up in the barn. At trial I led evidence to suggest he had more than one good opportunity to shoot and kill Sgt. Webb, the officer whom he eventually wounded.

The trial took place that fall before a judge and jury at the

Welland County Courthouse. The jury seemed as fascinated as I was with the variety and number of officers who were called in from the entire Niagara Peninsula and Buffalo, New York for the shootout and siege, and the staggering amount of teargas and other ammunition employed — at least twelve teargas canisters and over 450 shots from the variety of weapons. One of the early newspaper reports had commented on the number of holes in the sides of the barn, and that the ground around the barn was littered with teargas canisters and spent rifle shells. Why had the teargas not driven John Anthony out of that barn? He was finally captured because he had fallen asleep.

The psychiatrist gave evidence in support of the defence of automatism. My only gripe with the psychiatrist was his fee — $2,000, which was not helping our overdraft problems at the office.

The jury acquitted Anthony of attempted murder. But they did convict him of the lesser charge of wounding with intent. I was crushed, feeling I had let my client down. I had been going for the Perry Mason not guilty verdict. Anthony was taken from the courtroom back into the cells at the courthouse. I changed from my court robes and went down to the cells to talk to him. I was trying to frame an apology as I entered his cell. He was seated on the bunk bed of his cell. He looked up at me, and before I could say anything, he asked, "Do you think the Crown will appeal?"

John Anthony was a model client, polite, street smart and funny at times. He and his family were grateful for everything, and I had grown quite fond of them. I was surprised and pleased to receive a Christmas card from John Anthony from Kingston Penitentiary that Christmas wishing me greetings of the season and best wishes for a happy new year.

# CHAPTER 30

# *Juries*

I AM a fan of juries. Twelve persons from all walks of life who serve on a criminal trial (eight on a civil trial), twelve brains and different life experiences, who bring street and common sense into the courtroom and a citizen's sense of justice.

### November 22, 1963

The evidence in one of my criminal trials in Welland had ended, and the jury was sequestered, deliberating. It could go either way, and I was worried about my young client.

We all remember where we were when we heard the news. I was standing in a hallway of the Welland County Courthouse, on the second floor, looking out the window at a bleak November landscape. A senior sheriff came quickly down the hall, over to me. He had just heard the news, and was ashen. We were both stunned into silence, overwhelmed. John Kennedy. Gunned down by some lunatic assassin.

Suddenly, I had another grim thought, closer to home. The sheriff had turned and was moving down the hall. I called him back. "Sheriff, the jury must not hear a murmur of this until they have delivered their verdict to the court." The sheriff understood and agreed. The sheriffs are in charge of sequestering juries, and once in deliberation, no one is to contact the jury. A very tough rule.

The sheriff was an old pro, proud of his professionalism. No one communicated this awful news to the jury. The jury acquitted my client later that day.

I have always thought the outcome could have been different if the sheriff had not been so scrupulous about his job. Because that was the day it was hard to give any transgressors the benefit of the doubt.

## Women and Juries 1963

"Why aren't women allowed on juries?"

"Aren't they?" I said, with some surprise.

It was an evening in 1963 with a group of women in Niagara Falls. I was the guest speaker. Judy had told me that I would probably be getting requests to speak to groups, usually women, on legal matters. It would be my choice if I wanted to accept such engagements, but her advice was sound: you will find it good training; you learn when you prepare and give speeches, and it never hurts your practice.

This was one of the first of many such speeches. These evening talks were supposed to be casual, but I spent considerable time preparing for them.

The topic requested had been wills and estates. The question on juries had come out of the blue. I realized I had never seen a woman on a jury, even in Toronto. Why weren't there any women on juries, indeed? I said I did not know, but I would find out.

At that time, other than female witnesses, there were almost never any females in any capacity in any courtroom. Only a handful of judges in Canada were female. In the courtroom, a sea of males, the clerks of the court, the court reporters, all police officers, probation and other peace officers, security guards, court attendants and sheriffs. In the three counties in Southern Ontario, Welland, Haldimand, and Lincoln, all lawyers were male, with the exception of Judy, and then me.

I learned that in Welland County, jury panels were chosen from lists of property owners, and fifty-five years ago, there were few women listed as property owners. If a woman's name did come up as a property owner, the sheriffs told me they just struck her name off the jury list.

The importance of being a property owner was huge. It still is. In those days, the property was invariably in the husband's name. Joint ownership of property was rare.

After that, when I spoke to a group of women, I would ask them whose name their home was in. Almost without exception, they never knew. I would explain joint tenancy, something they might want to discuss with their husbands. After lobbing that delayed grenade into the discussion, I should have been hiring security, or at least have someone start my car for me.

On occasion, a day or two after such a chat with the women, a husband would accost me on the street or in the courthouse and ask me what the hell had I been talking to his wife about, and what business was it of mine whose name his house was in.

At another one of those evening talks to a group of women in Niagara, there had been another unexpected question about juries.

"How do you pick who you want on your jury?"

This was easy. I could relax on this one. I had just finished a jury trial. Besides, after your first year of practice, you know almost everything. It is so reassuring.

"Well," I smiled, "you may want youth, or maturity, or a professional, or a working man. You have only a name, address and occupation supplied, and you and your client probably know none of the jurors personally. So you rely on your instinct. If you just do not like the look of someone, you don't like the cut of his jib, you just don't trust the look in his eyes, you challenge, or reject that juror and he is out." It seemed like a worldly explanation.

"Is that why you rejected my husband this week? You didn't trust the look in his eye? You didn't like the cut of his jib?"

Oh Lord, she was hostile. My public speaking needed more work. Judy had been right — you do learn when you give speeches. My attention to juries also needed work.

## G. Arthur Martin

In my second year of practice, I had the extraordinary good fortune to do a one-week preliminary hearing in Welland with the incomparable G. Arthur Martin. It was a scrap metal fraud case of some magnitude. Two of the accused could hire the best, Martin and another eminent lawyer from Toronto. The third accused, less affluent, hired me.

That week was a seminar in criminal law for me. Martin spent considerable time every day with me, during and after the hearing. I have no doubt that he was making sure I did not screw things up for his client, or for my own.

Every day after court, the two senior lawyers and I would

repair to the best cocktail bar in town, wind down, and discuss the case. Some days, I was also included in dinner. My education continued. My admiration for this great lawyer grew. His respect for the law, the court, his utter courtesy in court, and his restraint in posing questions at a preliminary left an indelible imprint on me.

Martin might ask twelve or fourteen questions in a day. No more. He reminded me we were there to learn what the Crown's case was. We were not there to impress the provincial court judge or an imaginary future jury. Or give away our defence unnecessarily. We were there to get the information we needed to investigate further in order to defend our clients. Grandstanding at a preliminary hearing was never done, or justified.

It may have been during that week that I became aware Martin believed that you could do no better than pick the first twelve when choosing a jury.

## Choosing Jurors

Things did not improve for women on juries over the years, even when women were placed on the large jury panels, from which the jury for each case was picked. Most lawyers refused to have women on juries. Even some women lawyers took this attitude. In the mid-seventies, I had a spirited argument with Jessie McNeill, a fine prosecutor and lawyer in Vancouver, who told me she would never allow a woman to be on a rape trial jury. I argued that the ideal jury would be half women and half men, regardless of the charge.

In the late seventies or early eighties, there was an article in *The Vancouver Sun* where the reporter interviewed some well-known criminal lawyers. "How do you pick a jury?" They were asked. One told the reporter, "Never pick a teacher. You can't trust them." Another cautioned to "avoid hard-eyed women." Yet another affirmed, "Never have a woman on a jury, especially if sexual crimes are involved."

And what defence counsel would put an ex-policeman on a jury? I did, unknowingly. It was my last trial in Welland in 1966. A wonderful caring but naive Irish doctor and his wife were charged with sixteen counts of fraud in what was probably the first Medicare case to be tried in Ontario, or Canada. I knew my clients were innocent, but I was consumed with worry that the jury might not do the right thing. A finding of guilt on even one count would be the end of my client's professional life, let alone his personal life and reputation.

The trial took three weeks, unusual in those years. After the jury filed out to begin their deliberations, one of the court officers came over and said, "Nancy, we didn't want to tell you this during the trial, but the foreman of your jury is a former Sgt. of Scotland Yard." The foreman's former occupation would not have shown up on the jury list, just his name and current occupation. Sick with concern for my clients, I kept that news to myself.

After twenty-three hours of deliberation over two or three days, the jury came in with not guilty verdicts on all sixteen counts. My clients were vindicated. I was later told that the foreman had led the jury painstakingly through all of the evidence, to make sure they grasped it all, and led them to the verdict. So much for the wisdom on keeping police officers off juries. Later I thought, who better to judge credibility than a seasoned police officer?

The last jury trial I did before going onto the British Columbia Provincial Court bench in 1972 was defending a clean-cut-looking young man on an armed robbery charge. John Hall, now retired from the British Columbia Court of Appeal but then an experienced and fine lawyer, was prosecuting. We set about picking a jury. There were women in the jury panel, and the only challenges I made were to try and get at least a few women on the jury. John was relaxed about women on the jury, and we quickly ended up with eight men and four women

The judge adjourned court briefly to allow the chosen jurors time to make the necessary phone calls to homes and businesses. The sheriff in charge of the large jury panel came over and thanked John and me profusely, for 'allowing' women on our jury.

What John Hall and I had not realized was that this was the

last case and jury to be picked from the same large jury panel over a period of several weeks. With all of the preceding trials, every time a woman was called forward, either the defence lawyer or the prosecutor had rejected each and every woman. It had become very apparent to the entire jury panel that none of the lawyers would allow any woman on any jury. The sheriff knew he had a revolt brewing.

Our trial lasted two to three days. My innocent-looking client had a long and similar record of robberies; he did not take the witness stand. The evidence against him was circumstantial. The jury must have taken reasonable doubt to heart, and they acquitted my client. As I was leaving the courtroom, the four women jurors followed me quickly down the hall, and thanked me for letting them be on the jury.

Corrections with regard to juries evolved when women became full participants as jurors. Other corrections will occur, in our diverse country. But our jury system remains a pillar of our justice system and democracy.

# CHAPTER 31

## *Political Campaigning*

WHILE ARTICLING IN TORONTO, I campaigned enthusiastically for Mitchell Sharp, who later ran against Dalton Camp. Much later, after I met Camp and we became friends, I thought, how could anyone campaign against this amazing Canadian? Well, at the time, he was just another Tory who had to be defeated.

When I moved to Niagara, there was the same enjoyment in campaigning with like-minded people

When Judy had been firing out her initial and rushed instructions in those three hours on April 22, 1963 before she hurtled off to Ottawa, she had given me lawyer Jack Burnett's name and number as someone I could always call if I needed help. I did not call him often, but when I did, he always made time and never sounded hurried, remarkable because not only was he practising law at high speed and running Judy's campaigns, he was also establishing a new trust company. I had a crush on Burnett. He was young, attractive, smart, and funny. But so too was his wife.

Jack happened to be in court one day in the early months of my practice. I was defending a client on a criminal charge, and the case had not gone well. As I was walking out of the courthouse, completely dejected, Jack came up beside me, put his arm around my shoulder and said, "Nancy, I'm going to give you some advice. You are going to win a lot of cases, but every now and then, you will lose a few, as you did today. Just remember, when you lose a case, your client has two choices: he can either think you are the biggest asshole in that courtroom, or the judge is. Make sure your client makes the right choice."

I thought that was great advice — until I became a judge.

John Clement, another favourite young lawyer in Niagara, also gave early and interesting advice. Because I was doing a lot of criminal work, he told me to assume that my phones were bugged at all times, at the office and at home. When I voiced shock, knowing that bugging phones was not legal, John said of course it was not legal, but the police were probably doing it anyway, and I should conduct myself accordingly. I did.

It was 1963 and Lester Pearson's Liberals were back in power. Another election was coming up. Minority governments are like that — a lot of elections.

As Judy's campaign manager, Jack Burnett had Judy's total trust. As did her financial agent, John Matthews, another Niagara lawyer, as talented and wary as Burnett.

As the new arrival in Niagara, I didn't know anyone in the area, let alone the campaign, but was asked to join Judy's campaign financial team of ten. The only female. The boys told me it was a good opportunity for me to get to know people. They had a big list of donors, people and businesses, and part of that list now had my name on it. People would know I was running Judy's office, and that would get me in the door.

John Matthews presided over the financial team. Our committee met weekly over lunch at the Park Hotel, to check on progress, add additional names, and assign the best person to approach each donor for a campaign contribution.

One name on my list was Dr. Don Jamieson, a favourite local doctor, whom everyone called Jamie. The boys laughed as they agreed I was definitely the one to call on Jamie, a charming ladies man. He had generously donated $200 in the last election. When I came back with Jamie's donation of $400 for this campaign, you can guess their reaction.

There was mafia money around the Niagara Peninsula, and none of it was to find its way into Judy's campaign funds. At one of our lunches, Jack Burnett reported that he had just received and returned a sizable cheque, for $2,000, from one of the locals with a Mafia history and reputation.

There was only one way to approach anyone to give money to a politician around election time. In person. We all followed the same courtesy. A telephone call to see if the person had time for a short visit, and then the follow-up visit to the office or place of business. We took time out of our business day to make the approach mean something, and the results were seldom disappointing.

Our reward was simple. We all thrived on politics. We believed in Judy. We were committed Liberals, and it was fun. We raised a lot of money for Judy and the party. We bonded in the way that people do who believe in the political process.

# CHAPTER 32

# *Niagara Falls*

IN 1963, Niagara Falls, population 52,000, was regarded by some as a grubby tourist town. Few young lawyers could be lured there. It had the obligatory Wax Museum, Oneida built a tower, Lundy's Lane was only the name of a major street, the War of 1812 a mere murmur. Pollution reigned. Cyanamid plants gave off unpleasant odors. Green smog was frequently a wall you drove through to get to Welland, the county seat.

There were a lot of Italians, my favourite people; their restaurants — good; the Mafia — very present. The Falls themselves were spectacular. I began most days detouring by the Falls in the early hours before tourists swarmed, or late at night, after the artificial coloured lights were shut off and the tourists were gone.

I had first seen the Falls in February 1959, en route back to Toronto from a romantic dinner in Buffalo. (It's not easy putting romantic and Buffalo in the same sentence.) Hoarfrost and frozen mist from the Falls had coated every tree and twig. It was 2:00 a.m. and a full moon created a silver fantasy world. The lone policeman strolling by nodded with a smile as my boyfriend and I paid homage to this wonder of the world, kissing as we stood by the thundering Falls.

The Falls remain magic for me. They are book-ended by the Niagara River Parkway, a drive from Niagara-on-the-Lake to Fort Erie, along the Niagara River. The towns and villages of the area, St. David's, Queenston, Niagara-on-the-Lake, are set amongst orchards, and more recently, vineyards.

It was easy to embrace life in Niagara. You stopped at the mushroom farm on your way home. You waited for the thoroughbred racing season at Fort Erie. Charlotte Penny, our friend Dorothy Howes and I rented a cottage on Lake Erie one summer and pretended the brown lifeless water was okay to swim in. Who knew the cottage next door was about to be rented to four bachelors from Buffalo?

You drove to Lewiston, New York for the best steaks and lobster. You shopped in New York State just because you could; you ate beef on kimmelwick buns, drank beer at the roadhouses of New York State and skied at Ellicottville, New York, where there was always snow.

And on quiet summer days, you could take your lunch and book of flags and park beside the Welland Canal to watch the ships of the world move silently through the fields. It wasn't the Panama Canal, but to a prairie girl, it was close.

The Canal dissected the road from Niagara Falls to Welland, so one learned to allow extra time for a bridge raised in surrender to a ship passing through. The first time I encountered it, I panicked. Oh my God! What if I'm late for court. Then I saw everyone getting out of their cars, or just opening their doors to let more sunshine in, reading their newspapers, drinking coffee from a thermos, relaxed. Lesson learned: delays are to be enjoyed, not cursed; keep a book in the car.


The experience I was getting in Niagara was inestimable — opportunities I would never be getting in a big or small firm in Toronto. But much of my social life was still in Toronto. Jacquie had moved to Toronto to work as a nurse and share an apartment with me toward the end of law school; Sandra Lyons had joined us. Jacquie met and married the lovable and bright lawyer, David Sims. Sandra later married Hugh Lyons, David's best friend. So I was driving that Queen Elizabeth Highway to Toronto regularly, visiting them and my rascally friends from Osgoode days, including Pat LeSage and Burke Doran.

Pat LeSage was working as a junior prosecutor for the City of Toronto. He knew I was enjoying practice as a litigator, particularly in criminal law, and one day, when I was in Toronto in midweek, he suggested I meet Henry Bull, the chief prosecutor for those tough Toronto criminal courts. Pat said there were some vacancies, and this might be a good time to get hired.

I was curious to meet Henry Herbert Bull. I had seen him prosecute the Lucas murder trial. I was interested to meet him for another reason. A year after my Mother's family had arrived in the Yorkton area in 1882, a family by the name of Bull from Ontario came to homestead in Yorkton. The Bulls, respected early settlers, were close friends with my great uncles and grandparents. I wondered if Henry Bull was related to that pioneer family.

Pat took me into Bull's office and introduced me. A large man, Henry Bull filled the chair behind his huge spotless desk, a desk my cheeky friend Gary Lauk would describe as a desk that sleeps four. Bull's voice filled the room. That was even before he began to yell.

As Pat was introducing me, he told Bull I was practicing in Niagara, but that I was interested in prosecuting and looking for a job with the Toronto office. Bull looked at the two of us, a look of granite, and slowly began to rise up out of his chair, yelling in an increasing crescendo, while pounding his right fist onto his naked desk. "The day a female gets into this office will be over my dead body!" he bellowed. It was as if a small tornado blew Pat and me backwards out the door of his office.

We fled. There went my chance to bond with Henry over the ancestors. I was afraid LeSage would lose his job, having had the nerve to suggest I be hired. Pat later said the same thought occurred to him.

A year later, when I was ready to move from Niagara Falls back to Saskatchewan, Henry Bull died very suddenly. His successor, Lloyd Grayburn, telephoned me in Niagara and asked if I was still interested in working as a prosecutor in Toronto. There was a vacancy. He would like to talk to me. But my plans had been made to leave for Saskatchewan.

The words of Henry Bull rose, "... Over. My. Dead. Body...." I have tried to resist (unsuccessfully) the image of tap dancing on his grave.

I was enjoying life in Niagara and the law practice. But the desire to get more involved in politics and law reform was growing. I also missed the West, the wide open spaces of the prairies, the lack of formality I associated with Western Canada, the less orthodox approach to life.

My interest in politics became more focused. I wanted to be the Member of Parliament for the Yorkton-Melville Saskatchewan riding.

My ultimate intention to leave the practice was a problem for Judy, I knew. She was still in Parliament. I had given her a year's heads-up of my intention to leave. Our efforts to find a replacement were ongoing but unsuccessful.

My plans were to leave the end of June 1966. The bank was happy, the practice was in good shape, and I almost made it out of town debt free. But stuff happens. My Nash Rambler, an ugly looking wine-coloured heap that had replaced my yellow Morris Minor in 1963, gave up the ghost at 60,000 miles. I was happy to kick it to the curb. I needed a new car.

By this time, Lois had gone back to her family and Verna, a former secretary to Judy's dad and Judy, had come back to the office, and brought the gravitas that only the great duchesses of a law office can bring. She knew more than any young pup lawyer, was smarter and funnier than anyone, and knew everyone in town. She decided I needed help in finding a new car.

"What kind of car do you want?" she asked. I said that what I wanted and what I could afford were two different things. Verna Robbins persisted. What would you like? "Well, I'd like a Porsche or a Thunderbird, but I can't afford either. "

Verna reached for her phone. "Hello, Ralph. How are you? My boss needs a new car and is interested in a Thunderbird. Uh-huh. Uh-huh. Swell. I'll tell her."

"No, Verna", I was pleading. "Hang up the phone."

Verna smiled. "They have one for you to try out. They are going to bring it around. Should be here in a few minutes. That was the owner of the dealership. It is his wife's car, and it has only gone 7,000 miles."

About ten minutes later, a grinning young man leaped up the stairs to our office, handed me the keys to a car, told me it was parked out front, full of gas. It was Friday afternoon — no need to return it until Monday, no need to refill the tank, enjoy the weekend. Someone had driven behind him, so no need to give him a lift back to the dealership.

I went downstairs and fell in love. A 1965 Thunderbird, classic hardtop convertible model, turquoise inside and out. Just my size. The dashboard was like an airplane. Bucket seats with leather like butter. A mere $7,500. More than I earned in a year. But the bank liked me.

# CHAPTER 33

# *The Prairie Lawyer*

AFTER A TWO MONTH ROAD TRIP in the Thunderbird to Boston, Plymouth and Cape Breton, meeting Dad's family for the first time and attending a French summer course at Laval in Quebec City, I drove back to Yorkton, Saskatchewan to begin practising with Dad. Practising law in Yorkton often meant driving to courts in smaller centres like Kamsack, Canora, Humboldt or Esterhazy.

I love the prairies. There was no better way to begin a day, those drives, the endless sky, no factories spewing toxic air, green fields in the spring, meadowlarks in the summer, the rush of harvest in the fall, the pink and mauve light of winter days. I'm deliberately blocking out the winter blizzards and windshield bugs of summer.

## Gerussi in the Morning

My radio would be on — always on CBC — and I would wait for it. The sound of a phone ringing over the air waves. It rang, and I would start to smile.

It was the Gerussi radio show on CBC weekday mornings, called simply "Gerussi!" From nine until noon, Bruno hosted the most eclectic, fascinating radio I have ever heard. Music, politics, poetry, rants and recipes. And once a week, this nutty old farmer from Beamsville, Ontario would call in.

"Bruno!!" The raspy quavering voice yelled, rising and falling a couple of octaves in just that one word.

"Fred, is that you?" And so it began each week, in that slot just before 10:00 a.m. Fred Dobbs would rage to Bruno about all those idiots at Queen's Park, the Ontario Legislature, or the even worse ones on Parliament Hill in Ottawa. No one was safe. Farm produce prices one week, election nonsense the next. Whatever. Fred savaged the hypocrisies and venalities of the day with wicked wit, cackles of scorn, accusations of conspiracies, and shouts of indignation. He was sound on ecclesiastical matters: "If God wanted us to be metric, there would have been ten apostles, not twelve."

"I tell you, Bruno." and Fred was off again.

I knew I was not the only one sitting in a parking lot, late for an engagement, unwilling to turn off the radio.

That was years before I met Bruno. He later told me that the true identity of Fred Dobbs, first introduced to the public in 1968 on Bruno's radio show, was kept secret for six months. It was finally revealed; Fred was the alter ego of actor and radio personality Michael Magee — well known in Toronto. Magee was also an expert commentator on the sport he loved most, thoroughbred horse racing.

Bruno loved Magee and delighted in the irascible Fred Dobbs, the wicked satire. His weekly interviews with Dobbs were models of interviewer restraint. After the initial, "That you, Fred?" — like any well trained jockey, Bruno gave the bit to Magee and let him run. There might be the occasional, "That true, Fred?" or "You don't say," from Bruno, to let Magee catch his breath or wind up again. But basically Bruno surrendered the microphone to Fred Dobbs and Canada smiled.

An old poster advertising Bruno's radio show, salvaged by good pal writer and poet Gary Dunford proclaimed, "Gerussi! He may shock, surprise, annoy or amuse, but he'll never bore you!"

# CHAPTER 34

# *Kamsack Thursday 10:00 a.m.*

I T WAS THURSDAY, an autumn day, and I was headed for Kamsack. The poplars had turned yellow and the harvest was almost finished. I knew my case, an impaired driving, would not be called until later in the morning, so I could listen to Gerussi's radio program until 10:00 a.m., then go into the courtroom. The building also housed the local RCMP detachment and cells.

Kamsack is a picturesque prairie town in Saskatchewan, where the Whitesand River joins the larger Assiniboine River, the aboriginal and early trappers' highway through the prairies. I had just begun practising law with Dad, and although I was comfortable doing criminal and civil litigation, I felt I was the new kid in town, who had to establish her own credentials.

The courtroom was filled. Thursday was court day in Kamsack. Mostly aboriginals and RCMP officers filled the small courtroom. North of Kamsack are First Nation reserves, the Coté First Nation, the Keeseekoose First Nation and the Key First Nation.

The judge was a younger man, bright, with a sense of humour. He had practised with Dad for a short time before going on the bench. Growing up, he had been one of those older kids I had admired. Sitting in the front row of the courtroom, I took out my yellow pad to start a letter while I waited for my case to come up. It would be awhile, from the look of the court docket.

A couple of quick matters were dealt with, which I tuned out, and then his case was called. An older man, a native from one of the reserves who had been in the RCMP detachment cells overnight. The RCMP officer who was serving as clerk of the court called out his name.

The older man stood up on shaky feet, and was brusquely told to come forward. The man looked unwell, and confused. A woman got up from the courtroom and came toward the front of the court with great hesitation, saying, "He is my father. He does not speak English or understand much. Can I help him?"

Everyone was quiet in the courtroom. There was a nod of assent from the judge. The woman stayed beside her parent, very still. Where was the interpreter? You cannot conduct a case unless the accused understands every word that is spoken in the courtroom. That was so basic it never occurred to me that there were courts conducted otherwise. There was no court interpreter here.

No longer tuning out, I began to watch. The clerk/officer picked up the information and bellowed out the charges against the old man in rapid singsong fashion, words so familiar to the officer they had achieved a rhythm. Being drunk in a public place and drinking off the reserve seemed to be the charges, but I missed the exact words, they were spoken so quickly.

The man looked bewildered. His daughter murmured briefly to him, but she did not look as if she had caught all that had been read out so quickly.

"Do you understand the charges?" Silence. The old man's eyes were downcast, and he looked ill.

"Do you understand the charges?" More insistent this time. The daughter tried to murmur to her father, but he looked bewildered, humiliated.

"How do you plead, guilty or not guilty?" The confusion seemed to increase for the old man. The audience sat very still. They could not help their neighbour. Some of them were next. The miserable couple standing were on their own.

Irritation and impatience were beginning to show on the judge, and the police. It would be a long morning if this kept up.

"Note that as a 'not guilty' plea and present your case," instructed the judge. A police officer was called to the witness stand, sworn in and gave his evidence in a quick and professional manner to the court. He related when and where the previous night he had apprehended the accused, related how very drunk he had found him to be, and how he had placed him in the cells for the night.

The man and his daughter were still standing. They had not been invited to take a seat. There was no effort to ensure that the old man had understood the testimony of the officer or that it was fully interpreted; there were no pauses for any translation. The daughter murmured to her father, but not enough to match the words of the policemen.

"Do you want to ask the policeman any questions?" The look of confusion increased. A shrug from the judge. A look on the man that begged to be left alone, in a place far from the courtroom.

"All right, step down," the judge said, dismissing the police officer who had given the evidence. That was the evidence for the Crown. The Crown's case was closed.


I sat stunned. The accused had not followed everything, as far as I could see. And worse, I had failed to jump up and interfere as a " friend of the court."

"Do you wish to present any evidence on your own behalf?" Why were they were yelling every time the clerk or the judge spoke to him?

"Do you want to testify?" A shrug to the daughter, then some murmuring between the two, both looking confused. The impatience of the court was becoming more obvious.

"All right, come forward. Come and take the stand. Come forward." This from the judge, motioning for the accused to come ahead into the witness box.

The daughter gently pushed her father forward and he was waved into the witness box. The daughter stayed behind, still standing, unsure of where she should go, but no longer at her father's side, no longer talking to him quietly. The judge did not invite her to come closer so she could interpret for her father.

A Bible was thrust into the old man's hands, and the clerk/officer bellowed, "*Do-you-promise-to-tell-the-truth-the-whole-truth-and-nothing-but-the-truth-so-help-you-God?*" It was run off like a round from an M-16, all one long word. The old man's downcast eyes looked up briefly. The smarty officer yelled out the oath once again, even faster this time, if that were possible.

Silence from the man, and his daughter.

A questioning look was exchanged between the officer who

was prosecuting the case and the judge. A wry shrug from this judge, whose sense of humour I had admired. This was also a judge who enjoyed a close personal relationship with most of the police officers, a difficult position in any community, and something with which my Dad had expressed disappointment.

The accused stood there, seemingly unable to understand what he was supposed to do in the witness stand, still clutching the Bible that had been put in his hands.

Then the judge said it.

"Give him a mickey to swear on. He'll understand that."

The policemen all laughed, and so did the judge. No one else in the courtroom did.

The man gave no evidence. He was convicted. The judge said to him, "I've told you, every time you are convicted of one of these offences the fine goes up another five dollars. This time it is $65. In default of payment, five days in jail. Do you have the money to pay the fine?" The daughter told the court that her father did not, so the old man was taken back to jail.

Kamsack, Thursday, 10:00 a.m., where there was an absence of respect, fairness, due process and justice in a courtroom, by those entrusted with the law.


What was this about? Indians not being allowed to drink? This was 1966. I knew nothing about the *Indian Act*, a statute never mentioned at law school. On returning to Yorkton after my case finished, I stopped by our office and picked up a copy of the *Indian Act* to take home and read that evening. It was an epiphany. As fine a piece of apartheid legislation as one could hope to find in the world. One law for whites, another for subjugated Indians.

It was the beginning of my understanding that minority rights extended far beyond women's rights. I became aware of the *Indian Act*, but not the residential schools.

Residential schools were virtually unknown then to all but government officials, administrators of the *Indian Act*, the churches involved and the aboriginal communities themselves.

The enforced enrollments in those schools were still being mandated when I began practising in Yorkton. I knew nothing about them. The last residential school to close in Canada was in Saskatchewan in 1996, the Gordon Residential School.

My aboriginal clients never spoke of their time or treatment in those schools. The schools were never mentioned in *Pre-sentence Reports* ordered by the courts. The existence, mistreatments and cruel legacy of those schools did not become public knowledge or understood until decades later. That belated understanding continues.

## CHAPTER 35

# *The Gelding*

WHEN I BEGAN to defend native Indians, I had to learn some of their ways, and drop some of mine. In my culture, you were judged by a firm handshake and direct, steady eye contact. The young men I frequently defended had not been raised to judge a person by a handshake, and direct eye to eye contact would be considered by many to be rude.

There was a disturbing deference to white people and police on the part of my native clients. For example, a visit to the jail in Kamsack to see my young client:

"What happened, Billy?"

"I don't know. Sgt. Jones said I tried to kill Walter, so I must've done it."

"Do you remember what happened?"

"No. I was drunk."

No rush of excuses, no denials, only resignation. And acceptance of authority.

So you, the lawyer, had to become the investigator, locate the other party goers, and try and reconstruct the evening, while your client remained in the lockup, never able to qualify for bail.

On this particular mission of reconstruction, I had traced a young witness to one particular reserve. He was essential to my case, and I wanted to have a long talk with him. It would be more courteous to go to his home turf, and maybe more fruitful. Plus, few had phones.

The RCMP had cautioned me not to go alone onto the reserves, but I had found it an unnecessary caution.

The Thunderbird I was still paying for hummed along the road to the reserve, both of us happy to be on an outing.

There were no street signs, and house numbers were unnecessary on the reserves. Everyone knew where their neighbours lived. So I looked for someone to give directions.

Two young boys were walking down the dusty road. I stopped

and asked if they knew where I could find Joey. Sure, he was up ahead at the pasture. They pointed down the long road. I could see no buildings or persons. Would they like to hop in and show me where? Their grins widened, and they dove into the car.

The pasture was about a mile ahead. I could now see a crowd of men, no women, gathered in the field at the end of a rough approach running from the road to the pasture. The boys were giggling, and kept looking at me. Then they would laugh harder. It was the laughter of little rascals, but I was beginning to wonder about the trip. Something seemed out of the ordinary, and I did not know what it was.

Most of the men turned to watch me park at the edge of the approach. The Thunderbird seemed suddenly very flashy. No one approached me. The boys got out of the car and gave me a final big smile before running off to join the men. My apprehension increased, but I had come this far to do an interview, and I was not about to lose face by driving away.

Then I noticed a horse down in the midst of the men. Must be an injured animal. Several men were crouched over it. I got out of the car — just as a great shout erupted and something came flying through the air.

Then the men turned and grinned widely in my direction. And the horse stood up.

I had just witnessed my first gelding. My amused hosts suspected as much.

My witness came forward then, and we had a long informative talk in the car. My client was nowhere near as guilty as he had assumed, and the eventual trial ended well for him.

# CHAPTER 36

# *The Second Wave of Feminists*

ONE ADVANTAGE to being back in Yorkton was that I found more time to read beyond the law. Five daily newspapers including *The Globe and Mail, The Winnipeg Free Press*, and *The Halifax Chronicle Herald* helped fill my need to keep informed beyond my own community and province. It was part of preparing for my run at politics.

The politics of the prairies, grain prices, the Crow Rate, railways and the weather merged with the politics of minority rights, particularly women and, later, aboriginal, in my reading and public speaking.

### Betty Frieden and Margaret Mead

'Women's Lib' was about to become a public sneer. The American, Betty Friedan, had written her transformative book, *The Feminine Mystique*. Friedan spelled out the pitfalls of women being "protected." In her book, published in 1963, she wrote,

> Protectiveness has often muffled the sound of doors closing against women; it has often cloaked a very real prejudice, even when it is offered in the name of science.

My copy of *The Feminine Mystique* is a beat-up paperback. I read it with my clients in mind. She was putting on paper what I knew to be true. Not enough women were keeping all their options open.

It was an affirmation for me of the concerns I had for female clients who had come through my door, who had formed the basis of the speeches I had been giving since my first days of practice.

The existing laws and culture for women were destructive for women and men, in the many ways spelled out by Friedan, destructive for society as a whole. But first and foremost — for females.

Friedan took them all on, educators, social scientists, the advertising world, and especially Freud. She even threw some well-aimed dirt at everyone's favourite anthropologist, Margaret Mead. Mead was an influence on my early belief that nurturing is not a trait exclusive to females. Rather, it is a human trait, which led me to view joint custody favourably, an uphill battle in those early years of practising family law.

Friedan blamed Mead for glorifying women only in the traditional role — wife and mother. Although at times, Mead demonstrated a Manichaean view of women's capabilities.

Mead's exaltation of women's sexual and biological functions, with little recognition of women's potential and capabilities in fields where males dominated, such as law, medicine and religion, drew scorn from Friedan. Although Friedan complimented Mead on her own personal accomplishments in a male world.

Friedan was not the first to break such ground in that decade, but her influence and that of her book were powerful.

### Gloria Steinem

The glorious Gloria Steinem wrote a forceful article in 1962 on women having to choose between marriage and their careers. She continued such writing, and in 1972 co-founded *Ms. Magazine*, which, like *Chatelaine*, was fomenting reform for women's and minority rights, a magazine breaking trail. Articles on local and international issues ranged from domestic violence, female genital mutilation, abuse of women under the cloak of religion. Steinem, now in her eighties, has not slowed down.

*Canada's Report by the Royal Commission on the Status of Women in Canada* came out 1970, with 167 recommendations designed to better women's lives and their place in the economy, education, the work place, public life and family life. Almost fifty years ago, the men and women of that Commission recognized the need for national day-care legislation. We are still waiting.

In 1970, Lisa Hobbs, a brilliant writer originally from Australia, and then living in British Columbia, wrote *Love and Liberation,* a book many felt surpassed *The Female Eunuch*, written the same year by Germaine Greer. These books were bringing women's rights into the mainstream of what many referred to as the second wave of feminism.

It was time for a lot of laws to change. And there was a large group of women, and men, ready to ensure those changes were going to take place.

## Doris, Judy, Flora, and Barbara

I was having trouble telling a friend why I don't subscribe to *Chatelaine* magazine. She likes the way it is organized, all the great recipes, helpful hints, shortcuts. To me, it is a throwback to the early forties and fifties.

*Chatelaine* under the formidable lead of Doris Anderson, was an early inspiration for me. It was a magazine like no other in its time. And Doris was like few other women of her time.

She was born in 1921, an illegitimate child who lived with her mother who ran a boarding house to support them. Her parents married when she was eight.

Doris qualified as a teacher in 1940, and worked to put herself through university, graduating in 1945. She travelled from her native Alberta to Toronto to work in journalism.

In 1951 she began working for *Chatelaine* magazine, and by 1957 had become editor. And then the changes began. "... what I wanted more than anything was to be able to look after myself and make sure that every other woman in the world could do the same." She continued to work after her marriage and the births of her three sons.

As editor of *Chatelaine*, Doris Anderson gave her readers food for the mind. The magazine featured articles on the legalization of abortion, the prevalence of domestic violence, the need for reform of women's rights and other minority rights including those of Canada's Natives, the need to reform the federal Divorce law of Canada. The magazine and the editorials of Doris supported the push for a royal commission on the status of women that Judy LaMarsh and Laura Sabia were urging upon Prime Minister Pearson in the early sixties.

Her editorials were aimed at women who worked both inside and outside the home. They were usually non-partisan; they were aimed at law reform, at every level of government. Some readers felt that she was turning "a nice wholesome Canadian magazine into a feminist rag" (*Rebel Daughter*, p. 151). Circulation, which was 480,000 when Doris became editor, increased to 1.8 million by the late 1960s.

By the early 1960s, I had become a devoted reader of the magazine and fan of its editor, whom I had yet to meet. Like most, I turned to her editorial as soon as I picked up the magazine. Her editorials were concise, provoking, informative, ahead of their time.

All the injustices women were enduring in those years were spelled out in those articles and editorials. Doris commissioned the leading women writers of the day. That magazine helped to motivate and energize women across the country. Doris was a profound influence in the fight for women's and minority rights in Canada.

I don't recall when I first met Doris. Her friends included some of mine, including Judy LaMarsh and Flora MacDonald. Doris was a Liberal, so it was probably through that connection. We were friends before I left Niagara to return to Saskatchewan, and remained so until her death in 1985.

When I returned to Toronto for back surgery in January 1974, Doris was a welcome visitor during my three-and-a half months of hospitalization there. One memorable visit saw four amazing women sitting around my hospital room, passionately discussing how to get more women into Parliament. The foursome was Judy LaMarsh, Doris Anderson, Barbara Frum and Flora MacDonald. At one point, Judy barked at me to at least take notes, as I had nothing better to do lying immobilized in bed.

Flora had been sitting as a Member of Parliament since 1972 for the Progressive Conservative Party. Barbara's radio program, *As it Happens*, was the most influential radio of the day. Judy had left politics by then, and was doing a mixture of law, media work and writing. Her autobiography, *Memoirs of A Bird in a Gilded Cage* had chronicled her years and departure from Parliament in 1968.

Some years later, Doris and I shared, with Barbara Frum and

Barbara's mother, Mrs. Florence Rosberg, the sad honour of being pallbearers at Judy's funeral in December 1980. Probably one of the first times in this country there were only women pallbearers.

When Jim Dorsey, a friend and colleague from my days at the Labour Relations Board in Vancouver, told Ben Trevino, one of Vancouver's nicest lawyers, that six women had been Judy's pall bearers, Ben looked thoughtful and said, "I never realized Judy LaMarsh was a lesbian." Ahh, the times. Judy, who adored red-haired men especially, would have laughed.

After twenty years as editor of *Chatelaine*, Doris left the magazine in 1977. *Chatelaine* was never the same. Maybe the same need was not there, but I don't really believe that. The need for reform is still there, nationally, internationally, in domestic violence, which continues as always, all the problems of immigrant and refugee women, Indigenous issues, child poverty, elder abuse, you name it. The magazine has never regained its leading role in advocacy for these causes.

# CHAPTER 37

## *Politics in Yorkton*

THE YEARS FOR a lot of law to change were still to come. Meanwhile, it was the late sixties, and I was in Yorkton, practising law and hoping to enter federal politics. I had grown up watching the CCF campaign in Saskatchewan. They were masters at it. The day after any election, they started getting ready for the next one. I would try and emulate that kind of organization.

I obtained a large copy of the new riding, the Yorkton-Melville federal constituency. I spread the map out on the floor of my small apartment. There was only one way to approach my campaign for the nomination, poll by poll.

In the next year and a half, I visited the polls and many prominent Liberals during weekends and evenings. The riding, a large one, is urban and rural, including the cities of Yorkton and Melville. My Thunderbird and I hit the highways, the small dirt and gravel byways.

Often when I would drive onto a farm, the farmer would be getting off his tractor. I would get out of the car and say, "I understand there may be some bad Liberals in this area." That usually got a smile, and I would introduce myself, and tell the farmer that I was going to be running for the nomination for the federal Liberals in the next election.

On more than one occasion, the farmer would look at my car and say, "That's a pretty fancy expensive car." I would look at his new air-conditioned cab tractor and say, "I'll trade you for that tractor." That usually settled the status symbol pissing match, and we would get down to politics.

There is a predominant Ukrainian and Russian population in the riding, particularly in the more northern part. The farm women frequently were not fluent in English, and I had no fluency in their language; but almost always, as I was leaving the farm, after a glass of lemonade or offer of tea, the woman would press a homemade loaf of bread or a jar of jam into my hands, and then give me a long level look, and grab my arm in a tight grip. We might not have been able to speak the same language, but I was getting a message of encouragement that was unmistakable.

The myth was prevalent — women will not vote for another woman because women are so jealous of one another. That this myth had no basis became apparent within the first couple of months of working the nomination. The main political organization was in Yorkton, where the women, the backbone of every campaign, were incredibly supportive of me.

Lil Sharpe was the centre of the wheel of that federal Liberal organization. Her team of women were the troops before, during and after every election. I became a friend and a fan of Lil. At the time, it appeared there was only one other real contender for the nomination, Peter Deilschneider, a lawyer and the mayor of Melville.

Assuring myself I was campaigning, I began curling for the first time. Polio had prevented me from curling in high school. I loved the sport, and now bonspieled my way through many of the small towns in the two winters leading up to the nomination convention.

On the prairies, each town and village featured grain elevators and a curling rink. There may have been other buildings and businesses, but they paled in importance to those two. Those were the years before farmers would head south for the winter. Instead, they headed into the curling rink.

Every now and then I would drive to the big city for a weekend. The big city was Regina. My close friends there, Penny and Ted Malone, Donna and Mike Spooner and Ed Odishaw dispensed hospitality and political gossip. Ed, a lawyer, was Executive Assistant to Premier Ross Thatcher and Provincial Cabinet Secretary. On one of my early trips to Regina, Ed said that he thought they better get some Farm Credit work to me, as I would be taking time away from working in Dad's office to do my politicking. He was talking about patronage legal work, doing the mortgages that farmers applied for through the Farm Credit Corporation. That sounded promising.

When I got back to Yorkton, I told Dad that Ed Odishaw had

said they were going to be sending some Farm Credit work to our office. Dad laughed, and said, "The day Ross Thatcher sends any work to this office, I'll eat my shirt." Dad was a Liberal, but he had an issue or two with Thatcher.

Two weeks later, a letter arrived from the head of the Farm Credit Corporation asking if I would agree to do some mortgage work for them. This had effectively cut in half all of the Farm Credit work that had been going to another Liberal lawyer in town. I took the letter into Dad's office, and asked if he wanted to start with his white shirt, or a blue one.

Within one year, I had done quite a bit of work for Farm Credit, and at the end of that year received a letter advising me that I was the fourth most efficient lawyer on their behalf in the province. The work kept coming. Word later went out that I was sleeping with Odishaw, which is why I got the work. Ed and I, lifelong friends, were not romantic. The gossip was unfair to both of us, but I knew I could do nothing about it.

Before the Yorkton-Melville nomination date of May 8, 1968, there was a much more important contest, the federal Liberal leadership convention in Ottawa on April 6, 1968. I was not a delegate for our local riding, so I approached our local paper, *The Yorkton Enterprise*, and offered to write some reports from the convention if they could get me a press pass. The paper agreed, and I went to Ottawa with press credentials, to the annoyance of friends who really were press.

I also hitched a ride on a government plane. Judy had telephoned from Ottawa to tell me that if I could get myself up to Saskatoon on a certain date, there were spare seats on a government plane, and I could fly back to Ottawa with some VIPs being picked up.

The field of candidates to replace Lester Pearson as leader of the party and Prime Minister was impressive. It included Bob Winters, Paul Hellyer, Paul Martin Sr., Allan MacEachern, Joe Greene, Pierre Elliott Trudeau, and a young John Turner.

The rumblings from Quebec had been ominous for several years. When I spent the summer at Laval in Quebec City in 1966, I was astounded at the level of animosity toward '*les anglais*'. The separatist movement in Quebec seemed organized and strong, something many in Western Canada seemed not to realize.

One of the talents Lester Pearson had was recruiting the brightest and the best, (provided they were male). He had recruited the three wise men from Quebec, Pierre Elliot Trudeau, John Marchand, and Gérard Pelletier. Three impressive men devoted to public service, to the country of Canada as well as their province of Quebec.

When Trudeau first came to Parliament Hill as a new Member of Parliament, *The Star Weekly* magazine ran an article on him, complete with a picture of Trudeau getting out of his Mercedes convertible in front of the Parliament buildings. It was a great shot, and I had cut it out and put it on the wall of my apartment in Niagara-on-the-Lake. When Judy came for dinner one evening and saw the picture on my wall, there was no end of teasing.

Shortly after that, I was in Ottawa. Judy, ever the hostess, regularly had colleagues into her office for drinks after Parliament rose for the day. I joined her on the few occasions I was in Ottawa, as I did this time. And sure enough, one of her guests this time was Trudeau. I knew Judy must have told him that I had his picture on my wall. He was one the most charming people I have ever met, and graciously suggested that if I ever came to Montreal, I should call him and we would have dinner. To my regret, I never went to Montreal and took him up on his offer. Soon after that, I left Niagara to return to Yorkton.

By 1968, I was delighted to see that Trudeau was running for leader. Judy was then Secretary of State. She was a strong supporter of Trudeau for the leadership. She had written me to say that she was going to have dinner with Paul Hellyer, and how she would have to tell Paul, a long-time friend, that she would not be supporting him for the leadership. She wrote that she believed Pierre was the best candidate. Indeed, she was not only supporting Pierre, but had also encouraged her Liberal contacts in the Niagara Peninsula to do likewise.

However, something happened on the way to the forum,

three weeks before the leadership convention. My source was the late Joe Greene, the folksy Ottawa Valley politician and cabinet minister who confided the following tale out of a cabinet meeting.

Two judicial appointments to the Supreme Court of Ontario were to be made. The list had been narrowed to four lawyers, all men, of admirable ability and reputation. Trudeau was then Justice Minister. Judy, along with Paul Martin Senior, had strong feelings about the importance of party background and contributions, and argued that two of the four who had party affiliations and had been supportive over the years financially and otherwise for the party, should get the appointments. All four were of equal calibre, but the party support should tip the decision in favour of those two. Trudeau disagreed, strongly. He did not particularly care about the party at that time, and he said he would appoint the other two instead.

The fight was on. It took place in the cabinet meeting. Both Judy and Pierre had tempers. According to Joe Greene, it was like watching a quick tennis match, as the two began to hurl arguments back and forth. Finally, Judy, her temper having risen to the boiling point, got up and charged toward the door to leave the cabinet meeting. She turned around, jabbed a finger in the direction of Pierre and yelled, "You will not get my vote for leader, and furthermore, I will make sure that you don't get one goddamn vote out of the Niagara Peninsula." To which Pierre snapped back, "I don't give a damn."

And indeed, Judy did try to turn around the votes of her supporters in the Niagara Peninsula. Unsuccessfully. To a person, they all stayed with Trudeau. Meanwhile, Judy swung her support to Paul Hellyer in those final three weeks.

The night before the vote at the convention, Judy cooked dinner for one of her best friends, Ben Benson, then Minister of Revenue, and myself. I had just bought a suede coat in Ottawa, coincidentally the colour was burnt orange, which happened to be the colour of Trudeau's campaign. When I walked into Judy's apartment, she yelled, "You bought that colour on purpose!" I hadn't, but she was unconvinced.

Her powers of persuasion were not sufficient to turn either Benson or myself against Trudeau. We were both supporting him. It was a great and lively dinner. Judy was a superb host and cook.

Judy's belated support for Paul Hellyer led to the infamous story of Judy's comment that was picked up by the then-new technology, the directional microphone, at the convention. As a vote was going down, Judy and other Hellyer supporters were trying to talk Paul into dropping out of the race after the first or second ballot. It was apparent that Hellyer would not win, but Bob Winters possibly could have, if Hellyer had dropped out soon enough and most of his support went to Winters. That was the only chance of beating Trudeau at that stage of the voting. Judy, thanks to the directional mic, was heard to say, "Get out now, Paul, or that bastard will get in." That bastard was Trudeau. Judy was still mad.

That led to the myth that the two of them were long-time sworn enemies. Not so. They were a couple of talented but hot-tempered colleagues who'd had an unfortunate falling out at the wrong time. They made up in the months and years to come.

My belief was that Trudeau was the best choice for Canada at that time in our history. I had concerns over the possible separation of Quebec. My Maritime roots, thanks to Dad, have always given me a pan-Canadian outlook. Part of my heart lies with the people of the Atlantic Provinces.

My passion for the West has always dominated. I like to say I fell for Quebec on my first visit there, and have remained smitten ever since. And as a Westerner, I have indulged in the fake national sport of baiting Toronto and suspecting Ontario. Trudeau was unabashed in his nationalism and he had the ability to speak to and for Quebec. I believed the country needed him at that time. I was relieved when he won the convention and became our new Prime Minister. I would not have to hop scotch over a separate state of Quebec to get to Cape Breton.

My sister, Moira, was not happy with me. She had campaigned in earlier years for John Turner and become friends. She was not a delegate in Ottawa for the 1968 convention, but she was working in Calgary to support Turner. At the end, 195 people stayed with Turner right to the final ballot. They formed their own club, the 195 Club. My friend Ed Odishaw was a member.

On reflection, I guess I should blame Trudeau for my not winning the nomination in Yorkton in May 1968. Trudeaumania began, and suddenly, swing ridings like Yorkton were looking good for a Liberal candidate. There were some who did not want a twenty-nine-year-old female lawyer standing in their way should they decide in the future to become the member for Yorkton-Melville. At least that was my take on it. Also a feeling that I was not subject to their direction.

Shortly after the federal leadership convention, I had a strange visit. The visitor was Sally Merchant, then a well-known media and political figure in Saskatchewan. Today she would be known as the mother of Tony Merchant, a Regina lawyer who garners considerable publicity.

Sally's parents, Rita and Vinty Smith, were close friends of my parents. Vinty was the District Court Judge in Yorkton when I was growing up. Rita was an elegant woman, Vinty a man of charm and humor. When I was still young, they moved from Yorkton to Saskatoon, so I did not know their children. Sally was their daughter, considerably older than me.

One afternoon after work, Mother called from their house two doors down to say that Sally Merchant from Saskatoon had dropped in and she wanted to have a visit with me. Was it convenient for Sally to drop over to my apartment? I said sure, and Sally arrived at my door.

I would not have known Sally to see her, but with our shared family histories, I was happy to meet her. I offered her a drink, and she got very quickly to the point. "Why are you running for this nomination? No one has asked you to run, have they. What made you think you should be running ? No one else wants you to."

She continued, sticking right to the point, telling me in any number of ways that I had no business running for the nomination, no one had asked me to and no one wanted me to. She told me how different it would be if she were running, because she was extremely well known, because of her media work, and she had run provincially successfully. According to Sally, people naturally asked her to run because she was so well known, whereas no one knew me, and I had no credentials to run. And again, she emphasized, no one asked you to run. What makes you think you should be the candidate. I certainly did not have the fame and caché of a Sally Merchant.

That conversation left me speechless. Having delivered her message — and that is what it was — Sally departed. I felt angry and humiliated. I had been told in no uncertain way that I was a nobody, and very unwelcome in the nomination contest. The 'visit' had been short, maybe twenty minutes. No wonder she wanted to see me alone, and not give that speech in the presence of my parents.

To this day, I do not know why she was in Yorkton, nor do I know on whose behalf she was carrying that message. Sally was not a power in the Liberal party in Saskatchewan, although her daughter, Adrian, was then married to Otto Lang, the respected young Dean of Law from the University of Saskatchewan in Saskatoon. Otto was the candidate for the Saskatoon Humboldt riding. It was his first run at politics, which was successful.

One of my supporters from the northern part of the riding was a well-known farmer from Kamsack, John Konkin. John was one of Dad's favourite clients. He was tall, charismatic and brought a smile to your face when he walked into the room. I was delighted to have his support; that more or less tied up the northern part of the riding, as John was a Liberal with considerable influence.

But the unexpected happened two or three weeks before our nominating convention. John's son, Pete Konkin, a popular veterinarian in Yorkton, suddenly announced that he would be running for the nomination. That was bad news for me. There was no question where John Konkin's support and influence would now be going. To my knowledge, Pete had not been involved in politics publicly before. Nor had his father ever made mention that Pete would be interested in the nomination. I later came to suspect that as a small group of Liberals in Yorkton became aware that this sudden wave of Trudeaumania could put a Liberal in Parliament from our swing riding, I was not the Liberal they wanted. Were they behind the sudden candidacy of Pete Konkin?

At our nominating convention on May 8, there were a thousand people in attendance, an unheard-of number. If you looked at the number of signs for each candidate, there was no question who had the most. Lil Sharpe and the women had made sure that signs for me were everywhere. Including some buttons saying "I fancy Nancy."

There were five candidates in total, only three serious ones though. Peter Deilschneider, Konkin and myself. To my dismay, on the first ballot Dielschneider came first, Konkin second and I came third. The fifth candidate dropped off, and there would be a second vote. I did not want to see Dielschneider win the nomination. They had run a bit of a mean campaign against me, with sexual innuendos that I had not appreciated. And by that time I suspected that part of the convention had been rigged against me.

I told my Dad I was going to withdraw from the race, and throw my support to Konkin, whom I personally liked. I asked Peter to take a walk with me, as they announced that I was withdrawing from the race. Peter and I walked the length of the auditorium floor, my signal to my supporters that I wanted them to switch to Konkin. He became the candidate for Yorkton.

I went home and threw up every half hour for the next twenty-four hours.

# CHAPTER 38

## *May 9, 1968*

I WAS STILL FEELING ROCKY the day after the convention, and crushed. Any hope I might one day be a Minister of Justice and help bring in some progressive law reform was not going to happen.

Moira was in town, having come from Calgary to lend support at the convention. I went over to Mom and Dad's for lunch. Moira was angry with the outcome of the convention. Dad was quiet, he knew how hard I had worked. But Mom had a tale of two visitors she'd had that morning.

> There was a knock at the door and through the glass at the top of the front door I could see two tall, nice looking young men. I opened the door, and the tallest one introduced himself. 'Good morning, my name is Lorne Nystrom, and this is Irv Carlson.'

Jessie knew Lorne was the twenty-year-old NDP candidate for the Yorkton-Melville riding, and Irv Carlson was Yorkton's young provincial NDP Member of the Legislature, serving as Lorne's campaign guru.

"Oh boys, I have to tell you. You are at the wrong door. We're Liberals here."

To which Nystrom said,

> I know you are. We know whose door we are at, Mrs. Morrison. We came because I wanted to say how sorry I am your daughter Nancy lost the nomination last night. I have not met her, but I was looking forward to meeting her in the campaign. I've heard so much about her.

Mother finished her story by saying, "I didn't notice any Liberals at my door today, telling me how sorry they were that my daughter lost."

Dad and I swore Jessie voted NDP that election for the first and only time in her life. She admitted to nothing.

Later that day when I was back in my own apartment, the phone rang. It was one of the men from our Liberal campaign office. They had a big problem and needed my help. All the women had quit. The female campaign workers had served notice — they would not be working for this election. They had told the men, "If a woman candidate is not good enough for you, you don't need us either."

The women, who had been the core of my support, were the reason that an unprecedented thousand people had turned out for that nominating convention (unfortunately for me, not enough were voting delegates). Without the women, there would be literally no organization or troops to run the campaign.

That part of me that was tickled pink at such unqualified support had to give way to the political soldier.

The men asked, would I go and speak to the women, particularly Lil Sharpe, and bring them back into the campaign? I said I would go and see Lil right away. Then I made an offer they should have accepted. I volunteered to be the campaign manager. I liked Pete Konkin, and I knew the riding and poll captains.

Those boys weren't even ready for a female campaign manager, let alone a female candidate. But they did ask me to take over the twenty-nine polls in the City of Yorkton.

Lil agreed to bring the women back on board, and she and I ran those twenty-nine city polls with professional intensity that was lacking in the rest of the riding.

Prime Minister Pierre Trudeau came to Yorkton in June during that election campaign of 1968. Much excitement — Trudeaumania! I was looking forward to seeing him again. Our local (male) Liberal cabal set out the rules for this brief touchdown. The prominent male-only Liberals of the day would meet with Trudeau and then be on the stage with him. There would be no females allowed. I was told if they permitted me on the stage, then they would have to let all their wives too.

In disgust, I left town and went to Calgary to visit my sister.

In the end, Nystrom, just twenty-one, was elected as the youngest Member of Parliament. The only city in Saskatchewan to go Liberal in that election was Yorkton. Lil Sharpe and I won all our twenty-nine city polls, but it was not enough to carry the large riding.

After that, I swore I would never run again unless the Prime Minister came asking. Sixteen years later, in 1984, John Turner, my favourite Prime Minister, did just that.

# CHAPTER 39

# John Turner and Law Reform

*With John Turner in the 1984 election campaign.*

L AWYERS PAY ATTENTION to who the Minister of Justice is, because the Minister's policies and judicial appointments affect our work and clients.

John Turner was an exceptional Minister of Justice. Appointed by Pierre Elliot Trudeau in July 1968, Turner served as Justice Minister for four years, until his appointment as Finance Minister. Well-informed and highly intelligent, his views on and dedication to law reform were established before he entered Parliament in 1962, In Parliament, he encouraged the legal profession to press for changes.

Turner brought about bail reform, long overdue. For those of us practising criminal law at the time, the impact of bail reform on clients, clogged jails and courts was significant. He sought compensation for victims of crime, privacy protection from new technologies like wiretap and more equal access to our courts.

On judicial appointments, Turner began the consultation process with the Canadian Bar Association, where candidates were rated well-qualified, qualified or unqualified. Among his many nonpartisan judicial appointments to the federal bench was thirty-eight-year-old Tom Berger, a prominent NDP politician and superb lawyer. In 1970, he was responsible for establishing the Law Reform Commission of Canada, an independent body to provide government with ongoing expertise and recommendations on law reforms.

Once the Commission began its operation in 1971, I was one of the early ones through the door. I went to Ottawa in hopes of obtaining a job with the Commission. They were still unpacking boxes the day I was there, with Justice Tony Lamer, vice chair, apologizing for the chaos as we met for my interview. I told Lamer of my interest in law reform and that I would particularly like to work on family law and domestic violence. Lamer immediately shook his head and said they were not going to be doing anything in those areas. I returned to Vancouver.

Five years later, as Lamer was about to leave the Commission for the Quebec Court of Appeal, he arranged to have dinner with me in Vancouver, to discuss the possibility of my becoming one of the five commissioners. Moving to Ottawa for five years at that time was problematic, so it did not happen, but I continued to follow the work of the Commission with interest.

Meanwhile John Turner had resigned from Parliament in 1976, but as politics is like malaria, once bitten, never cured, he ran once again for the federal Liberal leadership, winning in June 1984 to become Canada' seventeenth Prime Minister. This was a prime minister I believed in.

# CHAPTER 40

## *Finlay, Dalton, and Flora*

A FTER MOVING from Ontario to Saskatchewan, I continued my association with the annual Couchiching Conferences, a thinkers' conference held at Lake Couchiching north of
Toronto — summer camp for adults.

I had discovered the Couchiching Conferences my first
summer in Niagara. A week's vacation disguised as a thinkers'
conference, in a serene lake setting with interesting people from
Canada and around the world. The conferences were casual, fun
and suited my modest income.

The second summer I attended one, 1964, the topic was
Order and Good Government. The line up included: Stanley
Knowles, Pauline Jewett, Davie Fulton, Woodrow Lloyd, Peter
Newman, Maurice Sauvier, George Nowlan, Stephen Lewis. I
won't say who it was who kept trying, unsuccessfully, to crawl
through Jewett's window. Rebuffed, he grumbled she must be
a lesbian.

The July 1967 Conference at Lake Couchiching was my
favourite. It was there I met my three favourite Tories: Finlay
MacDonald, Dalton Camp and Flora MacDonald.

At an intermission of one of the evening sessions, with everyone standing packed in the outer hall, I found my nose pressed
against the name plate of one Finlay MacDonald, a broadcaster
and a founding director of the CTV Network, from Halifax. He
was tall and handsome, with prematurely grey hair and a wide
smile. I told him I was a second-generation Maritimer.

"How is that?"

"My father is from Boularderie." That is an island in the Bras
d'Or Lake in Cape Breton, and you would have to be from there
to know Boularderie. Finlay beamed, and yelled, "Dalton! Get
over here."

That was Dalton Camp, the journalist, politician and pundit
who had many of us getting out our dictionaries at least once

or twice with each of his brilliant columns. Dalton hailed from New Brunswick.

Soon, Flora MacDonald joined us. Finlay had been born in Sydney, Cape Breton, and Flora in North Sydney, Cape Breton. We were almost family. They knew well where Boularderie was, Sydney being near the tip of Boularderie Island. Those three Tory Maritimers took me under their wing, in spite of my Liberal leanings.

That summer was the lead-up to the September 1967 Conservative Party leadership convention in Toronto, which Robert Stanfield eventually won. My three new friends were active in the campaign, optimistic their friend and fellow Maritimer, Stanfield, would win. On their advice, when I returned to Yorkton after Couchiching, I made bets with my political pals in Saskatchewan that Stanfield would win. Stanfield was virtually unknown in the West. The wagers went well. I cleaned up. I wrote Finlay to thank him for my gambling sweep. Finlay replied September 16, 1967.

> Dear Nancy,
>
> I was just delighted to receive your letter of September 13 recalling those happy, carefree days when we were young and used to play hooky from the NDP study groups by going to the old Couchiching swimming hole.
>
> Yes, the forces of good triumphed at the Maple Leaf Gardens. Modesty prevents me from telling you about the part I played at that time save to say that I was literally everywhere – issuing crisp instructions here, arranging a fast alliance there, in constant communication with our 397 floor managers – attending to every detail of our 33 spontaneous demonstrations.
>
> At the final moment of victory, our fearless leader, RLS, broke down and in a voice choked with emotion uttered those immortal words,

'Finlay how has one man got so fucking much talent.' Nancy, the imagination boggles when I think of the rewards that soon will be mine.

Dalton joins me in sending renewed assurances of our esteem and affection. You will recall that we warned you of the terrible, terrible mauling you will suffer at the hands of the Yorkton electorate should you run on the Liberal ticket. But knowing of your stubborn background, there is little we can say to deter you, so keep us advised of your plans and Dalton and I will be there. For gawd's sake keep it to yourself because our assistance might be misunderstood. But keep your eyes on those two dear, little old ladies in the long dresses, mauve hats and veils. That will be us. If that cover is blown, we will re-emerge as two of the local village drunks, a role we have come to play rather well since last Saturday.

I am taking the liberty of sending confidential copies to my favourite Grit and my favourite Tory.

Yours, Finlay

The copies were sent to Judy LaMarsh and Dalton Camp.

Less than a year later, things had not gone well for myself (that 'terrible, terrible mauling') or for Robert Stanfield. In a letter dated June 27, 1968, following the victory of Pierre Elliott Trudeau as Prime Minister, Finlay wrote,

Dear Nancy,

Your letter of last Sunday arrived the day after the election and only cheered me up a little. If I had the guts, I'd open a vein. When I surveyed my election bets through a bleary hangover, I viciously embarked upon a policy of entrenchment both at home and in the office.

My heart is in the casket with Stanfield and Camp. Bob could still come back (remember Lester P. In 1958 ). He would have to prove to be a very responsible leader of the opposition and one capable of being invoked if P.E.T. stubs his toes in the next four years.

Spoke to Dalton yesterday – he's laughing to fight back the tears – and I really don't know what the future holds for him. He really is no longer interested in being ever again a backroom boy but he has had two kicks at the cat and like you say, getting a seat in the House of Commons is not an exact science – time, tide, barometric pressure, too many intangibles, too many uncertainties. It's them gawd-damn voters you know.

Good to hear from you, have lots of fun skiing in Chile but for Christ's sake, be careful on that banana boat. It is not like them chivalrous Cunard White Star operations. If anything goes wrong, there is none of that fucking nonsense about " women and children first."

Yours, Finlay


Ever the loyal Conservative, Finlay was appointed to the Senate by Brian Mulroney December 21, 1984. That prompted more correspondence. I suggested the appointment was the only good thing Mulroney had ever done. Finlay responded that Brian had no choice, that Mulroney could not walk with Finlay hanging onto one leg, refusing to let go until he was appointed. Finlay wrote he was so happy he could put his foot through a Salvation Army drum.

Forced to leave the Senate in January 1998, when he reached the mandatory retirement age of seventy-five, Finlay kept active in his home province and had a home at Mahone Bay. I had usually seen Finlay and Flora and often Dalton on my infrequent trips to Ottawa, but my last visit with Finlay was at Mahone Bay in late 2001. He was in excellent form, as usual, but was worried about Dalton's health, as were we all.

Then suddenly, on March 2, 2002, Finlay died of a heart attack. I called Flora in Ottawa. She had just been speaking with Dalton, who was in hospital in Fredericton. Dalton was doing well, still feisty. Also still writing his sage columns. He was suggesting Flora visit and bring a notebook down and play secretary as he had some work to do. She was laughing at his cheekiness. Flora gave me Dalton's phone number at the hospital and urged me to call him.

That suggestion was serendipitous. Dalton and I had a wonderful long conversation that day. He sounded great, although his loss of the rascal Finlay must have been profound. His recall of a political visit to Yorkton when I was there was whimsical. Then sixteen days after Finlay's death, on March 18, 2002, Dalton died. Another grieving call to Flora.

When many in the Conservative party felt it was time for John Diefenbaker to be replaced as leader of the party, Dalton had been the designated hit-man. Flora and Finlay were ready to drive the get-away van. Dief never forgot, nor forgave. He once referred to Flora, the Conservative Member of Parliament for Kingston and the Islands from 1972 to 1988 as "one of the finest women to ever walk the streets of Kingston."

In 1979, Flora had been appointed Canada's first female Minister of Foreign Affairs, and later held the portfolios of Minister of Employment and Immigration and then Minister of Communications.

Flora, an extraordinary humanitarian and politician, died in Ottawa on July 26, 2015 at eighty-nine. In her late eighties, she was still quarter-backing her long time endeavours to bring education and assistance to the women and girls of Afghanistan. Her energy was amazing and her self-deprecating humour enriched us all.

# CHAPTER 41

# *Women and Sports*

WHILE I WAS practising in Yorkton, Dolores Lockhart, a friend and community organizer was planning a provincial Parks and Recreation conference. She suggested I join the conference as a guest speaker. The conference was being held in Melfort, Saskatchewan and Dolores wanted some female input in the male-dominated sessions. What should I speak on? Dolores said, "You'll think of something."

Soon after, I was in bed one weekend with the flu. My eyes were too sore to read. That left television. In the late sixties, Yorkton had only one television station, CBC. A friend, Linus Westberg, the director of the station, was a sports fanatic.

On this particular Saturday, I was not too thrilled with the television schedule. It was that time of year — the last of the hockey season, the beginning of the baseball and football seasons, full-out US basketball season with some overseas soccer and rugby thrown in. All sports, all day, all male. At least there would be the nine o'clock Saturday-night movie. At nine o'clock, no movie. Instead, a British soccer match. Not one female in sight all day, even as a commentator. A female commentator? In those days? *Hah.*

By 9:15 p.m., the flu forgotten, I was sitting up in bed, clipboard in hand, writing my speech for the conference, "Women's Role in Sports and Recreation."

At the conference, my indignation still fresh, I let it all out in my allotted twenty minutes, the lack of females in team sports and on television, the lack of a future in sports for females. While curling on the prairies was a sport for men and women, there was no advancement for girls or women. When I was in Grade 11, our Yorkton High School had a winning girls' curling team. My friend Jacquie Vaughan was on it. They won twelve straight matches across the province, no losses.

Our boys curling team did poorly that year, and lost out on

their chance to compete nationally. So did the girls. Because there was no national competition for girls.

After my speech, a man came up and asked if I remembered him. He had been the coach of that successful female team, and it still rankled him that he could not take those talented curlers into national competition.

Things are somewhat better now. Don't turn on the television if you want to see a lot of female athletes competing. Still mostly male. In golf and tennis, compare the prize money and media coverage between male and female athletes, and the prime times they are viewed, if at all. Although girls beach volleyball does get very favourable coverage.

Russian and other billionaires are not outbidding one another to own female teams. Fabulous endorsement deals seldom come to female athletes, unless they are gorgeous.

*Title IX* was passed by the United States Congress in 1972, to ensure "no person, on the basis of gender ... could be denied the benefits of any education program or activity receiving financial assistance." That improved access for young women to better equipment, coaching, facilities and funding in the US. Attitudes in Canada have changed, but it has been slow and uneven.

An article written November 22, 2013 in *The Vancouver Sun* by Daphne Bramham confirms the situation at that date — fifty years after my flu-clouded epiphany. "Young women athletes are still lacking equity and equal funding in sports in Canada," wrote Bramham.

She noted that few women were coaches and managers, that girls should have "equal access to the best playing fields, playing and practice times, funding and leadership roles." She ended her column by suggesting that Canada might set a better example, "for those parts of the world where girls can't play and women are hobbled in burkas."


Dad and Moira were avid football fans, with season tickets to the Regina Roughriders, later the Saskatchewan Roughriders. They were part of Rider Nation long ago. Moira and I played golf from the time we were kids. Saskatchewan was once said to have more golf courses per capita than anywhere in North America. I didn't golf much through university or in Niagara, but played a lot when I returned to Yorkton.

On moving to Vancouver in 1970, I was keen to keep playing, but ran smack into the world of men-rule-golf. I had moved to North Vancouver near the Seymour Golf and Country Club, so I went to join. The club manager was gracious in his welcome, and he explained the rules: all weekends and holidays were men's days; women were not allowed on the golf course until after 1:00 p.m. on those days.

I was astounded. I knew of no such nonsense in Saskatchewan. The manager assured me that as a female, I would enjoy the advantage of paying lower fees than the men. I said I would pay the same fees then — for the same privileges. No, not possible.

He reminded me that Tuesdays were ladies days, when the men could not play until after 1:00 p.m., unless a particular Tuesday was a holiday; then it was a men's day.

I pictured telling my boss, the red-headed tyrant Stewart McMorran, that I would be unavailable for court as a prosecutor on Tuesdays due to my golf commitments. Amused as I was at this thought, there was and is a serious side to limiting the membership of women in private golf courses and private clubs like the Vancouver Club. A lot business occurs there. It bars women from valuable business opportunities and contacts.

My practice and career did not require me to belong to such clubs. I just wanted to play golf at an affordable golf course close to my home. But women in business, in corporate law or accounting, in government or public service, in private or public corporations were and still are being shut out of the networking opportunities and bonding that occur when spending a day on a golf course, usually followed by time in the lounge and dining room.

Businessmen loved to ride the golf cart for four hours with then Presidents Obama, Bush or Clinton. Trump? It's complicated.... The chance to forge a deeper relationship and trust, pitch an idea, be invited to speak at a conference; all the inter-acting within a club that nominally appears to be merely social.

And those tax write-offs, for 'business expenses' — for the substantial club memberships, annual fees, business golf games and dinners, entertaining important clients — open to few women. We just help subsidize as taxpayers.

At least we didn't have to smoke the cigars.

Fifty years later, women are finally being allowed (I know better than to use the word 'welcomed') as members of Augusta National and the Royal and Ancient Golf Club of St. Andrews. And no, the votes were not unanimous.

# CHAPTER 42

# *Endeavour*

ENDEAVOUR IS A SMALL VILLAGE in Saskatchewan, and no village has a more apt name. In 1967, a fear was about to become a reality. The province was going to shut down the one-room school in Endeavour, which taught Grades 1 to 8. The order had gone out: beginning in September 1967, the sixteen students in Grades 7 and 8 in Endeavour were to attend the school in Sturgis, a larger town twenty-five miles away. Many students were already travelling twenty miles or more to get to Endeavour, so this would add twenty-five additional miles. The parents and citizens of the village were convinced that sooner than later, all the students would be bussed to Sturgis, and the local school would be closed.

So they refused to send their children to the Sturgis School, and lobbied the Saskatchewan Minister of Education for an inquiry to consider their concerns on sending their children to another district, and the whole issue of centralizing education. Their persistence was successful. A three-member board of inquiry was set up in late October 1967.

The parents and ratepayers of Endeavour had asked my father to represent them. His court calendar would not allow the time, but mine did.

Litigation lawyers obtain their information and briefing from the clients, and in this case, the clients were about 250 townspeople, organized, armed with facts, studies, statistics, and telling arguments on the harm the school closure would do to their children and their community.

Saskatchewan was moving away from the rural schools into bigger, central schools that served a large area. Bigger plant, more teachers, more facilities. Why couldn't the stubborn citizens of Endeavour appreciate all the advantages of the larger schools? There were amenities not possible in a tiny one-room school, where one teacher taught all eight grades. With a greater number of teachers, one could have more specialized teachers in the larger centres. The students would not be distracted by the lessons of the other grades. There were science labs, libraries, after-school activities of music, band, plays, organized sports teams, etc.

The men and women of Endeavour were not of any one political or religious persuasion. They were dedicated to public education. There was no one leader, but rather several leaders, men and women, with no sense that men must lead and women should follow. Nor did they, to my knowledge, question the wisdom of having a young female lawyer when almost all lawyers in the province were male.

We sat down around kitchen and dining room tables. From this tiny town in east-central Saskatchewan, they had researched throughout the Western world on the problems of education, the pros and cons of centralization; they were raising issues most of us had never considered. They were in the vanguard, caught up in a matter of principle as well as survival. All of this was done long before the age of computers and Google.

I looked forward to each session with my clients, involved in an issue that really mattered. First, they had to educate me, and then we had to educate the members of the inquiry.

The only negative aspects were the many dark and early winter morning drives to Endeavour. Then later to Sturgis where the hearings began November 15. The inquiry soon moved to Endeavour to accommodate the residents. For me, it was a hundred kilometres each way on those dark November and December dawns and dusks over roads often sheeted with black ice or obscured by early blizzards. I thought about the children they wanted to bus greater distances.

People lived, worked and raised their families around Endeavour because that is where they wanted to be. They cherished their rural way of life, the values they wanted to instill in their children, so they could go into the world as adults with the best possible foundation. To shut down the school in the village would have a profound effect on their way of life, and particularly on their small children.

First, there were the buses, school buses, those bright orange ones, devoid of most safety features. Children aged six to thirteen would be picked up from their farms around the area to be taken to Sturgis; for most, a drive well exceeding one hour each way, to give time for the many pickups involved.

Children would either walk to the road from their farm homes, or be taken by horse and sled or car to the road, to wait in the dark pre-dawn for the bus. For most, a 7:00 a.m. pickup. Then home by 5:30 or later. In the winter, this meant leaving in the dark and coming home in the dark. It also meant no time in the morning or before supper for the usual chores, and this was a crucial point.

Chores are an integral part of a child's life in a farming community. My clients smiled as they told me that the farm did not really need the working hands of the six and seven-year-olds to collect the eggs from the hen house in the morning before breakfast. But the young children needed those early lessons of responsibility and usefulness, the character-building aspect of chores.

The two to three hours of bussing each day for some children would mean little or no time for chores. Evenings would have to be devoted to homework after supper and a loss of family time. The older children did more meaningful chores around the farms, but the loss of labour was not the point. It was the loss of a way of life. Young children spending useless and even dangerous time on a school bus each day, instead of being home.

What was dangerous about bussing? My clients explained, and I have never looked the same way at a school bus since. The list of complaints about the buses was long. They were not driven by professionals, but rather by those who could not find full-time work on farms or elsewhere, often an older person or a single mother, drivers ill-equipped to handle flat tires or being stuck in the mud or a ditch or snow drift, far from phones or population. There were no spare tires on most buses anyway. One school trustee assured the inquiry that was because spare tires were dangerous to carry on a bus.

The buses were not equipped with any safety devices. No fire extinguishers, mobile phones or flares. No means to summon help if caught in a sudden blizzard, stuck with a load of children. No seat belts, of course, of any description. The heating was rudimentary at best, and the lack of adequate springs and proper suspension made a long ride uncomfortable and possibly unsafe by orthopedic standards.

These were not big comfy Greyhound buses rolling over smooth roads. The country roads were mostly unpaved, some described as dangerous with hairpin curves, some resembling a coyote trail. One father described the buses as too light and on one, the steering was in bad shape.

A Sturgis School Board trustee testified, "The bus drivers are always complaining, but I do not pay any attention to their complaints. The buses are regularly checked at unit approved garages." That was supposed to be done every three months, and witnesses said the work was performed by a journeyman and mechanic's helper.

The parents contended adults would not tolerate being bussed to their businesses in such conditions in the early morning. It would be important for them to arrive rested, ready to begin their work day. Why were children being so transported? The alternative was children going to their own school at 9:00 a.m., minutes from home, after a proper breakfast and time to do the morning chores.

Rural kids bussed to the larger schools pile onto their buses as soon as school ends, leaving no time or opportunity for the wider range of extracurricular activities that were touted as benefits for these children. No time to be part of a band, or in the school play or participate in team sports. They had to be on the bus to get home. An important part of the social life of the larger school was going to be denied to these farm youngsters.

What about the benefit of all those extra teachers and separate classes? My clients were firm about the intimacy of the one room school having special advantages for such young children. The teacher knows her students well. She knows which one has likely arrived without breakfast, and/or may go home to a meager lunch. Quiet arrangements are made. She knows which child may have a special disability, learning or otherwise. There is sometimes a home that has suffered a death, or bears the burden of an alcoholic or otherwise struggling parent or family member. Extra support and built-in counseling comes from a teacher on the spot, who understands. And from other students who share the wisdom and empathy.

The bigger school, and the vulnerable child were not a good combination, in the eyes of my clients. They knew some of their children needed special attention, and they knew help was more likely and reliable close to home.

In Endeavour, many children could skip to a home for lunch, and break their day, as the adults did, an advantage over eating a cold sandwich in a big school classroom or auditorium.

Educational television was not much of a reality in Canada in 1967, except for Ontario, where more funds were available. But the concepts of ETV, or educational television, and satellite transmissions were thoroughly explored by the citizens of Endeavour. They were ready for the information highway, and had studied the ways education could be brought to rural communities.

They talked of satellite science labs and travelling libraries, that would visit their communities. You cannot bus everyone, and there were more remote communities in need of such advanced facilities. Bring the facilities to the children through mobile units. Cheaper in the long run, they argued, and fairer to all those who live in outlying areas.

By taking the school out of the community, they argued, you've doomed the town. People would not move to a place or even stay where there was no school for their children. So if the man who owned the garage and the farm equipment dealership moved, there would be no garage. The same for the other businesses, and slowly, commerce would leave that town.

They had seen it happen to other communities on the prairies, and they knew it would happen to theirs over time as well. That domino effect that has occurred to so many rural villages and towns. It may not always be the loss of the school that triggers the demise. But in the case of Endeavour, the entire population was determined to keep their village, and not suffer the fate that was occurring throughout Saskatchewan and other rural areas of the prairies.

The inquiry heard the evidence and submissions, and on February 26, 1968 gave their report and recommendations to the provincial government that the school be retained in Endeavour, at least for a time. It was a sweet victory for those residents.

I left Saskatchewan in 1970, to move to Vancouver. Although I returned to our cottage north of Yorkton every summer, I had been afraid to go and visit Endeavour. Afraid of what I might find. I looked with grief at Tadmore, three miles from our cottage, a hamlet no longer, just a collection of houses, not all of them inhabited. Some for sale for years, with no buyers, at prices from $4,000 for a fully modern home.

The soul of Tadmore left a long time ago. Maybe when the garage or one of the two general stores shut down. Or the post office. Or the pool hall. Or when they took down the first and then the second grain elevator. It's hard to pinpoint a time, when death is so slow in coming.

What happened to the school in Endeavour? It remained open for about forty more years, closing June 2006. Endeavour remains a thriving village with more community activities than many larger towns.

# CHAPTER 43

## *Lotus Land Called*

AFTER THREE YEARS practising in Yorkton, I was beginning to get restless. Was it Jessie and her subliminal messages that it was time for me to go out and discover the world again? Vancouver was never far from my thoughts, and getting a job there as a prosecutor seemed like a good new beginning.

Over the years at the annual conventions of the Canadian Bar Association, I had routinely sought out the chief prosecutor of Vancouver, Stewart McMorran, enquiring about a job. McMorran's refusals were always courteous, if amused. The refusals were based on my gender. Women were not dependable, they went off and got married and had babies. There would be no women prosecutors in his office.

It became a game for me. I was getting fond of McMorran.

By 1970, my restlessness had gotten the better of me and I decided to leave Yorkton and move to Vancouver. To qualify to practice law in British Columbia, I had written six hours of exams, and was called to the British Columbia bar in January 1970 in Vancouver. While in Vancouver, I set up interviews with several people and law firms, with no success. I was looking to do labour law or prosecute in the criminal courts, the latter being a route for quick recognition and knowledge of the local scene.

McMorran was my first call. To my surprise, he had actually hired a woman a year previously, Wenda Deane, so the hurdle seemed less high. He was courteous as always, but there were no vacancies, and even if there had been, he wanted a commitment that I would stay at least three years. I knew I did not want to prosecute on a long-term basis, and told McMorran that I could not make such a promise. I said that if he ever needed someone on short notice, to let me know.

Other attempts to find a job were unsuccessful. One lawyer insisted it was easier for him to interview me at the Hotel

Vancouver where I was staying, rather than his office. I waited for him to call after he got out of court.

Instead of a phone call, there was a knock on my hotel room door, and there he was, bottle of scotch in hand, smile on his face. I told him I did not drink scotch, and the interview was over before it began. He never got through the door. I never got the job offer.

I returned to Yorkton. A letter from McMorran arrived in the middle of a prairie blizzard, near the end of February. There was a vacancy, and I could have the job, on my terms, without having to make a three-year commitment. I looked out the window at the howling landscape, and picked up the phone.

Some of the prosecutors were adamantly opposed to any females being hired. At least one, Eric Bendrodt, put his job on the line when Wenda was being considered. He would quit if McMorran hired her. It was never wise to throw a challenge at the Irish McMorran. Wenda was hired, and her supervisor was Bendrodt. He had a pet phrase designed to humiliate Wenda every time she would rush in from a quick adjournment to get some advice. "Ah, Wenda. What news of fresh disaster?"

Wenda would grit her teeth, tell him the problem, and Eric could supply the necessary help. He was quick and bright, but his sense of humour was often at her expense. He did not want her there, and she knew it.

Then the same challenge to McMorran when my hiring was discussed. Again, Eric reportedly put his job on the line. However, I was hired, and again, Bendrodt was made my supervisor. I never figured out if that was just McMorran being perverse. Probably.

After seven and a half years of defence work, and a lot of jury and other trials in Ontario and Saskatchewan, I was unsettled to find there were a lot of charges in *The Criminal Code of Canada* that were unfamiliar to me. The male prosecutors in the chambers court were having sport with the new girl by sending to my court all the rotten sex cases. A rite of passage obviously. Indecent assault, gross indecency, prostitution cases by the yard.

There were cases where I needed some help in learning the local charges, jargon and customs. When I went to get help from my kindly supervisor, Eric, he would sneer the same thing, "Don't you know anything?"

I was confirming his wisdom of never hiring females. Tiring of the abuse, I simply went over his head to a more senior prosecutor, Skip McCarthy, who earned my undying gratitude with his courtesy and help. I never sought help from Bendrodt after that. That was many years ago. We have both mellowed and are friends now.

Somewhere out there is a policeman, retired by now, who happened to be the young investigating officer on the first gross indecency offence that I prosecuted. He stood nearby as I scanned his report, five minutes before the case was to start. Volume and speed were the necessary skills of the day. The leisure that a defence lawyer might have was not available to a prosecutor, who might have to prosecute six or more cases in court on the same day.

I had minutes to read the report and interview the police officer before going in to begin the case. It was a charming story of a very private act in a very public place, in Pigeon Park, in the heart of skid row. I looked up from reading his report and asked the young policeman, "What's a BJ?" He couldn't believe it. He looked around for help. I looked at him impatiently, and repeated my question. "It is a blow job," he murmured, blushing. I said, "What?" "A blow job." He said again. "What the hell is that?" I asked.

The young cop was red in the face, and he knew I didn't have a clue what he was talking about. "It is fellatio," he murmurs, quieter. "How do you spell that? What is that?" I demanded. He told me.

I thought I knew most street language by then, but apparently not. Law school had been no help. The euphemism that our family law professor at Osgoode used for sexual intercourse was that the couple was, "... in bed together reading *The New York Times.*" Those were gentler times.

I have often wondered what that young policeman told his

buddies when he returned to the squad room that day. I'm sure for the next number of years, if my name ever came up in the newspaper, he would tell whoever he was with that I was the dumbest prosecutor he had ever encountered.

That may have been part of the reason I had repeated requests from friendly Vancouver City police officers to come up to the viewing room and see the porn films that they were confiscating. I had never seen one, and was curious. But I knew that once in the room, I would be watching the film and the officers would be watching me, having made book on my reactions. I declined the kind invitations.

At the time I was prosecuting, there were eleven female Vancouver City police officers. They were given desk jobs only, although paid the same as the male officers. I became friendly with some of the women. They resented not being able to use their training and do the same work as the male officers. Some of the male officers resented that they were getting the same pay.

I spoke to McMorran about the women, knowing he had a good relationship with the police chief and commission. Why couldn't these women be assigned the regular work of any police officer? McMorran was appalled at the idea. "Nancy, how would you feel if one of those women were shot and killed on the job?"

I replied that I would feel terrible, the same as I would if that happened to a male officer. McMorran shook his head and said, "I just don't understand you sometimes. "

But the best dust-up with McMorran was still to come.

# CHAPTER 44

## *"Take Off Those Goddamn Pants"*

"Isn't it true you once had to take your pants off to appear in court?"

It was the early seventies at a conference on Women's Rights at the University of British Columbia. The question was aimed at me. The previous day at the conference some irate young and radical women had rushed the stage, objecting to remarks of a well known feminist professor from Seattle, Pepper Schwartz. That had ensured more press were present on this day, the press no doubt hoping for more ink.

On that startling query, the cameras swung around.

The question was from a law student, Leslie Pinder, who had worked as a court recorder in Vancouver Provincial Court when I was prosecuting in 1970. (The same Leslie for whom I had written a letter of recommendation when she applied to law school. My letter assured UBC Pinder was more than ready for law school, but questioned if they were ready for her.)

As a court recorder, Leslie knew that the ruling god of all Vancouver City prosecutors and staff, Stewart McMorran, would never allow any females working for him to wear pants to work.

After prosecuting in Provincial Criminal Court for ten months, I had given my notice to leave the end of December, ready to begin a civil and criminal defence practice of my own. To ensure I would not be saddled with any trial continuations, I was assigned to traffic court at 475 Main Street for my last two weeks.

It was the Friday before Christmas, and I had a clothes dilemma. I was having drinks with friends after court, then dinner with a favourite date, and dancing after. No time to rush home after court to change. I needed the right outfit for court as well as my busy evening.

I had just bought an expensive navy blue French pantsuit,

tailored, with a tunic top. Perfect, I thought. I'll bring pearls for the evening. With my thoughts fixed on my after-work social agenda, McMorran's edict against pants never entered my mind.

By 9:30 that morning, I was in the courtroom negotiating a plea arrangement with the amiable Nick Mussalem, a few minutes before Judge David Moffat would enter to begin court. Suddenly the door at the back of the courtroom crashed open and in strode a red faced McMorran.

Jabbing a finger at me, he yelled, "No one wears pants in my courtrooms! Take off those goddamn pants!"

And out he stormed, never bothering to look back, to return to his office at 312 Main Street. Someone at 475 Main had ratted me out.

The court clerk and Mussalem were stunned silent, I was mortified. I excused myself and went into my tiny temporary office down the hall. And took off my pants. That left me with the one-piece tunic top. It was the day of the mini skirt, and believe me, this was a very mini skirt.

Back into the courtroom and the day proceeded. The pants came back on at the end of the court day. I never talked about the episode. Until that day at UBC, a couple of years later.

The press liked the way Leslie framed her question, and I still get asked about it, decades later. I can see the obit, "Judge who had to take pants off to appear in court, dies."


Court apparel for women continued to be a trivial issue for me. It gave my friend Bill McIntyre a laugh on one occasion. He reported that the gentle Peter Seaton, his friend and colleague on the BC Court of Appeal, had returned from speaking to law students at the University of British Columbia, where I apparently got him into trouble. In the question and answer session after his talk, a young female law student asked if it was permissible for women to wear pants with their court attire, rather than skirts.

Seaton, a lovely man and respected judge, told the class that that would certainly not be appropriate, that women lawyers in court must wear skirts. The trap was sprung. The mischievous law student then pointed out that Provincial Court Judge Nancy Morrison frequently wore pants when presiding in court. So why not women lawyers?

Years later, after leaving the provincial bench, in 1981, I went to Matz and Wozny, tailors for the law profession in Vancouver at that time. I had decided to poke a little fun at the pinstriped pants that the men usually wore in court by having a pinstriped skirt made. Matz and Wozny were aghast. No! Pinstripe was for men's trousers only. Never for a court skirt. I explained there was no law about all this. Then threatened to go down the street to another tailor. They gave a doomsday sigh and made the skirt, very unhappy.

Within a couple of years, pinstripe skirts for courtroom wear were popping up all over, significantly in Matz and Wozny ads.

# CHAPTER 45

# *You're One of Those, Aren't You*

I GREW UP believing that banks were good. (You know where this is going.) They were pleasant places where little kids were encouraged to deposit their nickels and dimes, people sometimes gave you candy, everyone smiled at you, and bank shares were really good.

I switched banks when I was eight, when the Bank of Nova Scotia came to town. That was Dad's Cape Breton chauvinism. Moira and I were given some shares in the Bank. In order to get the shares in my name, I had to declare my occupation and marital status; it would have to be "spinster." That caused chuckles from the bank manager, but not from me once I looked up the meaning of the word.

The dictionary defined: "Spinster — an unmarried woman, especially elderly, thought unlikely to marry, one who spins historically." Oxford confirmed, "It is now always a derogatory term, referring or alluding to a stereotype of an older woman who is unmarried, childless, prissy, and repressed."

No bank should piss off an eight-year-old.

Throughout university in Vancouver and Toronto, I banked at whatever branch was closest to the school. In Toronto, there was a small Toronto Dominion branch across the street from Osgoode Hall, where Dad would transfer funds from his TD account to mine.

When it was time for my call to the Ontario Bar in 1963, it was also time for me to cut the financial umbilical cord. I wanted to pay for my own call fees, about $300, my new court gown, vest and shirts, another $350, and take a two-week skiing vacation in the Laurentians before starting the practice of law. I was about to get my first loan, $1,000.

My male classmates, experienced in financial ways, counselled me. Just a straight 6% demand loan. No longer term, higher interest, or special loan. And deal with the manager, not the subordinates. The genial manager of my TD branch, where I had banked from 1958 to 1963, was happy to consider the loan. All looked fine, no problem. "We'll just have your father co-sign for you." No. Dad did not even know my plans. This was me establishing financial independence.

No co-signer, no loan, said the TD. My last ever dealings with the TD Bank. Down the street I went to the large main Toronto branch of the Bank of Nova Scotia. This should have been my bank all along. We had history. I still owned those shares. Voices echoed in that vast cathedral space. Soft voices, like in a church.

I felt small. This was a bigger bank than I was used to. I went up to a counter and announced I wanted to see the manager. Why? To obtain a loan. They pointed across the marble cavern to where they Scotia Plan Loans were dispensed, telling me that is where I wanted to go. No, I want to see the manager. I did not want the Scotia Plan loan.

The manager was away on holidays. Would I see the assistant manager? Of course. They called for the assistant manager, and he ushered me into his large office. He seemed delighted to meet me, was interested that I was about to be called to the bar, and did not blink an eye when I told him part of the loan was for a ski holiday at Mont-Tremblant. And that I had not yet begun work, but I had a job lined up in Niagara Falls.

He was writing some things on his desk, and then pushed some papers across for me to sign. What was this? He said that was my new chequing account, that he was just depositing $1,000 into it; and the paper confirmed the straight 6% demand loan. The account could be transferred to Niagara once I was in residence there. He told me to have a great time at Mont-Tremblant. This was not a typical experience for a woman seeking a loan in 1963.

When I was practising with Dad in Yorkton, I was lulled into the feeling that banks were friendly and benign. The local managers of all banks were great citizens, Rotarians, Kinsmen, etc. All men, of course, but that had always been the case. My feminist focus was not on the banks.

Then Gordon Wallace came to town, the young banker from

Winnipeg rumoured to fix the problems with the local Bank of Montreal. We became friends, and it was apparent that he would not stay a small city banker for too long. He was bright and ambitious, and ended up in Vancouver before I did.

When he was in Yorkton, Gordon was tasked by the Bank head office to interview university graduates in the four Western provinces for prospective bank talent. That was 1968. When he came back from his extensive interviews, Gordon had some serious concerns that he shared in confidence with me. *(I know, Gordon — but that was over forty-five years ago. It's time.)*

Before he began his interviews, he was instructed that no females were to be hired or even considered, even though he would be interviewing males and females at all the universities. He would know that; the women would not. The instruction and the duplicity concerned him. And the stupidity. Because he found that so many of the candidates who were outstanding were female. There was one in particular, a young woman who was such a complete package of brains, talent and personality that he called head office and urged they reconsider their policy of hiring no women. I think they considered a special position for her.

Gordon's discomfort was reassuring to me as far as my friend was concerned, but it was no consolation when it came to women's chances and standing in the banks. Either as employees or customers.

There were other bad bank moments in Yorkton. Mom had her own bank account. From an early age, she had counselled Moira and me always to keep our own bank account, even when married. Mom had inherited her old family home when her sister Jane had died years earlier. The old house had three rental apartments. That gave Mom independence that she valued.

One day when Dad was home for lunch, Mom said, "William, I was at the bank today, and there is almost nothing in my account." She was not about to deplete it, she had just checked the balance. "Oh", said Dad, "I forgot to tell you. Mr. Yee needed a mortgage and we took $10,000 out of your account." Mom wanted to know how he could do that without her signing. He murmured something to the effect that the bank allowed it. Of course it did. Dad was their lawyer, their biggest client, his trust account was huge, he did all his banking with the TD Bank, and his office was in their building. Jessie was not pleased, but the mortgage gave her decent interest and security. Dad had the grace to be embarrassed.

It was not until Dad died in 1979 that I learned more about another bank practice of the days. At Dad's funeral, Danny Eng, a popular Chinese restaurateur came and spoke to me.

> You know, many of us who are Chinese would not have been able to go into business if it had not been for your father. The banks would not give loans to us, to Chinese, so your Dad arranged private loans and mortgages for us. I began my restaurant, thanks to your Dad.

## You're One Of Those, Aren't You...

When I moved to Vancouver in March 1970 to take a job as an assistant city prosecutor at 312 Main St., next door was the oldest bank building in Vancouver, the Bank of Montreal branch at Main and Hastings. Many of us deposited our cheques there.

By December 1970, I had decided to set up my own law firm, and spotted office space I wanted in the barely renovated Gastown area. The only other female prosecutor in the province, Wenda Deane, (who had been the first one ever hired ) decided to join me in practice. An old friend from UBC days and a wise accountant and entrepreneur, Chuck Croft, drew up a business plan for me, which suggested a line of credit of $15,000 to cover first year operating costs, equipment and salaries.

Wenda also banked at the same Bank of Montreal, so we went to see the manager, whom neither of us knew. We were prepared to leave the bank and go down the street to another financial institution if we did not get what we wanted, the line of credit at 6%.

Dick Nelles was the bank manager. He welcomed us, complimented our business plan, and then did what old style bankers were so good at — chatted to find out more about us. Where was I from? Saskatchewan. Yes, he had been with the bank there, even in Yorkton briefly. He had not met my father, but knew of him. Wenda related her history, two years in practice, married to a radiologist, no children yet. I had been in practice for eight years by this time, in three provinces.

Nelles assured us the line of credit and interest rate were fine. "We'll just have your father co-sign for you, and your husband co-sign for you," as he looked first at me and then at Wenda. I smiled. "Tell me, when my male colleagues come in here for a loan, do you have their wives and their mommies co-sign for them?"

There was a moment of silence. Nelles looked at me, and then said, smiling, "You're one of those, aren't you." "Yes. I am." Women's Lib was a derogatory term at that time. It had not been said, but I knew what he meant.

Dick Nelles leaned back and laughed. "Of course I don't."

He became my favourite banker, and his file contained every article ever written about us. He was close to retirement. When he moved on, so did I.

# CHAPTER 46

## *One Alexander Street*

A RMED WITH our line of credit, Wenda and I needed to rent office space. I liked Gastown, in spite of the drunks on the street and pigeon droppings everywhere. It showed the promise of Toronto's Yorkville. One Alexander Street was a heritage red brick building at the square where the statue of Gassy Jack stood, backing on to the railway tracks, with a view of the harbour and the North Shore mountains. The lone tenant was Town Group, the developer/realtors who were developing Gastown and who owned the building.

Wenda and I went to see about a lease. The space we wanted was on the second floor on the north side of the building, overlooking the harbour and mountains. We met with a younger partner of Town Group, Bob Saunders, who was pleased with a law office going into the space. We came to terms on a lease. Smiles all around.

As we stood up to shake hands, Bob said, "All right, girls, I'll get the lease prepared for your bosses to sign."

My architect friend, Ross Kembar, liked the space, an exposed brick wall along one side, almost floor-to-ceiling windows on the north side overlooking the view, and ample space, although long and narrow. Wenda was a born interior decorator, and her ideas on colour and furniture meshed with Ross's concept of the space. He suggested exposed track lighting, something I had never seen in any office. Wenda agreed. We had soundproof glass partition walls, so our secretary and clients in the waiting area could enjoy the same view that Wenda and I had in our offices. Such open glass exposure for a law office then was most unusual.

Larry Killam of Town Group was nervous about these two women setting up a law office in his building. He kept telling me that the decor had to be first class, that this was a show building. When our office was finished, I teased Killam that I was going

*December 1970, Vancouver Sun. The picture that launched thirty-five complaints to the Law Society that Wenda Deane and I were advertising illegally*

Photo: *Vancouver Sun*

to charge a fee for all the prospective tenants he was bringing in to show them our place. They were great landlords.

I waved to the trainmen below, welcomed the new restaurants that started springing up in Gastown, watched the float planes take off and land in the harbour, and felt sorry for my Osgoode classmates stuck in concrete caves in Toronto.

While work on the office was under way in mid-December 1970, a *Vancouver Sun* reporter who covered the provincial court knew that Wenda and I were forming our law firm and wanted to do an article on us. There was no other female law firm in the province, and maybe not in the country at that time. I agreed to the interview, on the condition that the article not appear until after I had left the prosecutor's office, at the end of December. The reporter wanted a picture in our office, which was still under construction. He brought a photographer over. The only place to sit was on a construction hobby horse, where Wenda and I perched for the shot.

To my consternation, three days later, a huge picture of Wenda and me appeared on the second front page of *The Vancouver Sun*, with the article announcing the formation of our female law firm at "One Alexander Street in Gastown." I went to apologize to Stewart McMorran, but he did not mind. However, other lawyers did. Thirty-five lawyers from the lower mainland and Vancouver Island sent complaints to the Law Society of British Columbia, our governing body, that Wenda and I were advertising. It was against the rules of the Law Society for lawyers to advertise at all. The big photo was bad enough. But the address of our office under the picture and in the article was the nail in our coffin.

We had to appear before a discipline committee of the Benchers on these complaints. Dick Anderson, who later became a judge, was head of the three-member committee. He and the other two members did not take the complaints that seriously. They were interested in our plans for the practice, liked the photo, and wished us well.

Stewart McMorran kindly gave us some ad hoc prosecution work to do, and legal aid sent over some minor cases. Clients slowly began to come in to the office.

One Friday afternoon I was alone in the office, having sent our secretary home early. I was vacuuming, and the phone rang. It was a call from the head of Legal Aid asking if I was available to take the defence of a rape trial that was going ahead Monday in New Westminster in the Supreme Court of BC. The lawyer of record, Ken Young, had himself removed that Friday morning from the case, as he had not been paid. It then fell to Legal Aid to find a lawyer immediately, as the trial judge had said that Young could be excused from the case, but the jury trial would go ahead Monday morning regardless of whether the accused had a lawyer or not. The judges were tough in those days. This was Mr. Justice William McIntyre, whom I did not know.

In Ontario and Saskatchewan I had been defence counsel on at least four rape trials, plus many other criminal trials by that time. It was surprising to get the call from the head of Legal Aid as up until that time I was getting only minor offence cases. Given the late hour on this Friday afternoon, I suspected every male criminal law lawyer in town had been canvassed or gone skiing, before my name came up.

I said I would take the case if the accused was out on bail, so he would be available for me to interview and prepare, and if there was a transcript of the preliminary hearing. Those two conditions were met, and the transcript and file of the case were sent over by cab.

The trial began Monday morning in New Westminster. It lasted three or four days. Juries in those days were often reluctant to bring in a conviction of rape, knowing that the penalty was very harsh. (Later amendments to *The Criminal Code* made it easier for juries to find guilt within a range of lesser included offences, to suit varying degrees of culpability.) This jury acquitted the accused.

At the end of the trial, Justice McIntyre followed the time-honoured tradition of the judge taking counsel out for lunch or dinner, while awaiting the verdict. Just before that, he had called me into his chambers and, in effect, asked me who I was. He told me I had done the best cross-examination he had ever seen in a courtroom, a compliment I treasure as the finest in my career.

With few female litigation lawyers in the province, McIntyre wondered where I had come from. I explained I had been practicing for seven years in Ontario and Saskatchewan, that I was from Saskatchewan. McIntyre said he was from Moose Jaw. I told him that the only person I knew from Moose Jaw was Bill Grayson, a lawyer who was married to Betty Christopherson, my first cousin. McIntyre smiled and said, "Bill Grayson is my cousin."

They had both been in World War II, and both had gone to law school after at the University of Saskatchewan. Grayson, a revered war hero from the Juno Beach invasion, had graduated as the gold medalist.

So Bill McIntyre and I considered ourselves related, albeit remotely, and he and his beloved wife, Mimi, became almost family for me. Bill had met Mimi in England and brought her back as a war bride.

Shipped overseas in 1941, Bill was part of the invasion of Sicily in July 1943 and by December, engaged in Canada's famous battle at Ortona, the small Italian port town on the Adriatic. The Canadians won the terrible house-to-house battles with the elite German unit who had been commanded to hold the town. But the Canadian victory was at a terrible cost. Bill never spoke of the war, except once to say that Ortona was the worst Christmas imaginable.

When I was appointed to the provincial bench, Bill wrote me a gracious note, telling me that I would be a good judge, and counselling me to "pay no attention to those fellows on the Court of Appeal." A year later, Bill was appointed to the Court of Appeal. I wrote him a gracious note congratulating him on the appointment, and assuring him that I would continue to follow his advice with regard to the Court of Appeal.

After six years on the BC Court of Appeal, Bill was appointed to the Supreme Court of Canada in 1979 where he served for ten years. He retired in 1989 when Mimi's health became an issue, and they returned to live in Vancouver.

His biography, *William R. McIntyre, Paladin of the Common Law,* was by Prof. W.H. McConnell of the University Saskatchewan. He wrote that McIntyre saw *The Canadian Charter of Rights and Freedoms* "operating essentially as a supplement and occasional corrective, not as a rival to the common-law."

When on the Court of Appeal, Bill wrote a dissent in *R.v. Miller and Cockriell* in 1975. Miller and Cockriell had been found guilty of murder. The death penalty was still part of Canadian law. Their defence counsel, Joe Wood, had argued that the death penalty was an imposition of cruel and unusual punishment, contrary to the *Charter*. McIntyre agreed, and wrote his brilliant dissent. The year the case went to the Supreme Court of Canada, Parliament abolished capital punishment.

Bill died June 14, 2009. Mimi had predeceased him fifteen years earlier, and a few years before his death, Bill married a former classmate, Dorothy Parkinson, who had been a widow for many years.

I often think how lucky I was to be vacuuming my office that Friday afternoon, to take that case in New Westminster and meet Bill McIntyre, who became a mentor and a special person in my life.

# CHAPTER 47

# *Marjorie*

O NE OF THE ADVANTAGES of living in Vancouver was meeting so many other professional women. My friends in Vancouver included many in journalism, law and politics.

The gutsy Marjorie Nichols was one of those.

It was 1972, and Marjorie Nichols would pay only in cash. For everything, meals, hotels, travel. She did not believe in being tracked. She was a superb journalist, fearless, brilliant, non-partisan. As *The Vancouver Sun's* columnist and legislative reporter covering the new NDP government and Premier Dave Barrett, she was more than a thorn in Barrett's side. He finally yelled at her, "Fuck you!" in an infamous confrontation in the halls of the Legislature in Victoria.

The 'small c' conservative in her knew early the power of a government to track its citizens; while the rest of us embraced the cashless society, the wonder of credit cards, as we wrote blizzards of cheques, Marjorie paid cash. Prescient and paranoid. Lord knows her reaction to Facebook, Twitter, Instagram and Linkedin had she lived long enough.

Our mutual friend, newspaperman Patrick Nagel, had introduced us shortly after my move to Vancouver in 1970. After Bruno came into my life, he became part of her fan club. She called him Little Chief. Her visits to his home in Gibson's ensured the problems of the world were solved in exuberant late-into-the-night discussions, and ended with us tucking Marjorie into the spare bedroom.

Marjorie was hard wired with energy, political knowledge, and ethics. In those dreary budget lockdowns where journalists get to see the budget hours before it is tabled in Parliament, Marjorie was one of the few who raced through the pages with total comprehension.

In the early eighties, I organized a fundraising dinner in Vancouver for the Judy LaMarsh fund, to raise money for female Liberal candidates running for office. The entertainment was all

Photo: *Vancouver Sun*

*Marjorie Nichols, with journalists Robert Lewis,
Allan Fotheringham and Jack Webster in 1986.*

political. Nancy White, the satirical songbird from Ontario, and a panel of three media luminaries, Jack Webster, Allan Fotheringham and Marjorie Nichols. They were the best of friends. This was the first and only time all three appeared together.

Marjorie kept worrying about her material. She would call and read out some of it. Good enough? It was great. Those three loved one another, but they were all a tad competitive. They were a hit, with Marjorie the undisputed winner. Dr. Foth and Webster beamed like proud parents.

Marjorie's final job was in Ottawa, covering Parliament. Her life was cut short at forty-eight by cancer. Pamela Wallin was one of the special friends in Ottawa who cared for that amazing woman in her final months.

A day or two after Marjorie's death, on December 29, 1991, Bob Krieger of *The Province* newspaper in Vancouver had a political cartoon. It was St. Peter, calling out, "Okay! Everybody clean up your act! Marjorie Nichols is on her way!"

# CHAPTER 48

# *The Father*

HE WAS TALL, fair-haired, burly and distinguished. Very bright, he came from old Maritime stock, pedigree intact. To no one's surprise, he became a respected professional in his city, two or three degrees dripping off his letterhead.

His first marriage did not go too well. That wife arrived with two young daughters. In a rather ungrateful manner, she left suddenly after a couple of years. He had been an excellent provider and devoted stepfather. Who knows where the first wife went. He did not go looking.

His second wife was in awe of his brains and position. They gave the marriage a good try, and had a sweet baby daughter. But by the time the child was five, the second wife knew it was over. The marriage had not gone well. She and the young daughter left for another part of the country, and the father lost touch.

It was awhile before he married again. The third marriage produced another baby daughter. But this marriage was not going well. They separated, but remained in touch.

In the meantime, he had been thinking about his first biological daughter, now fifteen. He wondered where she was, and what she was like. Was that guilt he was feeling? He had given no support, financial or otherwise, to the second wife and his daughter for almost ten years.

So he hired a detective and found them quickly, in a city at the other end of the country. His second wife had remarried, but had recently separated from her second husband. The daughter had been very fond of her mother's second husband, and was grieving the loss of her stepfather. She was a sweet, fifteen-year-old girl, unsophisticated and young for her age. But bright academically, generous and interesting. And shy. Then her real father made contact.

There was anticipation, excitement, phone calls, gifts, the meeting, and then more visits. The young girl was overwhelmed having her real father back in her life. He courted her with flowers and phone calls. The second wife watched this love gratefully, seeing her daughter so happy.

Could she go and stay with her real father for the summer? Please? All right.

And then the painful request to the mother at the end of the summer. Dad wants me to live with him and go to school in his city for a year. The excitement of the renewed bond was too much to resist. The mother reluctantly agreed.

Thanksgiving weekend came, and the daughter went back to visit her mother. School is fine. New friends, assignments, teachers, all were going well. Dad's third wife and baby daughter were not in the picture. This was the mother's first Christmas without her daughter. It seemed easier to go away and visit friends rather than feel the loneliness. So she did not know about the phone calls.

Just before Christmas, the social workers began trying to call the mother. These were social workers from the father's city. When they could not reach her by phone, they wrote her a letter, saying, please call us as soon as possible. It is about your daughter.

The father lived in an upscale condo, and when his neighbors heard crying and beseeching by the young girl through the walls, they phoned the child helpline. Social workers called to check it out. The shy young daughter answered the door, and all their questions, and smiled, assuring them that all was well.

Time passed.

The nosy neighbours claimed to continue to hear things, and this caused another visit from the authorities. Both father and daughter were somewhat incredulous, earnest in their denials of any problems.

The social workers almost believed them. But they wanted to talk to the mother.

It was lead hitting her heart when the mother returned from her Christmas visit and opened the letter from the social workers. She called and heard the social worker's concerns. The daughter had not attended school at all, since early September. This was the end of December. School stories she had told her mother at Thanksgiving were fabrications. There were no classes, no teachers, no friends. Hanging up the phone, the mother's instinct kicked in. She had a phone call to make, to the first wife.

The first wife began to cry. "I always knew I should have warned you, especially after I heard you had a daughter." Then it poured out.

The professional creep, this father, during his first marriage, had kept first one young stepdaughter home from school, and then the second young stepdaughter, alternately, while the mother was at work. And he swore the six and eight-year-old little girls to secrecy for two years, as he persisted in raping them, time and again.

Finally, the first wife discovered the horror, and fled with her children. She never told anyone, and criminal charges were not laid. The father was safe.

The second wife took a plane immediately to the father's city. She met with the police, the social workers and a lawyer. They knew they had to get to the girl when he was not around. And they needed a court order to apprehend the girl, if necessary, without the father being alerted first. They needed an *ex parte* order, with no notice to the father. Courts are very reluctant to give such orders.

They got the order, very quickly, that same day. And then they went to the condo door when they knew the father was at work. The girl answered the door, and the mother reached out for her, crying, " I love you. And whatever has happened to you does not matter. I love you, I love you."

And the girl began to sob, and sob.

The mother took her home. There, a psychologist said it would be detrimental for the girl to testify about the repeated raping and incest, so the father was never charged.

The police wanted him, badly. So did the lawyer, and the social workers. They all pleaded with the mother. But she could think only of protecting her daughter, and she relied only on the advice of the psychologist.

That was a number of years ago. The father remained free, a respected professional.

His daughter from his third marriage would be older now.

# CHAPTER 49

# *Being a Judge*

I NEVER WANTED to be a judge. It was never my dream, never my ambition. Growing up in Yorkton as I had, with a father who was a lawyer, there were many opportunities to meet and know judges. Our local county court judge, Andrew Kindred, lived next door. The Court of Queens Bench judges from Regina came regularly on the assizes to preside over cases set in Yorkton.

The legal profession in Saskatchewan was small and collegial. Many lawyers were Dalhousie graduates in the earlier days, and almost all were friends of my father. With a large law practice, Dad's cases were often the majority of cases to be heard. Which meant the judges could not socialize with Mom and Dad until all Dad's cases were finished in that particular assize.

Of those judges who came to Yorkton to sit, when I was still in school and university, I had my favourites, especially Hully Davis and Emmett Hall.

From an early age, if you had asked me for a word association for judge, I would have said "lonely." Some of this would have come from hearing my Mother say, on more than one occasion, "Poor Hully, he was eating his dinner alone again at the Holiday Inn." The judges seldom brought their wives with them. Yes, the judges were all male.

It did not seem like a job of joy to me.

But as a young lawyer, it was a pleasure to appear before certain judges.

Judge Johnstone Roberts presided over the Niagara Falls Magistrate Criminal Court when I began practising law in Niagara. He was one of the finest men in our profession. He brought brains, courtesy and respect to the courtroom. If you had prepared your case well, he never failed to praise your work, even when you lost your case.

Roberts, tough but fair, also brought empathy to his court. It was 9:30 one morning and the adjournments and guilty pleas were being called first. The courtroom was crowded with lawyers and their clients. A man by the name of Smith was called; Mr. Smith stood up and lurched forward. He was drunk. He was not represented by a lawyer. The practice of many judges would have been to instruct the sheriff to take the impaired accused to the cells to sober up overnight.

Most of us in attendance that morning were waiting for that scene, Mr. Smith being yarded out of the courtroom down to the cells. However, not so. Johnstone Roberts was not that kind of judge. "Mr. Smith, I don't think you are ready to deal with your case this morning. Am I right?" Roberts spoke slowly with courtesy. Smith seemed to straighten up a bit and looked at the judge and answered, "Yes."

"I understand. Mr. Smith. I am going to ask that you leave the courtroom now and go home. I know that when you come back tomorrow morning at the same time, you will be ready to indicate to me what course you would like your case to take at that time. Would you do that?"

"Yes, sir. I will. Thank you."

"You're welcome, Mr. Smith. I look forward to seeing you tomorrow morning."

Mr. Smith left the courtroom with a lot more dignity than when he had entered. Not one person in the courtroom dared snicker. I happened to be in the courtroom the next morning, and Mr. Smith did indeed return, this time sober, and was met with the same courtesy from this profoundly wise judge.

Long after Johnstone Roberts retired, I was back in Niagara Falls at a gathering where Charlotte and Bob Lewis had ensured he would attend. I had the chance to tell him what an influence he had had on my career. It was never lost on me that judges are instrumental in training lawyers, in ways good and bad.

In defending a client in a criminal case, you spend a lot of time in preparation and getting to know your client well, so that in the event that your client is found guilty, ( by some misguided judge...) you are able to speak to sentence to obtain the most favourable result possible.

After speaking to sentence, I remember regularly feeling sorry for the judge. I had pleaded every conceivably good aspect of my client, how good he was to his grandmother, how he volunteered to help the disabled, how he rescued small puppies and kittens, how he had overcome illiteracy, how many foster homes he had been shuffled to and abused in, etc.

I would sit down and think to myself, as I looked at the judge, *I wouldn't have your job for all the rice in China.* I tried my best to make sentencing very difficult for the judge. The thought of being one of those judges never occurred to me. I liked being in the courtroom as a lawyer.

Then one morning in late September 1972, I received a telephone call from Rosemary Brown, who had been elected in August as an NDP Member of the Legislature for British Columbia. She was a member of the new NDP government of Premier Dave Barrett. Rosemary and I had met working together on *The Vancouver Status of Women*, which had arisen from the 1970 *Report of the Royal Commission on the Status of Women*. We were friends, but not as close as we would later become.

Rosemary was excited, "I have great news. Alex MacDonald, our Attorney General, has agreed to appoint you to the bench as our first appointment to the Provincial Court."

I was stunned. "Rosemary, I am too young to die." I was thirty-five. It was Rosemary's turn to be stunned.

Rosemary, an early and tough advocate for women's rights had been pressing Premier Barrett and the cabinet to make their new government's first judicial appointment a female. The cabinet agreed, but they wanted the appointment to be nonpartisan, not an NDP member. Alex MacDonald had told her that he wanted the names of four women lawyers. Those were provided to him, and he indicated he would appoint me. I had never met MacDonald, but I did fit the bill, female, and a known Liberal, never NDP.

Suddenly it was an advantage to be a female in the law profession?

Many believe being a judge is the ultimate honour for a

lawyer, and that is true. My respect for the judiciary was profound. But for me personally, it signalled a life isolated from many friends in my profession. It meant full stop to all political involvement and activities, and a loss of independence in determining my own work and recreation schedules, where I would work and with whom. I didn't want to think what it might do to my social life.

I told Rosemary I did not want to be appointed, explained why, and thought that was the end of it. I was also about to drive to the Chilcotins for a week-long holiday.

The week away was great. I returned Friday evening, October 4, 1972. As I walked into my home in North Vancouver, the phone was ringing. It was a frustrated Judy LaMarsh yelling, "Where have you been?" I reminded her I had taken a week off to spend at a lodge near Riske Creek in the Chilcotins. Judy barreled on.

> You always said you would give your left arm to meet Bruno Gerussi. Well, we're going up to Gibsons tomorrow. He has invited me to his place there for Thanksgiving, and I said I would only go if I could bring a friend. So we are catching a ferry tomorrow afternoon to the Sunshine Coast. We are taking your car.

My heart did a sudden flip.

Judy had just moved to Vancouver for a year of broadcasting opposite the legendary Jack Webster on a rival station. She had arrived to find no one had made any arrangements for her first program, due the next morning from 9:00 a.m. to noon. In desperation she phoned Bruno who was in Gibsons filming *Beachcombers*. They were old friends, and she had been on his radio program a number of times. He was happy to come on her opening program, arranging with the director to film around him while he roared over to Vancouver in a water taxi and back after the end of the show. It was during a break in the show that

Bruno invited Judy for Thanksgiving. She accepted, with the condition that she bring a friend. Judy was matchmaking.

I had first seen Bruno in 1960 when I was in law school in Toronto. A group of us had gone to Stratford to see *Romeo and Juliet*. Bruno's Romeo was unforgettable, as was Bruno. I had followed his career — saw him in *Coriolanus* in 1961 at Stratford, and knew of his switch to radio after his young wife, Ida, had died suddenly, leaving Bruno with two young children to raise. I had been a big fan of his CBC radio show; Bruno's show transformed radio in North America in the mid to late sixties.

The next day, October 5, was the beginning of Thanksgiving weekend. Judy had told Bruno that she and her friend would be arriving in a turquoise Thunderbird. Ever the tease, she deliberately did not reveal the gender of her friend. Ever cool, Bruno later admitted, curious as he was, he refused to ask. He told Judy to look for his orange BMW that would be parked at the end of the road leading off the ferry, and to have the Thunderbird fall in behind the BMW; he would guide us to his place.

Judy was not familiar with the ferry system, but I knew that the last ferry left Langdale on the Sunshine Coast at 8:30 p.m. to return to Horseshoe Bay and Vancouver. That meant that we would be staying overnight, either at Bruno's or at a motel. I told her we would have to pack an overnight bag.

I still remember that inner flutter driving off the ferry down the ramp and seeing the orange BMW parked up ahead with that well-known face peering out the window. Bruno pulled his car out in front of us and we followed him down a winding road to a charming house he had rented on the waterfront. Bruno's two children had remained living in Toronto, as he had come out to British Columbia that first year to begin filming *Beachcombers*. However, they were visiting their Dad that weekend. Tina, sixteen, Rico, twenty, and his partner and future wife, Patsy Berton, were all at his home.

Bruno, the generous host, was pouring huge drinks for everyone before dinner that first night, rum and coke, Judy's favourite. The conversation was spirited, everyone contributing. Bruno's children were worldly and independent, and we all became combative over the new show which was the rage of the day, Archie Bunker and *All in the Family.*

Long a fan of Lenny Bruce, Bruno delighted in the fearless issues and tough language featured on the show, language considered impolite, racist, off colour. Both he and Judy as well as Tina, Rico and Patsy all agreed that bringing that language out into the open demystified it, took the sting away, showed prejudice for what it was. I remember sitting cross-legged on the floor, leaning forward and pounding my fist on the rug, trying to take on all five of them, arguing that such language would perpetuate itself and become acceptable in everyday language. I didn't mind the swearing, it was the racial slurs that had bothered me. To say I lost the argument would be an understatement. Bruno did not mind my swearing in the least. His language could peel paint.

Judy and I ended up staying the weekend. The attraction between Bruno and me was immediate and mutual. After dinner that Saturday evening, Bruno came with me out to my car to bring in our overnight bags. It took us a while to bring in the bags.

The suggested appointment to the provincial court bench was far from my mind. However, in the several weeks that followed, Rosemary persisted. She was aided by our friend, Gary Lauk, also recently elected as an NDP MLA. Lauk reminded me that I had been making a lot of noise, giving speeches on women's rights, advocating for more women to be appointed to various government and non-government positions, and if I was not prepared to put my money where my mouth was, why should anyone else. That was probably the most compelling argument. Except I had not been advocating for myself, but for women generally who were consistently frozen out in every profession, government and business.

At the time, I was in practice with some frisky left-wing lawyers, Bill Deverell, Frank Harrop, Josiah Wood and Wayne Powell. They were good lawyers, fine company and the only law firm that ever asked me to join them. They were great fun to practice and be with.

They were also pretty good on feminist issues. Although there was that time they were hiring a new secretary. The interviews were on a Saturday morning, with coffee breaks at the Normandy Café below the office, where I joined them as they reviewed the candidates.

"Great knockers on that last one," enthused one. It was 1971, and I told them in no uncertain terms that such observations were reprehensible. They seem chastened.

At the next coffee break, after the final interviews, one candidate was the favourite. The partners discussed her skills, work ethic, experience. "And," beamed the naughty Frank Harrop, "Did you notice? She's got great references!"

I did not want to leave practice, but eventually agreed to take the appointment, promising myself that I would give it a year, and if I did not like it, I would return to practice. I was sworn in as a judge of the Provincial Court of British Columbia in December 1972, the third female judge in the province. I was to sit in the criminal court in Burnaby.

Bruno and I had been dating for just over two months when I was sworn in. My Mom and Dad and sister Moira were present for the swearing in, as was Bruno. From the beginning, Bruno had encouraged my taking the appointment. Attending a judicial swearing in ceremony was new for him. What to wear ? He was not fond of wearing a suit and tie. I assured him it would not matter. He always dressed with style. He showed up in a dark brown turtle neck sweater and a classic brown check suit. He brought me his first-ever gift, a carved wooden plaque, nine inches by seventeen inches, modern in design. He had not carved it, although I was soon to learn how much he loved carving and sculpture. He later carved an exact copy of the plaque for himself. The original has stayed on my office wall from that day forward.

One of the older provincial court judges from the Vancouver Main Street Provincial Court came to Burnaby for my swearing in, Jim Bartram. His affectionate nickname was Jungle Jim.

He was older, wise, a thoroughly decent man and judge. I did not know him personally, although I had prosecuted briefly in his court at Main Street in 1970. I was pleased he had made the effort to come to my swearing in.

During the small reception after, he came over to congratulate me and told me I would be a good judge.

Then Judge Bartram added, "Do you mind if I give you some advice?"

"Of course not."

"When you err — and we all do at times — err on the side of mercy."

Unlike today, there was no orientation course for newly appointed judges. You just went and sat on the bench your first morning and began making mistakes, all on your own.

Before the appointment, I had met with Lawrence Brahan, then Chief Judge of the Provincial Court. There were two conditions that I felt strongly about: that I would continue to give speeches on women's rights, but would be careful not to speak about matters that could possibly come before the courts; and second, I would not gown. Brahan seemed surprised by the two conditions, but agreed they would not prevent my being appointed.

The thought of having to gown every day of my working life as a judge was too much. I always hated what I called the costume. The 18th-century stiff starched winged collars, so unlike anything anyone would sensibly wear, the vest, hot and uncomfortable, topped by the flowing black robe. Provincial Court judges in British Columbia had not always gowned, and there was no law saying one had to. So for my nine years on the Provincial Court, I never wore a gown in court.

Harry Boyle, the journalist and lawyer of legendary wit and compassion, appointed to the Provincial bench shortly after, also declined to gown. Claiming a dispute over red or black buttons on the judicial vest was unresolved, Harry said he would gown when that was settled.

I did some really dumb things that first year on the bench. They were mistakes that could mostly be corrected. Being a female meant you were pretty visible. The two other women judges in British Columbia were Winifred Murphy who sat in the Provincial Family Court in Vancouver, and Patricia Proudfoot, who sat in Provincial Criminal Court in Vancouver. There were no federally appointed women judges in the province.

People would sometimes show their shock when they came into the courtroom and saw a female judge. During lunch breaks, sheriffs would frequently ask one of the judges to speak with a class of students on a field trip to see the courts. On one occasion, I walked in to meet a Grade 4 class. As I entered, there was a collective gasp from the students. I went over to them and said, "Why did you all gasp when I walked in? You thought only men were judges?" They giggled, the sound of a stereotype being smashed.

I was not prepared for the major surprise that ambushed me on becoming a judge. Very shortly, I realized that I loved the work. There was enormous satisfaction for me in the role of an adjudicator. For one who had been so happy in the adversarial role of a courtroom lawyer, I had not anticipated this. In my new job, I did not have to take sides, indeed, I should not and hope I did not. I still did not like being a judge, or called a judge, or referred to as a judge socially, which was isolating. But the actual work of a judge was more fulfilling than I had ever imagined.

Meanwhile, I know the senior prosecutor in Burnaby, a veteran of many wars in the courtroom, had to be sitting at his desk with his head in his hands, near tears, in disbelief over the illegal and too-soft sentences that I was handing out in those early months. The lessons of those first few months have stayed with me. It was a given that my former partners and close friends in the profession would not appear before me. The danger is not that you will show preference for your friends; the danger is that you will lean over backwards not to, and therefore place their clients in greater jeopardy.

Bill Deverell phoned one day to see if I was available for lunch. I normally worked through the lunch hour, but was happy to take a break and see Bill. We went to a nearby restaurant, and it soon became apparent that Bill was on a mission. I was being too tough on some of the lawyers who appeared before me. Bill told me that I was expecting a level of expertise from some of the lawyers that was unreasonable, and, in effect, a level that none of us, including me, met. I can still feel the flush that came over my face as he delivered the message. I knew he was right, and in trying to overcome my own uncertainties, I was not being fair to a number of counsel who were appearing before me.

It takes a good friend to deliver a message like that. And live. One of the problems of being a judge is that you seldom get feedback. You never know what happens to people after they appear before you. You do know when you have royally screwed up; the Court of Appeal lets you know.

When I was appointed, Judy LaMarsh said, "Now they have put a sock in your mouth." She knew, as did I, that judges do not and must not get involved in politics.

With Bruno in my life, the loneliness of being on the bench that I had feared was alleviated somewhat. But he could never be a sounding board. No one can. Being a trial judge is not a team activity. It is a solitary job.

As I settled in, things were going well, although I suspect that senior prosecutor was still sobbing, "Oh God, why me?" into his tea. Good prosecutors are tasked with keeping new judges out of trouble.

A lot of shoplifting cases ended up in our courts. One of my first as a judge in Burnaby was a sad middle aged woman who appeared in court alone, no lawyer, no relatives present. She did not want to get a lawyer, she was terrified her husband would find out about the charge; she just wanted to plead guilty. The value of goods taken was not large, she had never been charged before, and the penalty would be a fine.

I accepted her plea of guilty, and attempted to find out more about her, before imposing a sentence. She had children, but they were no longer young. I asked her if she worked. She replied, "No, I am just a housewife." She stood in court, defeated and depressed, accepting that her life as a housewife did not constitute work.

I was dismayed by my question and her answer, and never asked that question again of any woman. The question became, "Do you work outside the home?" I knew, as well as any other woman, that work inside the home is never-ending, physically demanding, seldom recognized, too often thankless, never salaried, and absent any holiday time or pay, sick day benefits, pension benefits or short term and long term disability benefits.

### *Murdoch v. Murdoch*

That unfortunate woman was reflecting not only how many in society viewed the role of a housewife, but how the law and the courts did. But that was about to change, thanks to a rancher's wife, Irene Murdoch, in Alberta. She was bringing an action in the courts that would ultimately change family law in Canada.

By the early 1970s, the lack of property rights for married women, which had so stunned me when I began practising in 1963, still presented a stacked deck against wives. The courts, including the Supreme Court of Canada, were continuing to sock it to them, as most assets were confirmed to belong only to the husbands.

The provinces had begun work on legislation to recognize the contributions of married women to the acquisition of family assets, but such work was in the beginning stages. Then along came *Murdoch v. Murdoch*, a 1973 decision of the Supreme Court of Canada, that would shine a glaring spotlight on the brutal inequality.

*Murdoch v. Murdoch* was an application by Irene Murdoch, a rancher's wife, for one half of their family assets, including their home ranch, all equipment and other assets. This property and assets had all been registered in the name of the husband. The Alberta trial court dismissed her claim, stating that the wife's work "was the work done by any ranch wife," and their marriage was that of a normal husband and wife. Her contributions entitled her to no claim on the husband's assets.

The facts in Murdoch were pretty interesting. The parties had been married for over twenty-five years. The first four years had been spent as a hired couple on a ranch, where the husband broke the horses and looked after the cattle, and the wife did the cooking for the work crews and assisted her husband in his work. Their joint wages had been put into the husband's bank account.

They then bought a property which they operated as a dude ranch. Around this time, the husband began as an employee of a stock association, working for it during the day, and for five months of the year, he was away from home. He remained so employed until they separated in October 1968. The wife had performed all of the work and operation of the dude ranch during those five months when the husband was away, and worked in company with the husband when he was there. She took guests on pack trips, fishing and hunting hikes, as well as the other necessary work around the ranch.

At trial, she described her work:

> Haying, raking, swathing, mowing, driving trucks and tractors and teams, quietening horses, taking cattle back and forth to the reserve, dehorning, vaccinating, branding, anything that was to be done. I worked outside with him, just as a man would...

She also made lunches for the crews, taking the lunches and gas out onto the field. When the husband was asked on discovery what his wife did while he was away on his other work, he stated, "oh, just about what the ordinary rancher's wife does. Most of them can do most anything."

Trouble came in 1964 when the husband wanted to sell the ranch, but could not without the wife's signature because of the Dower Act. The wife put a caveat on the property to prevent the sale. In 1968, she refused to remove the caveat, and, in the words of the court, "a physical clash ... resulted in the hospitalization of the wife...." The parties separated that year.

The wife, denied her claim of interest in any of the family assets, was awarded monthly maintenance of $200 a month. Custody of their son was given to the husband.

As a final swipe, in spite of evidence of financial contributions made by the wife for the purchase of the household appliances and furniture, she was not allowed to take any of those items with her when she and her husband separated.

The Alberta Court of Appeal upheld the trial court's decision. Then the Supreme Court of Canada, in October 1973 upheld the Alberta Court of Appeal. However, Justice Bora Laskin wrote a compelling dissent in the Supreme Court of Canada judgment. He took issue with the trial judge's view that this was a normal husband and wife relationship. He found the wife's contribution, and physical labour to be anything but ordinary. Laskin reviewed the contributions of this wife over the twenty-five years of marriage — the physical labour and financial contributions.

He found a remedy for the wife in equity. "I would declare that the wife is entitled to an interest in the Brockway property and that the husband is under an obligation as a constructive trustee to convey that interest to her. "But this was a dissent so the majority decision of the Court ruled — the wife received nothing but her monthly maintenance of $200.

This powerful dissent set wheels in motion. The case received wide publicity and was a turning point in Canadian law for dependent spouses. Legislation in the provinces began to follow until today, where there is a presumption of equal entitlement to family assets. Too late for Irene Murdoch.

Condescension to females, immigrants, aboriginals, and other minorities happened too often in the courts. Occasionally, it came from judges; other times judges did not do enough to curb it.

In a case before me in Burnaby, a South American girl of nineteen years was testifying as the complainant in a sexual assault case. I'll call her Anna Gomez. Defence counsel was Ken Young, an experienced criminal lawyer who achieved considerable success in such cases. I admired his skills, but I took issue with one or two of his ways in the courtroom. He was very good at using a calming, soothing tone of voice when cross-examining a nervous female complainant.

On this occasion, he was leading her quietly and confidentially through his cross examination, leaning close to her, his elbow resting casually on the edge of the witness box in which she was sitting. It was a small courtroom, and he was standing too close to her. I said, "Mr. Young, I'm going to ask that you stand a more appropriate distance from Ms. Gomez." Young, always respectful of the court, nodded and immediately stepped back.

His cozy tone continued, and with uninvited familiarity, he continually called the complainant by her first name, Anna. "Tell me, Anna, what were you doing at that time?" and "Anna, can you tell me where Mr. Smith was at that time?" and "Now Anna, isn't it true that..." I finally said to the witness, "Ms. Gomez, Mr. Young's first name is Ken. If you wish to call him by his first name, please feel free to do so."

Ken broke into a big smile, threw up his hands in mock surrender and said, "Point taken, your honour. Point taken." Ken Young died far too early. He always served his clients well, and was a welcome presence in the courtroom.

Other than my own errors, there were no major problems in the courtroom. My belief that courtesy breeds courtesy seemed true in the courtroom. The same was not always thus outside the courtroom.

The television show *Laugh-In* was popular at that time, and Goldie Hawn was a favourite. I blame her for that awful phrase that made my life hell on social occasions every time I walked into a room, and some idiot would scream, "Here come da judge!"

That paled in comparison to what one drunken lawyer whom I hardly knew said to me at a Vancouver Bar Association dinner a few months after my appointment, "You know, I've never fucked a judge."

# CHAPTER 50

# *Bruno*

**M**Y RELATIONSHIP with Bruno brought a great change to my life. I had never had a partner before, or lived with anyone. He was smart, loving and funny. He was a feminist, and did not have a racist bone in his body. Few realized Bruno's tough background.

Born in 1928 in Medicine Hat, Alberta, Bruno was young and small in stature, a child in school when the rumblings of World War II began. Once Italy joined the war on the side of the Axis, he was mocked by his young classmates on two fronts, for being desperately poor, and for being Italian.

Bruno's father suffered from mental illness. This oldest of three sons described his father as a Renaissance man in many ways. He was a skilled stonemason, an artist and a talented violinist. He also spent time in Crease Clinic, a facility in New Westminster, BC for the mentally ill, receiving whatever treatment was available at that time, unable to work and support his family during such periods. That left the family destitute at times. They lived in what Bruno described as a shack in New Westminster, close to the paper mill — the same mill where Bruno began working on the dangerous green chain at age fourteen, while still attending school.

Bruno was very forthright about his father's illness. Early in our relationship, he told me about his growing up, and at one point he said, "I made a resolve that I would never be mad." His determination and hope was that he would never succumb to mental illness.

He described how his father would come home from work sometimes in a dark and explosive rage. His father, who had great strength, would smash his fists into the walls of their home, punching holes in the walls. Then he would burst out of the house and begin to run down the nearby train tracks. A six-year-old Bruno would run with him. His father would run and run, until he could go no further, then slowly turn around and walk back, the six-year-old by his side. Bruno said, "My father never touched my mother, or us kids."

There were many times the child ran with his father, down those tracks.

One of the reasons Bruno did not seek his future in Hollywood was his belief that he might end up typecast as "a little wop gangster." Having been called wop throughout his childhood, he was entitled to use that word, which he did, cynically, in self-deprecation. He was also called "slop pail" as a kid. The family home had no water, and it had to be carried by pails to the house. Bruno knew poverty up close and personal. But he grew up with a fierce pride in his family and in being Canadian, a Canadian of Italian heritage.

In her book, *Western Lights*, our friend Lisa Hobbs wrote a chapter on Bruno. On his introduction to the theatre, she wrote:

> The first time he stepped onto the stage in a school play Gerussi felt a quiet shock of recognition, a sense that he was standing for the first time on his own territory. 'I knew I had something out of the ordinary. It's a kind of energy, charisma. An audience senses it in an actor. The actor senses it, a sort of power line between himself and them. It's either there or it isn't.'

I don't ever recall Bruno expressing any desire to be rich. To be an actor in those early days, (and even now) in Canada, you worked at your profession because you loved it, not because you were going to become wealthy. You took whatever jobs you could get, wherever they were available. It might mean travelling to the far north, and it certainly meant travelling to a lot of the smaller towns across Canada, and sometimes into the US. He and his close friend from Stratford days, the incomparable Douglas Campbell, had formed The Canadian Players Company.

Having married his high school sweetheart, Ida, at age

twenty-one, and then having two children, Bruno had to work wherever work presented itself, in order to support his family. He would say, "You go where the work is." But he still resisted moving to the US.

Bruno had many reasons for not moving to the United States to further his acting career. The time he spent at the renowned repertory theatre in Seattle furthered his professional skills, and also enhanced his deep-rooted pacifism. His political instincts were honed at a young age. His parents had lived in Italy during the First World War. His mother had passed on stories that left no doubt that war represented horror, never glory.

There was another reason for Bruno's feeling of unease when it came to the United States. During his three years in Seattle, the Korean War was on, halfway around the world. As a student living in the United States, Bruno was eligible for the American draft. He did not respond to the invitation, and by the time he returned to Vancouver, he was apprehensive that he might be on the American radar as a possible draft dodger. And indeed, they came looking for him.

One day the RCMP knocked at his mother's door in New Westminster, accompanied by an American officer. They were looking for Bruno. He was not home at the time, and the two officers had to contend with Bruno's mother, the feisty Teresina. Bruno was stunned that the Canadian police had been complicit in helping the Americans track down a Canadian citizen to help the Americans fight one of their wars.

I don't think he was ever on any list. He never had any problems going back and forth into the United States, and even laughed that Prime Minister Lester Pearson had offered to assist if Bruno ever ran into any problems. But the hint of paranoia was there.

I first became aware of that on the first trip Bruno and I took out of Canada. We were to spend New Year's week in Maui. Neither of us had ever been to Hawaii. It was 1972, and in those days, all you needed was either a passport or a copy of your birth certificate to travel to the United States. Our flight was with Canadian Pacific Airlines, and we were due at the airport

*Bruno and me on holiday.*

around one o'clock on the Saturday before New Year's. The day before, Friday, Bruno was in Gibson's, packing, and I was doing the same at my home in Deep Cove.

In the early evening on Friday, Bruno called, somewhat frantic. He could not find his passport nor did he have a copy of his birth certificate. They were probably in his home in Toronto. He had telephoned someone he knew at Canadian Pacific, who said not to worry, that all he needed was, and here, Bruno had trouble finding the words, "...some kind of stat... a stat..".

I asked, "A statutory declaration?"

"Yes. But it has to be signed by a notary public, "and here, his voice rising in concern, Bruno added, "I don't know any notary publics."

"Well, you've been sleeping with one for the last three months."

Bruno was delighted to learn that all practicing lawyers were also notaries public. I told him I was going to ask him a bunch of questions and I would draw up a statutory declaration the next morning in my office. He would have the proper document when we boarded the plane. He studiously gave me his answers on a series of facts, when and where he was born, when and where his parents were born, when and where they were married, when and where his two brothers were born, where he lived, that he had a valid passport and where it was, and so on.

My secretary did not work on weekends, unless we had a trial to prepare, so I went to the office early Saturday morning and typed a two-page document. It was a useless document, of course, but it recited nothing but true facts, and by the time I put the blue backing on it, got the red seal out and took my notary seal home for the official swearing-in of the document, that statutory declaration crackled with authority.

Bruno drove over from Gibson's later that morning. I had him read carefully through the document . Then I explained that he would have to swear to God that all the facts in that document were true, and sign to that effect. He solemnly agreed and swore the necessary oath. I got out my notary seal, and crushed the metal seal onto the superfluous red seal that I had attached to the document. I folded the declaration, placed it in an envelope and handed it over to Mr. Forgetful. His relief was palpable.

We sailed through customs at the airport; no one asked to see our papers. Bruno was almost disappointed.

That was not the first or last occasion when I had to dream up a strange "legal document" to appease some pettifogging bureaucracy.


Although this was early in our relationship, by this time I had realized that Bruno, organized and disciplined when it came to his craft, was nonchalant when it came to his own papers. On our return from Hawaii, I sent for four copies of his birth certificate, wallet sized. I gave him two and kept the other two, with one always in my wallet, along with my own birth certificate, just in case. It was still there when Bruno died, twenty-four years later.

Before our trip to Hawaii, Bruno met my parents for the first time when they came to Vancouver for my swearing in, prior to their trip to Palm Desert. Moira and I were to meet them there. But I told Mom and Dad I would not be going, that Bruno and I had plans to go to Hawaii for that week over New Year.

They knew who Bruno was, of course, but it was going to be tricky introducing Bruno to them. He was older, Italian, an actor, and possibly sleeping with their thirty-five-year-old daughter. The waves of approval were not flowing my way. Mom and Dad had seen Bruno in *Coriolanus* at Stratford in 1961 when they had driven to Toronto for my graduation from Osgoode. I had said they must see this young actor in a performance. As we left the theatre, Mom had remarked, "When that young man is on stage, you see no one else."

We were scheduled to have dinner with Bruno soon after Mom and Dad arrived in Vancouver. Before they met, I asked Mom and Dad to listen to the record Bruno and Tommy Ambrose had done called *Fuzzy Love*, a combination of songs sung by Ambrose and poetry read by Bruno. My parents were suckers for poetry, all literature, in fact. The poetry and maybe some of the songs were written by Bruno's whimsical talented friend, Gary Dunford, who

*Is that a 'maybe' I am detecting?*

had written such magic poems for Bruno's radio show.

*Fuzzy Love* did its job. Dinner that night was long and fun. Bruno fell for my Dad. He had Dad talking about himself, which seldom occurred. The next day, Mom remarked that Dad told stories that evening of his youth and early years that she had never heard.

Allan Fotheringham wrote, as a blurb years later for the cookbook I wrote — *Bruno: Love in the Kitchen*

> Companions for twenty-four years, they could not have been a stranger mixture: Bruno with his lusty, irreverent, Shakespearean shouting, Ms. Morrison with her clear and logical legal mind, a pioneer as a feminist judge...

In fact, we were not that strange a pairing. We were alike in many ways. For those who check the signs of the zodiac, we were both Taurus. Our homes were our havens. Our mutual love of cooking we inherited from formidable mothers. Long before we met one another, we both thrived on entertaining, throwing dinner parties, delighting in spirited conversations over the dinner table. We were both serious readers and political junkies.

When we met, Bruno was forty-four, I was thirty-five. It was easy and natural to accept one another as we were. When we travelled, neither of us had a clue how to travel light. We travelled just short of the Elizabeth Taylor standard of multiple steamer trunks. We just emptied our closets into however many suitcases we could find. The constraints of our work did not allow much foreign travel, but we did break the winters with trips to Mexico or Hawaii. The Island of Kauai was our favourite. Neither of us was in continuous exploring mode, no bucket lists. If we found a place we liked to stay or eat or golf, we kept going back, becoming part of the community.

Bruno read multiple daily newspapers, magazines, books. Our favourite fiction author was Pat Conroy. We shared the same sense of humor, stayed up late to watch *Saturday Night Live* and I envied his story-telling and ability with accents.

In politics, Bruno supported the NDP, while I was a Liberal, but it was obvious we both leaned left on social issues. His passion for and knowledge of politics had served him well during those years on his radio show. He knew all the players, the issues. Always, he brought his passion and energy to the table.

As a radio host, he was a good interviewer. Informed, he knew how to listen. His interest in others was genuine, and he believed it was his role to make his guest look good, not himself.

It was an experience to be with Bruno when politics unfolded on television. Years ago, when George H.W. Bush nominated Clarence Thomas to the Supreme Court of the United States, (it was 1991), Anita Hill testified at the Senate nomination hearing. The US Senate hearings on the Thomas nomination had been reopened after a report by the FBI was leaked to the press, involving Anita Hill's allegations of sexual harassment by Thomas during the time that they had worked together.

The Senate confirmation hearings for Thomas took place around our Thanksgiving weekend, and Bruno and I were glued to the television set, meals eaten in front of the television, Bruno mocking the proceedings. We were appalled at the treatment to which Anita Hill was subjected. Anita Hill was discredited and Clarence Thomas moved on to his reward of a lifetime job as a judge of the Supreme Court of the United States, where he sits to this day.

While watching political moments with Bruno was not always a quiet experience, sharing a home was. The solitary part of my life found a natural partner in Bruno. We were both comfortable to share long quiet periods. We did not always live under the same roof. I had my own home in North Vancouver, Deep Cove, and later, in West Vancouver. Bruno bought his first home in Gibsons, BC in the third year of filming *Beachcombers*, and he later bought a townhouse in Toronto for his family and for the periods that he spent there.

He had a summer cottage on Snake Island in Lake Simcoe, used primarily by his children. I had my family cottage at Crystal Lake north of Yorkton. We spent long periods at the cottage in Saskatchewan, where Bruno was one of the locals, playing Wednesday evening men's golf with the guys. Bruno knew all the local golf courses.

Because of court, most of my time at Gibson's was on weekends. We lived more in Vancouver, particularly after *Beachcombers* ended in 1991.

There was a four-year period when Bruno and I were not together. A few months before Bruno turned fifty, I discovered that he had been seeing a young blonde woman who lived at Gibsons. The affair had been going on without my knowledge for months. I was devastated, and immediately broke off all contact with Bruno. His lack of honesty was the worst part of the betrayal. I experienced rage that I did not know was in me. I even reverted to sleep-walking, something I had done infrequently as a child.

Our restaurateur friend, Umberto Menghi, was busy during those four years keeping Bruno and me separated in Umberto's Vancouver restaurants. If I happened to be in Il Giardino having a meal, and Umberto spotted Bruno about to enter, Umberto would rush out saying, "No no, you can't come in. Nancy is here.

Come, we will go to another of my restaurants."

Many times over those four years, Bruno would be drunk, late at night, and my phone would ring. He would tell me he loved me, and I would ask about the girlfriend. He would say he did not want to talk about that, but that ended the conversation as far as I was concerned. And on any number of other occasions, it was my turn for one of those late night calls. After a dismal night on the town, I would come home and phone Bruno. He was always gentle and loving on the phone, even though I would be yelling at him like a bad-tempered fishwife. I must've been a disaster as a date with others during that time, because I know all I did was talk about Bruno.

I missed him terribly, but had told him that if we got back together, he would have to commit to a monogamous relationship, and that he would have to give up smoking. My asthma had returned after being in remission for twenty years. But more important, I did not want to lose Bruno to cancer.

Bruno was not fond of ultimatums, but for me, those two conditions were crucial.

Our lives were not the same without one another, and we did get back together in 1981, shortly after Bruno's remarkable mother died. Our relationship from then until Bruno's death on November 21, 1995 was a gift. We grew closer with each year.

Bruno's love of carving blossomed when he found more time. It also made my gift giving easier. When I was in Whitehorse sitting as an *ad hoc* provincial court judge, or later, as an arbitrator, I added to our collection of Maureen Morris' beautiful bird sculptures, carved from discarded antlers. These exquisite works by this renowned artist, who now lives in Atlin, BC, were Bruno's favourites.

In the early 1990s, I was in and out of Yellowknife frequently on arbitrations. On one occasion, Bruno drove with me to Yellowknife, where we acquired an amazing sculpture by Bill Nasogaluak, a talented Inuit carver. Bruno stayed on in Yellowknife for a few days to enjoy that thriving city. Years later, when I wrote our cookbook after Bruno died, I described Bruno as a rebel, romantic, wise, sexy, wickedly irreverent, direct and funny. He was all of that. Our friend Vicki Gabereau had the best line, "He was the least dull man I ever met."

And now it can be told. He didn't like Frank Sinatra. Frank Sinatra came to Vancouver. He filled the local arena. It was toward the end of his career, and he was a massive legend. Our dear friends, Tony and Diane Pantages, were huge fans of Sinatra. You seldom walked into their home that ol' Blue Eyes was not crooning on their stereo. Tony had arranged four tickets for the Sinatra concert. They were great seats, on the floor, close to the performer.

I had never been a bobby socks type who had swooned when Frank crooned, but I had always liked his music. And later in life, was amused at the Rat Pack shenanigans.

It was not until I read Paul Anka's autobiography that I fully understood Bruno's antipathy to Sinatra the person. On Sinatra's talent, there was no question. But Bruno despised Sinatra the person. The famous Italian who gambolled with the mob. Who gave credence to the stereotype of Italian gangsters.

I don't think Bruno ever met Sinatra. That night after the concert, there was no question of going backstage. Bruno respected Tony's admiration of Sinatra, and he was too fond of Tony to diminish the flame of a fan by growling about Sinatra's off-stage lifestyle.

# CHAPTER 51

# *Labour Relations Board &*
# *Chief Justice Nemetz*

I N MY EARLY MONTHS on the provincial court, I telephoned
Judge Nathan (Sonny) Nemetz of the BC Supreme Court, a
leading labour mediator and arbitrator, often called on to settle
the most difficult disputes in the country. My call was to congratulate him on his appointment as the new Chief Justice of the BC
Supreme Court and to say that if he ever needed a junior judge
on one of his labour inquiries, to keep me in mind.

I had met Nemetz after I arrived in Vancouver. He was a fan
of Bruno, one of the many who chastised Bruno for making him
late as he would sit in his car waiting for a segment of Bruno's
radio program to end before shutting off the radio and going into
the courthouse.

Although Nemetz never admitted to this, I credit him with
a phone call I received in 1973 from a young professor at UBC,
Jim Matkin. I did not know Matkin. He had helped draft the new
Labour Relations Code for British Columbia, and was a friend of
Paul Weiler, who had just been named head of the new Labour
Relations Board, set up under Barrett's NDP government.

When I met with Matkin, he told me I was being proposed
as one of the three vice chair of the new Labour Relations Board.
That I would remain a judge, but would be seconded by the
Ministry of Labour from the Attorney-General's Ministry. I told
Matkin that I had limited labour law experience. My only labour
client had been the Newspaper Guild, and that was thanks to
my journalist friend and Guild member, Simma Holt. I had done
grievances on behalf of the Guild, but otherwise, my practice was
civil and criminal litigation. Matkin said he was aware of that.

I told him that it would not be possible for me to take on the
job, which was to begin in December 1973. I had back surgery
scheduled for January 11, 1974, in Toronto, where I would be in

hospital for three and half months, and then in a walking cast for another couple of months. Matkin said he was also aware of that.

His information network was a lot better than mine.

I asked him if Nemetz had suggested my name, and Matkin, while not denying it, indicated that the names of other lawyers with labour law backgrounds had been considered too identified with either labour or management. They were looking for someone more neutral, and my background in civil litigation, especially family law, was seen as positive.

It was an exciting opportunity. The offices for the new Labour Relations Board had been leased, but no staff had been hired. That was to be my task in December before leaving for back surgery. Val Chapman, who had been secretary to the chair of the former Labour Relations Board, became my new secretary and soon, close friend. Between the two of us, we went over hundreds of applications for some thirty-five staff positions for the new Board. I spent December interviewing and hiring.

While practising in Yorkton, through the CNIB, I had been reading legal textbooks for a blind law student at the University of Saskatchewan. The CNIB in Regina had provided a suitable recording machine, and warned me not to make jokes as I read the textbooks word for word into the machine; the humour would not be appreciated by a student listening to the tape. (I broke the rule rarely, but once, while spelling a case name, I could not resist saying, "S — as in soap-dish," channeling comedian Shelley Berman.)

In 1970 when I moved to Vancouver, I volunteered to read for the CNIB, but was told that more professional readers were engaged at UBC for that purpose. However, my interest in the CNIB led to the hiring of one of our favourite young employees at the Labour Relations Board.

Two positions to fill were receptionists. I telephoned the CNIB in Vancouver to give them the job descriptions, suggesting they might have a candidate capable of filling one or both of these positions. The man I spoke with was surprised and pleased. He said they had a young woman, twenty-one years of age, who would fill the requirements ideally. She had lost her sight shortly after birth through an error in the drops placed in her eyes. She was intelligent, well-educated, and had a personality that shone. He was right. She was wonderful. I hired her after our interview. Our Vice Chairman in charge of administration at the Board was dubious that she would be able to handle duties as a receptionist, but he eventually came around.

I resumed my duties at the Board in the summer. My back surgery had been successful. I had regained over four inches of my original height, thanks to Dr. John Kostuik, my orthopedic surgeon in Toronto.

The word "genius" should never be thrown around casually, but that's what the chairman of the Labour Relations Board, Paul Weiler, was and is. He was young, extremely bright, down to earth, at home with everyone, staff, colleagues, the press; he transformed the labour bar in British Columbia with his encouragement and mentoring. He brought out the best in everyone. He brought progressive labour law to British Columbia, with precedents that are still followed in Canada.

The three vice chair of the Labour Relations Board were Ed Peck, who came from the management side, Jack Moore, from the IWA, the International Woodworkers Association, and me. The additional board members, numbering fourteen, came half from labour and half from management. They were the labour leaders in the province, extraordinary colleagues.

Of the eighteen Board members, I was the only female. There were a few Women's Lib moments. We met frequently in the beginning, in the boardroom. If I got up to leave the room, my seventeen male colleagues immediately rose to their feet. When I came back into the room, they would rise again until I sat down.

This needed a correction. So I thanked them for their courtesy in standing when I entered or left the room, saying I was from the same school. I had been taught to get to my feet when a woman entered the room, and also when someone older entered the room. We needed to make a deal. With the exception of

Weiler, who was six months younger than me, I pointed out that the rest of the members were all older. Our solution — I would not rise to my feet when any of them entered the room, and they would remain seated when I popped in and out.

Frank Rhodes was with the Ministry of Labour in those days, and he reminded me of the following, years later. My first cheque arrived from the Ministry of Labour, and apparently I sent it back. This was 1973 and the cheque was made out to 'Miss Nancy Morrison.' My letter stated that I had learned that the marital status of my male colleagues was not set out on their cheques, and that I would appreciate it if they would be consistent, either reveal my male colleagues' marital status on their cheques, or remove it from mine. I don't remember doing that, but Frank assured me I did. That was when many of us were promoting the use of the more neutral 'Ms.'

It was fair game to troll the government or private clubs, but I never wanted counsel, parties or witnesses to feel uncomfortable with me chairing a tribunal hearing. The indomitable lawyer, Mary Southin, was the only other woman in the province then chairing labour tribunals. I knew some were worried about how to address me. I was on leave from the bench, but not sitting as a judge.

At the beginning of a hearing, I would tell counsel and parties to call me whatever felt comfortable for them. The unions often preferred 'madam chairperson', a bit cumbersome; management usually used 'madam chairman'. I assured them any form of address was fine with me. And it was. They had enough to worry about in a labour dispute without having to tiptoe around that feminist sensitivity.

Other feminist sensitivities did arise, and one of the first involved bathrooms. Of course. There was this little dust-up at the Board over bathrooms. The office plans for the Board were being drawn up in December 1973 for the two floors that the Board would occupy. The hearing rooms and our executive offices would be on the third floor, with the balance of the offices where most of the staff would be on the second floor. There were two bathrooms on each floor. The administrative vice-chair and

I crossed swords. He decreed that the two bathrooms on the hearing floor would both be male-only bathrooms, and on the second floor, one bathroom for men and one for women.

I personally had no problem going down a flight of steps to access a bathroom, but I was incensed at the assumption that there would be few if any women at the hearings; that all the lawyers would be male as would all the parties and witnesses. The admin vice-chair dug his heels in, and so did I. Weiler resolved it quietly in favour of equality, and my impulsive threat to quit over a bathroom issue dissolved. To my delight, the influx of unions comprised mainly of women, such as the BC Nurses Union, SOR-WOC, AUCE, and others began flooding the hearing rooms.

Every Christmas, MacMillan Bloedel, the forest giant, gave an elegant Christmas party at the Terminal City Club for those in the labour community. As members of the new Labour Relations Board, we received invitations. I hated missing out on such a legendary party, but my written RSVP explained to the hospitable Gordie Towell that I would like to attend, however, I had a policy of not entering premises that did not allow women as members. The three influential private business clubs in Vancouver all barred women from membership. Weiler smiled when I tried, unsuccessfully, to talk him out of attending.

A lot of my assignments on the Board, made by Weiler, were in the hospitality industry. As a chair, I sat with two other Board members, one from labour and one from management. We called them wingers, or sidemen. They were my teachers. They were leaders in their fields, wise and experienced.

A typical hearing would start and often, at some point in the day, one of my colleagues would lean over and murmur that this might be a good time to take a break. One or both of the wingers would have sensed this was a good time for them to sit down privately with each side, outside the formality of the actual hearing, and see if a resolution to the dispute could be reached. Their instincts were usually rewarded with a settlement. I would go to my office to work on other matters, and then be advised maybe an hour later, maybe a day later, that either a settlement had been reached, or it had not; in which case the hearing would resume.

I would not have been privy to any of the informal discussions that had taken place.

Two of my favourite colleagues were John Billings from Forest Industrial Relations and Angus MacDonald from the Steelworkers. Weiler had us travelling all over the province on hospitality industry disputes. We had to impose more than one collective agreement, when, on occasion, management had found out which employees were organizing, fired most of them, and then tried to rebut unfair labour accusations. The irrepressible lawyer, Bob Gardner, often represented Local 40 of the Hotel, Restaurant & Culinary Employees & Bartenders Union. John Billings and I would almost have to lock Angus MacDonald in his room to prevent him from going out and partying with Bob and Local 40 during our hearings.

Flying around the province did not decrease my fear of flying. As my favourite Powell River wit, Stewart Alsgard, said of the experience of flying into Castlegar, it is an exciting approach, "flying over all those broken fuselages".

In December 1975 Barrett's NDP government was defeated. Bill King had been the Minister of Labour throughout its tenure. I had never met King. That December, he came to the LRB offices after the government defeat, a brief visit, to thank every member of the Board, executives and staff, saying, "You made us look good." He had never set foot at the Board before or interfered in any way.

I was later told that when the Board was first formed, King had received a delegation from the BC Federation of Labour after it was announced I would be a vice chair of the new Board, demanding I be removed. "She is no friend of labour," King was told. His response reportedly was, "She is an independent thinker."

After three years on the Board, I returned to the provincial bench, concerned that I not be away too long from the other disciplines of criminal and civil law. I left with great memories, the itch for labour law somewhat scratched, my admiration for Weiler undiminished, and one interesting nickname.

A well-known restaurateur, possibly not a fan, referred to me as "that fucking feminist." I had never been involved in any of his labour disputes.

After returning to the bench, I had lunch from time to time with Sonny Nemetz, always at his table at the Four Seasons. Though small in stature, he was a force. Those lunches featured numerous interruptions as people dropped by the table to talk to Sonny. It was no secret he was on a first name basis with pretty well everyone in the country.

Nemetz had broken a few barriers in his day. He was the first Jewish Chief Justice in the province. It became an embarrassment for the exclusive men-only, white-gentile-only, Vancouver Club, that the Chief Justice of the Supreme Court in the province was not an acceptable candidate for membership.

So in 1977, Nathan Nemetz became a member of the Vancouver Club, sponsored by the then Lt. Governor, Walter Owen, and the Chief Justice of the province, John Farris. Other Jewish members followed, but male only.

Women were not welcome as members of the Vancouver Club. Female guests were barred from even entering the premises before 5:00 p.m., and then had to enter only by the side door, never allowed to pass through the stately front door entrance, or enter many of the rooms.

When my friend, Bill Rand was married he had his elegant reception at the Vancouver Club, where he was a member. He had to make a special appeal to the Board of Directors of the Club to allow his female guests to enter the front door along with the male guests.

Bill knew that Cheri Lemiski and I, among others, would never attend if we had to bow our way in through a side entrance. It was a grand party, where Doug and The Slugs rocked the dance floor. Cheri, Jane Auxier and I, late in the evening, explored the rooms forbidden to all females, regretting we had neglected to bring a camera to record as we lolled in the overstuffed leather chairs.

In speeches, I frequently criticized the private clubs for their discrimination against women. One of the nastiest letters I ever received was from an august member of the Vancouver Club, telling me how wrong and stupid I was. It was hand written on beautiful engraved vellum stationery. His penmanship and grammar were impeccable.

On one of our lunches, Nemetz said he should have been more alert sooner to the exclusion of women from the Vancouver Club. Sonny Nemetz liked and actively promoted women. He once told me he could not get me appointed to the British Columbia County or Supreme Court (his idea, not mine) — that Ottawa would not make the appointment because of Bruno. We were not married. At the time, that seemed like another good reason for Bruno and me to continue our status quo.

Although in late 1973 we missed a cruise we wanted to take when the P&O Cruise Line refused to accept us as passengers unless we registered as Mr. and Mrs. Bruno Gerussi. We laughed and made other travel plans. Even as a teen, I had informed my parents I would never adopt a husband's name and give up my own.

Bruno and I shared respect and affection for Nemetz. Our last visit was when we ran into him in Hawaii shortly before Bruno died. Nemetz was again a silent benefactor when he and Bill McIntyre decided I should have the Q.C. (Queen's Counsel ) designation after my name.

Recently, Pat LeSage told me this anecdote about Nemetz. As an associate chief justice and later a chief justice in Ontario, Pat was in that exclusive club of chief justices and associate chief justices who make up the Judicial Council of Canada. Around 1984, LeSage was on a small sub-committee with Nemetz and Bora Laskin, then Chief Justice of Canada, the first Jewish justice appointed to the Supreme Court of Canada.

Sonny asked Bora, "Now, what about judges' salaries?" (There was no formal procedure to set salaries for federally appointed judges at that time.) Laskin replied that he would be meeting with the prime minister or the minister of finance the next week.

Sonny said, "Don't go into that meeting without me present, Bora. You negotiate like a gentile."

# CHAPTER 52

# *"It's a Broad!"*

I'VE BEEN BLESSED with excellent hearing. I had no idea how good it was until I joined the staff of the Prosecutor's office in Vancouver. As a municipal employee, I was required to have a physical examination, and that included my first audio test.

At the Vancouver General Hospital audio testing lab, I was sitting in a chair with headphones on and instructed to repeat back what the lone technician behind the glass wall was saying to me over the headphones. Her voice got progressively softer until it was a faint whisper. She came out from behind the glass and asked if I would mind doing the test again. Not a problem. A couple of other white coats had joined her behind the glass wall. More whispers over the headphones.

Out came the technician again. "Do you mind if we do this all once again?" She smiled reassuringly. Go ahead. More white coats — it was getting crowded in the little booth behind that glass. After the third test, a man came out and introduced himself as an audiologist. "Are you aware you have extremely acute hearing?" I wasn't.

"Is that why I find myself having to leave a loud disco dance floor, much as I love dancing?" He told me I must find that physically painful with my hearing. I know I drove Bruno crazy with the radio on so softly he would ask why I bothered to have it on at all.

One busy day in the mid-seventies in Provincial Court in North Vancouver, a man opened the door at the back of the crowded courtroom and entered with his (male) lawyer. As he looked up and saw me on the bench, the man murmured in astonishment to his lawyer, "Holy fuck! It's a broad!" in a whisper I was never intended to hear. He did not look thrilled.

On a long case, I would often caution lawyers at the beginning of the trial if there was something that they really did not want me to hear, to wait until I was out of the court-room to say it — that their whispers would more than likely be heard by me.

While I never had trouble hearing in a courtroom, I often caught jurors leaning forward trying to hear a witness. So I would ask the witness to please keep their voice up. Also for the clarity of audio recordings. I am sure there were litigants and lawyers thinking — poor judge — she should get a hearing aid.

# CHAPTER 53

# Speaking to Sentence (Court Vignettes)

WHEN I WAS prosecuting in Vancouver, two defence lawyers invoked the same thought when either walked into the courtroom: "I'm going to learn something today. I just don't know what it is yet." Those two lawyers were Larry Hill and Josiah Wood.

Larry Hill belonged in a Damon Runyon tale, smart, streetwise and ethical and deceptively casual. He came into court one day to defend a run-of-the-mill case. Or at least I thought it was run-of-the-mill. Larry sat down at the counsel table, first courteously acknowledging the judge. Then instead of opening a court binder, he pulled out a small matchbook, opened the tiny item and laid his pen alongside. He had no other books, papers or writing material with him at the counsel table.

I called the first policeman to testify, carefully going through the evidence with the experienced officer. Larry, pen in hand, made a tiny note on the inside of his tiny matchbook, then indicated he had no questions for the officer.

Rarely in such a case would I examine the second policeman, but would call the officer to make him available for defence counsel to cross examine if they wished. However, Larry was making me nervous. Was I missing something? So I called the second policeman, who had been present with the first officer at the time of the arrest, and he gave the same account, only in his own words. Again, Larry made a little notation on the inside of his matchbook cover, and again indicated, "No questions."

I told the judge that was the case for the Crown. Larry carefully closed his tiny fold-over matchbook, stood up and told the judge of a new and precedent-setting case that had just come out of the Supreme Court of Canada that morning, *R. v. Piche*. The case had yet to reach our prosecution office; it was one of those cases that changed the way police evidence would be gathered and given in the months and years to come. My evidence could not sustain a conviction.

Larry courteously nodded to the court and me as he and his client left the courtroom.

Josiah Wood, known to all as Joe, was the finest lawyer I ever saw in any courtroom. When he ambled casually into the courtroom, most people smiled. The court officers liked him, the police respected him, the judges were delighted to have him in the courtroom, and the prosecutors knew they were probably going to lose their case. Joe was wonderfully smart, and as a defence counsel, he was able to bring not only his impressive grasp of the law, but also his easy manner into the courtroom. He was always prepared, he knew the law inside out, he never misled the court, his respect for the judge and everyone else in the courtroom was exemplary.

Joe seldom lost a case, but if he did, or if, rarely, his client pleaded guilty to a lesser charge, Joe spoke to sentence more effectively than almost any other lawyer. He knew his clients well, and he obviously liked them, warts and all. By the time Joe finished telling the court all about his client, I, the prosecutor, was ready to strike a medal for this poor accused. I did not have to; the judge had already been won over.

Joe went on to become a Justice of the BC Supreme Court and then a Court of Appeal judge, writing a number of precedent-setting judgments. He later served as a provincial court judge on Vancouver Island, forging valuable relationships with First Nations within the judicial system. He died too soon, June 9, 2014, at age seventy-three.


When I later exchanged my days as a prosecutor and defence counsel for life as a judge on the provincial court bench, submissions on sentencing yielded surprises, drama, and sometimes even laughs.

A case before me in North Vancouver in the mid-seventies involved a Canadian Pacific Airlines pilot on the Lima, Peru to Vancouver run, charged with importing and trafficking in cocaine. Significant quantities of cocaine from Lima were cached by the pilot in ingenious areas of the airplane, and detected only through a combination of luck and good police work.

It began as a trial, and after a few days of evidence, the lawyer for the pilot announced there would be a change of plea, to guilty on the trafficking charge.

Defence counsel began speaking to sentence. He explained that his client, at a relatively young age, had gained a reputation as an excellent pilot. He outlined the pilot's personal background, never in trouble, that he was married, and came from a distinguished family, and he listed the accomplishments of the pilot's father, grandfather and great-grandfather. Counsel said, "Unfortunately, my client is the end of the line for his family, as he has only two daughters."

No matter how much a judge tries to keep a poker face through court proceedings, there are times when you fail miserably. I know this had to be one of them. The pilot had been watching me carefully throughout, and when his lawyer made that statement, the pilot started to laugh. So did I, and so did defence counsel.

In spite of having no criminal record, the pilot received a tough sentence from me. Fairly early into serving his sentence, I was consulted, as the sentencing judge, on whether I had any objections to him being moved from a maximum-security prison to a medium- or minimum-security prison. I had none.

A year or so later, a parcel arrived at the North Vancouver courthouse for me. It had been ripped apart by the RCMP before being delivered to me. It was a beautiful pottery bowl, with a well executed lid. But it had been wrapped in a box that had contained a kettle. The police were nervous about the box, as the previous year a young Asian couple were killed when a bomb in a booby-trapped electric kettle exploded. I'm not sure if the box was chosen randomly, or with a smile.

In prison, the pilot had become a skilled potter, and had sent me this gift, with a note, "from one of your contrite accused." One of the RCMP narcotics officers brought it to me, smiling and saying, "This is just the right size for a hash stash, your Honour."

On another day in North Vancouver, a young defence lawyer, Leo McGrady, admired for his gravitas and good looks, treated the court to a seminar on how to speak to sentence. His client was one of the young men who was in the distribution chain that had been set up by the CP pilot to traffic the cocaine.

The accused pleaded guilty at the beginning of the proceedings, and McGrady had booked a day to speak to sentence. He began to call witnesses to testify about his twenty-three-year-old client. The young man sat beside Leo at the counsel table, looking miserable and anxious. He had never been in trouble with the law. His mother was seated in the first row of the small courtroom, sobbing quietly.

One of the first witnesses called was a high school teacher, who said the accused was a good student, always respectful, hard-working. He was not at the top of his class by any means, but he worked hard, completed his assignments, and was liked by fellow students and teachers. He had never been involved in trouble during his school years, and the teacher had been shocked to learn of his charge of trafficking in cocaine.

The young man had gone to work for a small company after high school, and his employer was in court to testify. The employer, in business for many years, said that the young man was an excellent employee, in all respects. He had worked for him for several years; there was never a hint of any problem, not with drugs, absenteeism, sloppy work. He was a fine young man, and yes, the employer realized the accused would have to serve some time in jail, but he had assured his young employee that his job would be waiting for him when he got out of jail. The sad mother continued quietly to cry into her handkerchief. The employer stepped down.

Other witnesses were called to fill in the picture of a young man caught up in a drug culture where he did not belong. The last witness McGrady called was the young man's father. He was tall and dignified, well spoken. In response to questioning, the father told the court what a fine son this young man was. That from an early age, he had always been there to help his mother, as well as others; that he had never caused a moment of trouble in the home, that he and his wife had always been proud of him. They had no idea he had been involved in such activities. He had been living on his own the last few years.

"Have you talked to your son about this crime when you learned of it after his arrest?" McGrady asked. The father affirmed that they had indeed talked about it, and his son had told his parents everything that he had done.

Then McGrady asked, "Do you think your son has true remorse for what he has done?" This reserved, composed businessman suddenly broke down completely and cried out, "Oh God, yes!" The young man, watching his father in such agony, also broke down, tears streaming down his face. The effect of this father's distress was overwhelming, for everyone in the room, including me.

"We'll take a short break."

McGrady gave speaking to sentence the time and importance it deserved. His advocacy was reserved, skillful and ultimately, effective.

# CHAPTER 54

## *Learning Disabilities*

AFTER LEAVING THE Labour Relations Board in 1976, I sat in Provincial Criminal Court in North Vancouver. Dealing with juveniles in trouble with the law was the most troubling aspect of my work.

One week, four pre-sentence reports mentioned the problems each of four young offenders were having, in part due to their learning disabilities. I knew nothing about learning disabilities (LD), and by the time the fourth report hit my desk, knew it was time to find out more.

I telephoned Peter Sievenpiper, our excellent probation officer in North Vancouver to ask some questions. One of the young men was twenty-one, up on a robbery charge. He and his pregnant young girlfriend had tried to rob a store, the young man with a gun. Robbery, a serious offence, signified jail time. He had a long juvenile record, stretching back years. But unlike so many who came before me, he was never alone when he came to court. His parents were always there, concerned, wondering where they had gone wrong — well-educated and caring parents, who were not giving up on their son.

Meanwhile the parents of the young pregnant girl probably wanted to kill him, for any number of reasons. The girl had never been in trouble before.

I felt a sentence of two years in jail was called for, but should it be two years less a day or two years plus a day? There existed a crucial distinction. Two years less a day meant incarceration in a provincial jail, the other meant two years in a federal prison, neither option attractive to the accused.

This young man could not read. His history was sad. He failed in almost every year in elementary school. So he was still in Grade 4, for example, when his pals and peers were in Grades 8 and above. He was small in stature, desperate to be with his peers. So he began stealing to ingratiate himself and get to stay with the guys his own age. First candy, smaller stuff, then booze and cigarettes, eventually cars and drugs.

His schooling was a disaster, and he was not a very good thief, although apparently an enthusiastic one, not given to discouragement despite being caught repeatedly by the local RCMP. His record grew, along with his frustration.

After one stint in prison for a few months, he was offered a job in a warehouse by an employer willing to give someone with a record a chance. The kid worked hard. The employer was pleased, and eventually promoted him to receiving in the warehouse. More pay, better job. But what the young man failed to tell the employer, or anyone else, was that he could not read. So when the bills of lading came in, he had no idea where to consign the goods. Within weeks, the warehouse was in chaos, and the young man was fired. Still no admission of not being able to read. Kids and adults who would rather admit to theft or robbery than to being illiterate.

Soon after that, the young couple, with no money, committed the robbery.

When I called Peter Sievenpiper, I told him I was considering two years, and wanted to know in which prison system, federal or provincial, could this young man get the most help to deal with his problems of LD. Peter laughed, the laugh or cry kind of laugh. There are no programs in any of the prisons, he advised. The kid is doomed in either system.

He also told me where to call for information on LD — to the Association of Parents with Children with LD. I called and introduced myself, saying I would appreciate as much information as they could recommend. I was soon buried in material they sent. What I read stunned me. Seventy to ninety percent of all juveniles in trouble with the law in North America at that time had some form and varying degree of LD. There were apparently thirty-eight different kinds of LD, dyslexia being the most recognized by the public. But there was little public awareness of LD in those years.

If all those juveniles in delinquency had such trouble with LD, many of whom were illiterate, and unwilling to even acknowledge this, didn't that mean that our prisons are filled with the same statistics of those with serious learning problems? No real stats on that. But to me, that seemed only logical.

Then it clicked — all those years of criminal defence work I had done in three provinces, where a pre-sentence report would be prepared on my client, where I would give the (usually) damning report to my client to read. Then after he had read it, I would ask, *is that all true? Is there anything that needs correcting?* And almost always, just a nod of affirmation that the information contained in the report was okay. At times I might ask, *even the part about you beating up on your sister?* No, he would quickly say, "I never did that. I would never hit a woman."

How many times did I stand back in quiet deference to let my client read a damning report, unaware they were pretending to read, leafing the pages over in correct timing, when in fact, the accused did not have a clue what was on the pages. And never once did a client say to me, "I cannot read."

How many times in the courtroom as a judge had I asked a person if he or she had read the pre-sentence report or other document and been assured that they had? How many had been going through those same motions of pretending to read? How often as lawyers and judges have we failed to be alert to such an overwhelming problem in our society and justice system? We assume everyone can read as we do. The statistics say how wrong we have been, and still are.

I gave this young man two years less a day. It meant his family could visit him more readily in a provincial prison. But the next day I was told that he was swarmed in prison, knifed severely several times, and had to be rushed to the hospital where they were able to save his life. He was regarded as a snitch, or a rat — someone still trying to ingratiate himself with his peers — and was almost killed for it.

Thanks to him, I began to learn more about LD. There was an interesting profile that kept presenting itself. Kids with serious LD — there are varying degrees — were generally brighter than average, very good at hiding their lack of learning, often manipulative in socially acceptable ways, quick to learn alternative ways to acquire the necessary knowledge to cope in a society that assumes everyone reads and writes with ease.

Then it dawned on me, that was my sister, Moira. She hated school, and was masterful at getting her information elsewhere, radio, television, from others. She could read and write, but avoided both when possible. Decades ago, her close friend in Toronto, Meg Corrigan, who taught children with LD, assessed Moira and told her she was a classic. Moira would help Meg read some of the student essays when their words posed problems. For example, Moira said they spelled "Europe" as "Urop" As Moira said, "How the hell else would you spell that?"

When computers came along, Moira was in her element. She helped others in her real estate office with the new skills, which came to her so easily.

Meanwhile, back in North Vancouver, I heard of a low profile resource for these kids in trouble. It was a small school in Vancouver, housed in portables, called 'Step Up', for boys and girls in Vancouver who were on probation, ages thirteen to seventeen. Most of these kids had been thrown out of numerous schools for their behaviour. Up to ninety-five percent were assessed with significant LD of some kind or other.

There are some unsung extraordinary heroes in our country. One of them was Bernie Agg, a retired probation officer. He began Step Up. His background included three years in the Army and twelve years as a psychiatric nurse at Woodlands, a school for troubled youth on Vancouver Island. Around 1970 he attended a workshop on learning disabilities, and the penny dropped. These were his kids. He believed he knew a better way to help young kids who were written off.

In October 1971, Bernie Agg began a small project to test his assumption that youths judged by the system to be "incorrigible" could be induced to attend a program where they could and would learn. He began with five tough boys, "the worst" in his caseload. His rules were simple:

1. No one could be kicked out of the program, regardless of their behaviour.
2. There would be no threats, only inducements.
3. No threats of being sent to the Detention Centre (for youth) or court.
4. Each youth would be paid 50 cents a day for showing up.
5. The program had to be interesting enough for them to want to attend.

He obtained a warehouse for them to meet. Dr. Marg Csapo, who taught special education at UBC, gave of her time and expertise, and provided university students to volunteer their time to tutor these challenging kids. Slowly the City of Vancouver came on board, as did the Ministry of Education and the Attorney General. The school eventually was established in portables near City Hall.

The school's name and logo 'Step Up' was selected by competition among the students themselves.

Step Up rewarded good behaviour with lots of positive attention, even if the good conduct was as minimal as sitting at a desk, or picking up a pencil or handling a book. Bad behaviour was ignored or gently stopped. The good behaviour got all the attention. This was new for these kids.

Each student went through a thorough assessment for learning abilities; their rates of LD were huge. Each student had their own workplace, tutor or worker. All volunteers were trained.

My favourite feature was their treatment of homework. No one was ever assigned homework, unless they asked for it. If they completed homework, they were paid for it. So, often on a Thursday, as the weekend loomed and money was needed for a movie, homework was requested. They were working for the same incentive that most do, money.

The school was concentrating on the basics, reading, writing, arithmetic. These most-difficult of young students were responding. Where the general rate of recidivism with people in trouble with the law and re-offending is often as high as eighty-five percent, Step Up was around twelve percent. This is astonishing success with kids almost everyone had written off.

We were able to slide a few of our North Vancouver students into Step Up, even though it was for Vancouver students. I had met Nona Thompson, a gifted teacher there who made sure she hugged all these kids often and told them how proud she was of them. Words most had never heard.

The school became privatized in 1984, but still operates with a low profile; a non-profit, always in need of more volunteers. It is continuing proof that education, understanding and prevention are a better answer to crime than giving up and locking them up.

Bernie Agg, Marg Csapo, and Nona Thompson were special people working their magic under the radar, trying and usually succeeding with kids who needed encouragement, not more punishment.

# CHAPTER 55

## *Building Bigger Prisons*

I N THE MIDST of having my driveway paved one June day, Jim Ferguson of Monarch Paving and I were talking about kids who get in trouble with the law. He coaches skiing to youngsters, and said, "There are no bad kids." I agreed. I have never met a bad kid. I have encountered ones who have done some very bad things.

I still check the *North Shore News* for names of youngsters who appeared before me when I was a Provincial Court judge in North Vancouver, hoping not to see their names, hoping they have been able to overcome their early problems of drunken homes, incest, abandonment, addiction, cruel physical abuse, you name it.

Sometimes, after a day in juvenile criminal court, or sitting on a protection/apprehension case, I would drive home feeling useless and defeated by the lack of tools and resources available to us in the courts to help young people in trouble. I would tell myself I should quit the law, buy a big house, hire a housekeeper, and offer some of those kids a home. Bake till you're batty, have cookies that were available when I grew up. Tell them how wonderful they are, as you were told all your life. Not what miserable little rats they are, as they have been told all their lives.

That day in June, I thought of a youngster who I will call 'Jack.' In the late seventies he was about thirteen, and had committed dozens of B&Es. (Break and Enter.) Serious charges, and his angelic appearance got him into places he never should have been. The police kept picking him up and taking him back to his beautiful but dizzy young mother, with the usual side trip to the cells and juvenile court.

On every court appearance, Jack's mother would appear, tell me again that she was sure Jack would not do it again, and that she had found a new dad to replace the one that had deserted them many years before. That all Jack needed was a dad. The latest new dad was always someone who had been on the scene for a few days at most, but she was sure this was the one. Jack would be standing in front of the court, with the look of someone who has heard that many times, but also that protective look that said, *don't say anything to hurt my Mom.*

We had tried every resource existing to try and keep Jack out of trouble, and finally he was in custody in a group home under strict supervision. On his regular reporting trips to the court, the reviews from the group home workers were encouraging. So much so that Jack was going to be allowed to go on a week's summer camp with others, still closely supervised; an outward bound trip that often helped young kids. Or at least gave them a week of camping they had never had a chance to experience.

The night before they were all to leave, Jack leaped out of a second-floor bathroom window to run away, but broke his arm badly in the fall. He was in hospital getting pins and screws to repair the break. He would be in hospital for at least a week. The social workers guessed that he was terrified of the coming trip and responsibilities.

I drove home that Friday with the familiar thoughts about the uselessness of my role with these young people.

I was going out with friends that evening. Before I went, I baked a batch of chocolate chip cookies, and arrived at the hospital, cookies in hand for the sad delinquent.

After that, Jack would sometimes come and sit in the court, just to say hello. In my remaining year or two there, there were no new charges. I am sometimes asked what has been the hardest part about being a judge. It's the kids. They stay with you.

During my years on the bench, I have often been asked (accused), "You're not one of those bleeding heart liberal judges, are you?" To which I reply, "You bet. One of those." And I add, "Come and sit in our courts for a while."

Or read the papers. An article on an aboriginal teen suicide in Alberta. A fifteen-year-old who tried five times to kill himself before being successful, He had been in and out of government care until age ten, then was made a permanent guardian of the state. In the last five years of his life, from ten to fifteen, he had eight different case workers and thirteen foster placements.

I wonder whatever happened to the shy young aboriginal girl in care, finally adopted as a pre-teen by a well-meaning single woman, who brought her back saying it just was not working out. The official return into care took place in my chambers with the girl, her case worker and the woman, and all the child could do was look down at the floor, beyond even tears.

Or the twelve- or thirteen-year-old who was turned in to the police by his parents because he had again stolen money out of his mother's purse. The parents were sitting in court behind the slight youngster, who was standing before me. The prosecutor laid out the charge, and the mother stood up suddenly and told me what a total failure this child was, "He isn't of our blood anyway. He's adopted. He has never been any good." The father nodded in agreement. The boy, still standing, was weeping silently, tears streaming down his face.

I have sent to prison young and older males for crimes committed, men with long records and personal histories that defy belief. The juvenile and adult records and family histories come before me as a judge when the pre-sentence reports, compiled by the probation and social service workers, were filed. And with submissions and evidence tendered by counsel for the Crown and defence.

One young accused had a juvenile record for a number of property crimes. By the age of nineteen he had been in fifty-six foster homes. He had been apprehended by child welfare at the age of one when it was discovered he had been raped by his father. He was assaulted both physically and sexually in more than one of the many foster homes.

I found a thirty-one year old man guilty for his part in an ill-conceived drug-fueled bank robbery that was right out of a script for Larry, Curly and Mo. The total take was $345, except the dye pack blew up right outside the bank. He and the female co-accused were apprehended shortly after.

His early years were horrific. His father was unknown. He was savagely abused by his mother as an infant. He was locked in a room for days on end as an infant, tied up and repeatedly submerged in water, his hands were held to burn on stove elements. This torture was by his mother and her boyfriends.

He was finally taken into care at age five, diagnosed with ADHD and from age five to eighteen he was in fifty-two foster homes. In seven of those homes, he was physically and sexually abused. One of his foster homes was that of Donald Bakker, then a well-regarded justice of the peace. The same Donald Bakker who later gained infamy as Canada's first convicted sex trafficker, a pedophile known for his sadistic sexual treatment of children in Thailand and women in Canada.

In 2000, a twenty-year-old young man on a fifth robbery charge was before me for sentencing in Supreme Court. In addition to the defence lawyer's submissions, the accused had written a letter to the court on his own behalf. The letter was well written and showed keen intelligence. His youth record began at age twelve and was one of the longest records I had ever seen.

The word 'tragic' would not begin to describe this young man's personal history. Many foster homes and years of sexual abuse in six of those homes, including the home of the same Donald Bakker.

I know there were judges other than me who had to think, *how would society like me to punish this youth or man? To really teach him a lesson. What more can I do to him that will beat what has already been done?*


Our need for universal child care, more resources and trained workers to help these kids has long been a national disgrace. Early child care is imperative to assist those who need it, parents unable to handle the care of their infants for all the reasons that we know: a mom so young she is still a child herself, substance abuse problems, domestic violence, sexual abuse, poverty so dire that kids are sent to school without breakfast or lunch. We know the value of early intervention to help families and to assess children, whether their problems are nutrition, learning disabilities, mental or physical health, or abuse.

Instead of building a national child care network, we have been building bigger prisons.

There are some better moments in sentencing young offenders. *The Criminal Code of Canada* spells out the principles of sentencing. Two of those principles instruct that an offender should not be deprived of liberty, if less restrictive sanctions might be appropriate, and that all available sanctions other than imprisonment that are reasonable in the circumstances should be considered.

I have never thought jails solved much. Some criminals obviously must go to jail, some for long periods, and a relative few, for life. I believe in restorative justice and rehabilitation, and an offender being given the opportunity to compensate his victims and/or community. The more community involvement in our justice system, the better. Wherever appropriate, I would suspend sentence, place an accused on probation for two or three years, and often order, as a term of probation, multiple hours of community work service, sometimes 200 to 400 hours.

As a judge, I soon realized that while I might make an order for two hundred hours of community work service, it was up to the probation services to direct what, when and where that work service would occur. How about cleaning up the local parks, school grounds, hiking trails? No, that is union work. Why not help an elderly couple stay in their own home by assisting with outdoor maintenance, cleanup chores and gardening? Well, the temptation to case the joint might be irresistible.

It was frustrating not knowing where or how an individual would spend his or her hours of community work service, and sometimes disappointing I did not have the ability to suggest or direct. There was one exception.

In the late seventies, Howard Bradbrooke, a smart young defence counsel on the North Shore, was representing an aboriginal youth from one of the First Nations in North Vancouver. The circumstances were ideal for probation and community work service. In speaking to sentence, Bradbrooke stressed the favourable attributes of his client, his youth, lack of any significant record, close ties to his community and his talent as a carver, a prized art and tradition in the West Coast aboriginal culture.

Indicating my intention to suspend sentence, and order probation with two-hundred hours of community work service, I made a proposal: if the elders on his reserve would agree to supervise the community work service, I would order that the young man spend those two-hundred hours carving, under supervision. One half of his completed works would be donated to the craft shop on the reserve, and the young offender could retain the remaining half.

Court was adjourned to the next morning for Bradbrooke to canvass the elders for their agreement to participate. The elders agreed and the order was made.

Decades after I left Provincial Court in North Vancouver, I was told that in the late seventies, during the mainly volunteer construction of Presentation House, a venue for local theatre and other community events, those overseeing the construction were grateful to receive an ongoing supply of new helpers from our North Vancouver Court, serving out their community work-service hours.

# CHAPTER 56

## *The Sublime Blanche MacDonald*

*Blanche*

---

I T WAS A SURPRISING YEAR, 1972. As my appointment to the bench had demonstrated, suddenly there were slots for token females, in the law profession and elsewhere. But just one at a time.

On the personal side, when Judy LaMarsh came to Vancouver for her year of broadcasting, she could not believe how slack we Western types were. She called us Lotusland. Those long exhilarating Friday afternoon lunches, sometimes around the outdoor pool of the Bayshore Hotel. When the women got together, Allan Fotheringham dubbed us the Wolf Pack: Judy, LaVerne Barnes, Rosemary Brown, Lisa Hobbs, Hannah Smith, Marjorie Nichols and Blanche MacDonald. No one lunched with the ladies better than Dr. Foth. These friends were extraordinary, visionary, funny and tough.

The sublime Blanche MacDonald, with the gift of making everyone she encountered feel special, was beautiful, loving, smart and a born entrepreneur. She was also a Cree Metis, proud of her identity and heritage. By age twenty-nine, Blanche had established her eponymous modelling and fashion agency in Vancouver in 1960. That business has continued in various forms long after her early death in 1985 from cancer.

Blanche was committed to women's rights and the rights of aboriginals, particularly women. On March 7, 1978, Blanche and Pauline Jewett, a former Member of Parliament and then President of Simon Fraser University, appeared before the Royal Commission on the Incarceration of Female Offenders. The Commission was set up by the BC Government following serious allegations of sexual misconduct, fraud and other complaints occurring at the Women's Prison at Oakalla.

Blanche and Pauline were presenting a brief on behalf of an ad hoc Citizens Advisory Group. Their stated concerns were "the needs of women in prison with special emphasis on the Native Indian women." Their objective was to facilitate the integration of these women into society and their communities after incarceration. Their brief suggested "the majority of women's offences can be categorized as either lifestyle-related or self-destructive offences, e.g. prostitution, alcohol and drugs."

They were seeking more community involvement to assist these women, including re-entry homes where needed. Their brief stated:

> It is a truism in Canada that native Indian people are vastly over-represented in our prisons, far out of proportion to their numbers in the general population. The question of why this discrepancy exists has never been a subject of enquiry..."

This was 1978, forty years ago.

Their recommendations included "a community based residential facility staffed by native Indian women" and that native Indian women be encouraged to apply for such positions. Also that there be an affirmative action program for all staff with ongoing in-service training and job upgrading skills. It was the stated hope that the objectives would develop positive feelings about being native and being female by encouraging an identification with native culture, and contact with other women who could serve as positive role models. There was a recognition that these women needed to increase their knowledge of health, nutrition, parenting, financial matters, education, job training and access to other services.

> We have focused our attention on the problems of native women in prison because we felt that inadequate attention was being paid to their condition.

There were eleven women in this ad hoc group that Blanche, Pauline and others spoke for. The group included three social workers, two lawyers, a sociologist. Four of the eleven were aboriginal, including Blanche.

I was having dinner with Blanche and Pauline the day the *Royal Commission on the Incarceration of Female Offenders Report* came out in June 1978. In spite of Pauline's famous shepherd's pie, it was a grim evening. Still sitting as a judge on the Provincial Court, I was not involved, but very interested. I was one of those tasked with sending people to our prisons. The Commission wrote:

> This Commission is not convinced that there is a problem of great magnitude regarding native women in the prison system.... The Commission does not see any special problem presently surrounding the incarceration of native women.

For Blanche, those findings were particularly galling. She had worked with women in the prisons and in her community; she knew the problems. She knew these women at a deep and personal level; these were her sisters, her aunties, her grandmothers.

A few days later, in the British Columbia Legislature, commenting on the *Commission Report*, Rosemary Brown rose to point out the problems faced by native women in prison, cultural isolation, discrimination against natives, the misleading statistics on who is identified as native, and the disproportionate number of native women in our prisons.

When Rosemary spoke to the Legislature on June 8, 1978, she said, "The whole impact of the justice system on Native Indians of both sexes is one that's always been a disgrace in this country." My friends were tilting against unforgiving and overwhelming windmills.

Later in June of that year, I accompanied Blanche on a trip to Haida Gwaii, home of the Haida Nation, then called the Queen Charlotte Islands. We flew into Skidegate for the historic raising of Bill Reid's carved totem pole, *Tribute to the Living Haida*. It had taken Reid, the renowned Haida artist and carver and his assistants two years to carve the gigantic pole. We all watched in awe as dozens of men manually raised the totem pole before the longhouse in the Village of Skidegate. A potlatch followed that evening. It was an unforgettable experience.

It was a Friday, May 11, sunny and warm. It was Blanche's birthday. I called to wish her happy birthday. "Is anyone taking you out for lunch?" No? "Lets' go to Umberto's Il Giardino. My treat."

I called Rosemary Brown to join us. Back in practice at this point, I cancelled my Friday afternoon at the office. It was going to be one of those Lotusland Friday lunches. Then Blanche called to ask if her older brother, Wylie Brillon, could join us. Wylie, a successful fisherman out of Haida Gwaii, was in town. Blanche adored him and it was easy to see why.

It was a splendid lunch. We were almost the last to leave the restaurant. As we sat in the near empty restaurant, it suddenly occurred to me: "I'm the only white person at this table."

"That's right, Nancy. How does it feel?" said the wicked Rosemary, leaning forward with a now-you-know smile.

# CHAPTER 57

# Mr. Scott

IWILL CALL HIM Mr. Scott. The RCMP had picked him up the night before, driving, very drunk. For someone so small in stature, the high number he had blown on the breathalyzer was astounding. He had spent the rest of the night in the jail cells of the courthouse, and when he was brought up into the courtroom at 9.30 a.m., he was in bad shape, probably still impaired. He was also physically disabled, on permanent crutches.

The charge was impaired driving, and the prosecutor advised that Mr. Scott had three previous convictions for the same offence. I asked Mr. Scott if he understood the charge, and if he had a lawyer. Mr. Scott said he understood the charge and wished to plead guilty. He could not afford a lawyer. With a fourth conviction of impaired driving, there was a mandatory substantial jail sentence. He was looking so unwell I did not consider him capable of making a rational decision at that time, so I told him I was adjourning his case to the next day, and urged him to seek the advice of a lawyer.

The next day, Mr. Scott appeared, the red flush on his face replaced by a white pallor. I asked him how he was feeling, and he said he was feeling better. Had he had a chance to speak to a lawyer? He shook his head; he had not, he just wanted to plead guilty and get it over with. I explained to him what the possible penalty could be, substantial jail time, and that I felt it was important that he get some legal advice before entering such a plea.

Crown counsel indicated that Mr. Scott worked as a skilled tradesman at a location miles from his home, a job he had held for twenty-five years.

A two-year jail sentence would obviously end that job. I asked Mr. Scott if he was married. He nodded. Did he have any children? He had four children. Did his wife or any of the children drive? Getting answers out of Mr. Scott was not easy. He was not a talker. But it eventually came out that his wife suffered from a chronic illness, she did not drive, and all four children were young, well under the driving age.

Mr. Scott worked only the midnight to dawn shift. Because of his wife's illness, this meant he could help with the children during the day. Two of the youngest children had serious medical conditions and disabilities.

The consequences to Mr. Scott, his wife and four children on him being sent to jail for his fourth conviction of impaired driving were obvious. He would lose his job, his wife, unable to care for the four children alone, would probably be on welfare, and the conditions of the two young children could mean institutional or foster care for them. The family would pay heavily for his excessive drinking.

I told Mr. Scott I was not prepared to accept his guilty plea that day, and again suggested he speak to a lawyer. I adjourned the matter over for one week.

A week later, Mr. Scott appeared, and a tall, well-dressed younger man appeared alongside him. Mr. Scott looked better. The younger man stood up and said,

> My name is Dave, your honour. I am from Alcoholics Anonymous. Mr. Scott came to see us for the first time last week after his appearance in court. He has come every evening since, and he has not had a drink since that time.

I asked Mr. Scott if he had consulted with a lawyer. He had not. He still intended to plead guilty.

AA does not work for everybody, but for many, it gives them back their lives. Mr. Scott was going to get another adjournment, whether he wanted one or not. I kicked it over for one month.

In they came a month later, Dave and Mr. Scott. Dave had good news. Mr. Scott was still attending the AA meetings every evening before he went to work. He had been sober for over a month now. Dave, his sponsor, was much more verbal than the silent Mr. Scott. I asked Mr. Scott how he was feeling, and he indicated he was feeling much better, thank you.

Things seemed to be going well, court was busy that day, so I suggested this was not the day to take a guilty plea, and I adjourned the case for three months. The prosecutor of the day was happy to get another case off his list, and Dave and Mr. Scott left the courtroom.

Mr. Scott and Dave appeared three months later, Mr. Scott still resigned to his fate, Dave still earnest and informative. Mr. Scott had now been sober for over four months, was still attending the AA meetings nightly, and Dave reported that Mr. Scott had an ability to reach and counsel some of the younger men who came to the meetings, ones in their late teens and early twenties. "He is someone they seek out and listen to."

Mr. Scott had a healthier glow to him, and even appeared to be standing taller, although permanently wedded to his crutches. Another busy day in the courtroom, Mr. Scott was still without a lawyer, and I felt another adjournment coming on. Another happy prosecutor with a shortened list when I adjourned Mr. Scott over for another three or four months.

With each reappearance of David and Mr. Scott, the adjournments became longer. The reports from Dave were nothing but positive.

This went on for almost three years. It was now 1981, and I had decided it was time I left the bench and returned to private practice. What about Mr. Scott? To send him to jail now pursuant to the existing mandatory sentence would serve no one, including the pubic.

The chief prosecutor for our court during those years was Don Celle, another of my favourite Italians. Celle was quick, smart, full of common sense and humour, a former colleague from prosecuting days. I called and told him I had a problem. I laid out the saga of Mr. Scott. His next appearance was due in two weeks. Celle said he would look at the file. Because there was often a different prosecutor in court, depending on the day, he and his office had no particular reason to be aware of these subversive adjournments.

The two weeks elapsed. I heard nothing from Celle. Mr. Scott and Dave appeared in court, as scheduled. And there was Celle in court, instead of one of his junior prosecutors. Mr. Scott's case was called, Celle stood up and advised the court that he'd had a chance to go over this unusual file, and that he had spoken with the arresting officers. He was aware of Mr. Scott's personal circumstances surrounding his job and family, and his conduct since the offence. In view of all the circumstances, Celle said the Crown was entering a stay of proceedings. That meant the case would not be going forward, and Mr. Scott was free to go.

The Crown could bring the matter back before the court, and would undoubtedly do so if Mr. Scott were ever caught driving impaired again. Dave smiled, Mr. Scott looked solemn, as usual. I wished him good luck, and thanked Dave. I wanted to give Celle a hug. And you wonder why I like Italians.

# CHAPTER 58

## *Judy*

I T WAS 1980 and Judy LaMarsh was back in Ontario, her year in Lotusland a pleasant memory. She was in Toronto, doing some writing, some sporadic broadcasting, not much law. We kept in touch. On my last visit to Toronto, I had been surprised to see a much slimmer Judy.

Her weight loss, unexplained but significant, delighted Judy. She had battled weight always, far too fond of the double martinis, large glasses of rum and coke, and fabulous meals, her own and those in the finest restaurants. But here she was, able to fit into clothes long left hanging in the closet, and better still, able to buy new ones for the slimming figure.

Her weight loss was, of course, too good to be true. The diagnosis was cruel. Pancreatic cancer, with its vicious survival chances, less than two percent. The doctors would try to operate.

Judy wanted to know, how long do I have? She was told, once they opened her up, they would know more. If they could operate and remove some or all of the cancer, she might have more years. If they saw there was nothing they could do, six to twelve months at the most. The surgery would be long, if hope was indicated. If not, only about half an hour. They would do what they could to make her as comfortable as possible.

As soon as Judy awoke in the recovery room, her eyes roamed the room until she found a clock. It had been the half hour open-and-close surgery.

"First I get on with the business of dying and then back to business of living," she announced.

Her will was made. Her instructions were clear. She asked the doctors for only one thing: no pain. And she wanted to die at home, in her rented townhouse in Toronto, not in a hospital. She didn't say it, but the meaning was there, not with strangers.

Her amazing spirit and passion continued. Friends were welcomed, fussed over, plied with food and drink. Conversations raged on as always — politics, the news of the day, the world and its struggles. Laughter seldom left her home. Judy was forthright about her terminal condition. So no one felt uncomfortable. Least of all her.

Judy had no money. She was heavily in debt, primarily to Revenue Canada. She had not really been able to work for some time, and there was no other source of income available for her. Earlier in her illness, my intuitive and generous Vancouver lawyer friend, Bill Rand, one of many under Judy's spell, knew Judy's finances were nonexistent. She had been talking of writing another book, so Bill made her an offer. He would give her an advance of $10,000 in return for a percentage of the book profits.

Bill knew, as we all did, that Judy did not have the time left or stamina to write that book, but she did not question the offer, and the deal was struck. I think we even had it papered. I bless Bill for his deceptive and loving gift, which Judy proceeded to blow through, as was her wont. My first duty on my next visit from Vancouver was to go to Holt Renfrew and buy three or four feminine lovely and expensive nightgowns for her.

A sometimes daily visitor to Judy's bedside was Barbara Frum. They had grown up down the street from one another in Niagara Falls and were friends. Barbara's hugely popular CBC radio program, *As It Happens*, was never missed by Judy. When the show was over each evening, Barbara would head home, but took to dropping in to visit Judy en route.

Barbara said she did not dare wind down until after her visit with Judy, as Judy would be full of questions and observations and the discussions were spirited. Then Barbara could continue on home and finally relax.

As Judy's condition worsened, it became obvious that visits from friends, staying over for a week here or there, were not enough to meet the needs of our friend, who was growing weaker by the day. Barbara called me with a timely solution. Barbara's late grandmother had had a housekeeper/caregiver at her home in her final months, and that woman was now available. The cost would be $96 a week.

As Judy's illness became known, so many friends of hers and

mine had asked, *what can I do to help?* Nothing at this time, I would say, but maybe later. I had told Barbara of these calls and offers. So when it was time to hire the housekeeper, knowing Judy could not afford the cost, Barbara and I agreed that now was the time to contact those friends to say, if you still want to help, here is how.

We agreed that no one would pay for more than one week. Barbara would be the banker, cheques would be made out to her. So the calls went out, and the $96 cheques came flooding in. To each donor, Barbara hand wrote a note of receipt and thanks. Given her star status, then and even now, I know some of those notes were prized and saved. Judy never asked how the housekeeper was being paid, and we never said.

When the end did come for Judy, there were about three payments still in Barbara's account, which were donated to Judy's funeral expenses. Barbara and I had been cautious not to collect too many donations in advance, knowing Judy was nearing the end.

Even with her amazing career and social agendas, Barbara again found time to hand-write notes to each person who had sent a cheque, thanking them again, and advising them of the amount left in the account, and where that small surplus had gone.

In the meantime, we had all continued to visit. Those of us from afar came and stayed in one of the spare rooms, dancing to the dictates from the bed. Fielding all the calls from well-meaning strangers who insisted on more brown rice for Judy, special prayers, you name it. If you were staying for a week, Judy demanded you go out for lunch or dinner with your friends. She beamed when the friends began and ended the visits at her place.

Judy's diagnosis was no secret. Some overdue honours began coming her way — including the Order of Canada. And one from the Niagara Falls library. And that prompted Judy's favourite letter.

As Judy was dying, she received this letter from Pierre Trudeau, which she kept beside her bed until she died. She called it her love letter from Pierre. And indeed, it was. She laughed and said that she knew Pierre had written the letter, because no one else would have dared put those words on paper on his behalf.

June 23, 1980

Dear Judy,

I am delighted by the tribute you are being paid by the citizens of Niagara Falls. When I think of all you have done for that community, for Ontario and for Canada, I remain constantly impressed.

When you were a Cabinet Minister, you played a very direct role in developing the Canadian social security programme which is now the envy of the world; and who will ever forget your magnificent direction while Secretary of State of Canada's great centennial celebration.

Happily, after you left politics you continued your relationship with the public as a successful lawyer, a top rated broadcaster and a best-selling author. Through it all, you have remained in the forefront of the women's rights movement.

You have always believed that part of being an involved Canadian is to be an involved partisan. Thankfully, you have always been a partisan of the Liberal Party. Your by-election victory in 1960 in Niagara Falls under Mr. Pearson — a government which, as I have already indicated, you served with great distinction.

At the leadership convention in 1968, you were a key player, albeit on the other side. Indeed, your vivid reference to me at that convention has already become part of the Canadian political folklore. Like most Canadians, I have admired your colourful and frank style, which has always been accompanied by an ongoing sense of dignity and a large measure of good humour.

You were kind enough to indicate your support for me at the time of the last election, but more importantly, in 1979, which was not a vintage year for us Liberals, you were right there in our corner.

Whatever your personal commitments have been, you have always been available for Canada, for the party and for your friends who are legion in this country.

So, Judy, this is a love letter, and I expect the last person in the world you expected a love letter from was me.

Thank you for everything. Please keep right on being your own true self, which is the real reason you are being honoured at the Library tonight.

My very best wishes, Sincerely, Pierre

As the cancer took its murderous toll, Judy was in terrible pain. Doctors who had once called on her as Minister of Health and Welfare, were nowhere to be found. Her old friend from Niagara Falls, Dr. Tom Jamieson, often came and visited, and did what he could. But there was no one in Toronto making house calls.

I arrived for one of my week-long visits during that time, which was also the opportunity to give the housekeeper a week off. Crabby after the flight from Vancouver, tired at that time of the night, and horrified at the sight and plight of Judy, in terrible pain, bedridden and helpless, I answered a call on her phone, standing in the kitchen, a floor below Judy's bedroom.

A sweet-voiced woman was calling to see what help they could provide to Judy's family. She was apparently with an organization that tried to help the caregivers. "Help her family!" I yelled. "What about helping this woman who cannot even get a doctor to the house. Who has nothing to alleviate her pain except some damn Demerol which is making her throw up. The family doesn't need any help. She does!"

I know I ranted more, rude beyond belief in my rage.

Suddenly the woman's voice changed. She became very businesslike. Told me to get a pen and paper and take down this doctor's name and phone number. I was to call him immediately at the hospital. He would be there to help Judy.

I took down the name and number and hung up in disbelief, but did as she had advised. This doctor at one of the top hospitals in Toronto was paged, came on the line, listened to me briefly, got Judy's address and said he would be up to the house shortly. And he was. This was 1980. I think he must have been an oncologist. To my regret, I cannot recall his name, and to my shame, I never got the name of that angel who called and was on the receiving end of my verbal abuse.

Shortly after he arrived and was seeing Judy in her bedroom, the doctor handed me a prescription and told me to go to Sunnybrook Hospital, which was not that far away, to the pharmacy there, and have the prescription filled. It was for the Brompton cocktail he said. At the hospital, the prescription was filled without any questions, no ID needed to be produced on my part, and, here, I am not exaggerating, I was given a small demijohn of clear liquid, which I later learned had enough morphine and other hallucinatory drugs in it to turn on an entire block.

The doctor was gone when I got back. He must have given Judy something for her awful pain, because she was back to normal, not crippled in agony. She was to begin 'the cocktail' immediately, so I got one of her Rosenthal crystal liqueur glasses for the occasion. Judy agreed that was appropriate.

Later in the week, Judy asked if she was slurring her words. She was. You did not dare give Judy a dishonest answer. Not then. Not ever.

"Yes, you are. But you are not slurring your thoughts, if that is what is worrying you." She seemed content with that, giving me that look of hers, that said, *okay, you can get away with that this time....*

On one of my later visits, Judy was in full planning for her funeral. Chief Don Harris of the Niagara Falls police had sent word that there would be a full police escort for her funeral. That delighted her. Then there was the discussion about pallbearers. I had an inkling Judy was going to opt for women pall bearers.

"What would you think about being an honorary pallbearer?" she asked me. "Well, I wouldn't do it." I replied. Judy was startled. "Why not?" "Because, if I am going to be a pallbearer, it has to be the real thing, not an honorary one." I knew the list was going to

*Six pallbearers, clockwise from top: Edith Duggin, Doris Anderson, Pamela Walker, Nancy Morrison, Florence Rosberg, and Barbara Frum.*

include Doris Anderson, Barbara Frum and Pam Walker, Judy's most recent associate young lawyer while in practice.

Judy said she didn't think we could carry the coffin. I reminded her she had not weighed herself lately. Indeed, she could not get out of bed at all, so that was a safe observation. She had lost so much weight she reminded me of a freight train still roaring down the tracks, but the engine had lost all the outer mountings, just this fierce and unstoppable engine blasting on.

"We are putting Boris on the back end." I told her. That was Doris Anderson, the tallest of the group. Judy smiled, and it was settled. Six women pallbearers: Barbara Frum, Doris Anderson, Barbara's mother from Niagara Falls, Florence Rosberg, Ede Duggan, a lifelong friend of Judy's, Pam Walker and myself. Judy's final instructions on the pallbearer question, "I want you and Pam on the front end."

"Why?"

"I want youth out front."

Her funeral instructions did not end there, of course. She was an Army veteran from WWII. After enlisting, Judy had learned Japanese and been a Japanese translator during the war. She wanted a bugle playing *The Last Post* at the cemetery. "And find someone who can play the damned thing properly. Every goddamn funeral I have ever attended, they buggered up *The Last Post*. If that happens at mine, I am coming back to haunt you all."

She was also coming back to do the haunt thing if we did not throw the best wake ever held in Niagara after the funeral.

Then there were the bagpipes. Judy came from Huguenot ancestry. Her close friend, Jack MacBeth, shared my Scottish background. On this particular visit, Jack had come to spend some time with Judy. He was splendid company. He had worked for and with Judy for years in the political arena. They had been on the Truth Squad together, been howled out of the theatre in Halifax together when Diefenbaker yelled back at the fearless Squad. Jack still feared Judy.

"Ask her about bagpipes at the funeral," said Jack, as I was heading up to Judy's room. "You ask her," I said. Nope, he wouldn't. I had to.

So as Judy and I chatted about different things, I casually said, "Judy, what would you think about bagpipes at your funeral?"

"That's MacBeth, isn't it," she smiled. And that was it. Jack got the bagpipes.

Judy made it so easy for all of us to say goodbye to her. She shared everything, with her innate generosity, with her frank acceptance of dying.

They gave Judy six to twelve months. She lived almost all that, twelve months, dying October 27, 1980, just short of her fifty-fifth birthday, in the arms of her dear friend Ede Duggan. Ede and Dick Duggan had been friends with Judy's parents, and lifelong friends with Judy. It was as close as one could come to dying in the arms of one's mother.

# CHAPTER 59

## *Resigning from the Bench*

IN THE mid-1970s, I met David Suzuki when I was asked to introduce him at a British Columbia Bar Association luncheon. His topic was startling: the future legal implications of reproductive technology. This years before Baby Louise was born in July 1978, the first child of in vitro fertilization.

David was a man ahead of his time, and on that particular day he opened up the troubled soon-to-come world of human reproductive technologies, and the unforeseen legal problems on the horizon.

Later, in 1980 and 1981, I had the opportunity to lecture in Family Law at the University of British Columbia's Law School for two semesters. It was a learning experience for me, and probably the hardest work I've ever done. It demanded a lot of research and preparation, and I was still full-time on the bench. The students were bright and often a step ahead of me. It offered a valuable break from judging, and a renewal in thinking for me.

The family law curriculum was fairly standard, but Suzuki's lecture had remained with me. I wanted to explore the future legal implications of the new technologies with my students. The only material I had were media clippings of the occasional first cases in the United States. At that time, it was all questions and no answers. And certainly no law, other than hints that might be gleaned from animal husbandry legislation.

*Who owned leftover fertilized eggs? What was done with them? How far could ethical experimentation go? Would a child be able to trace her ancestry? Did she have a legal right to do so?* The questions continue as science progresses: how to control sperm banks, surrogate mothers, the sale of eggs, the dilemmas of multiple pregnancies. Laws on human reproduction have been slow to enact, precedents maybe too quick to establish, but science continues to leap forward, with law scrambling to catch up.

One of the many reasons I left the provincial court bench in

1981 was the lack of opportunity then for judges to take a working sabbatical — that sometimes necessary time away. I was disappointed not to be accepted as a lawyer in residence at UBC Law School for a year at the end of my ad hoc teaching.

That step back from the bench helped me decide it was time to resign as a judge and return to private practice. There was still some street fighting to do. I missed being involved in the political issues of the day, and missed the freedom of private practice. Bruno and I were apart at this time, and socially I knew I was becoming more withdrawn.

I also believed it was not healthy for me, at forty-four, to know what I would be doing for the next thirty years. We all need change and new challenges. It was time to leave. My Chief Justice, Lawrence Goulet, urged me to stay another year so that my pension would vest, at ten years of service. It was wise counsel but I did not heed it, and sent in my letter of resignation in May 1981.

# CHAPTER 60

## *Back in Practice*

WHEN I LEFT THE BENCH IN 1981, there were no phone calls to come and join a law firm. Nor did I expect any. I was not one of the boys, and I would not be coming in as a pliant junior associate. My billing capacity would be unknown for them and me. I had no background as a team player, boasted no credentials from an appropriate private school, fraternity, football or rugby team, and was certainly not a member of the cherished all-male private clubs.

David Barrett's NDP government had appointed me to the provincial bench and then seconded me to the Labour Relations Board. In the minds of many, could I be more left wing?

I began scouting office space in the Gastown area. On the verge of signing a lease, I ran into my friend, Glen Orris, an excellent lawyer whose office was at 123 Main Street, on the cusp between historic Gastown and the notorious skid row. He said, "You're not going to practice alone. That's not right. You need people around. You are going to come and join us." He and Terry LaLiberté and Paul Myers had been sharing space, and Myers had just left to join the provincial bench. So I took over Paul's office, complete with sliding glass doors on to a cedar sun deck, my office for the next fifteen and a half years. We were later joined by Robbie Burns. That informal office-sharing arrangement gave me camaraderie, sounding boards, fun and lifelong friendships.

There were adventures. Our Christmas parties reached a zenith the year one of the (male) provincial court judges emerged from the bathroom wearing the clothes of one of the (female) court clerks, and she emerged wearing his.

Christmas giving became Christmas taking the year someone stole from my office my poster size black and white photograph of Doukhobor women hitched to and pulling the plow in Saskatchewan just after 1900. The lone male in the photograph was guiding the plow.

Our office was one block from the provincial court jail. One evening I was at my secretary's computer in the outer office after everyone had gone for the day. Robbie Burns was in his office with a client, door closed. Up the stairs came a tall, sad-looking man holding out a clear plastic bag containing a wallet, a watch and a few other personal items. He had just been released from the nearby jail. The bag was sealed, and did I have some scissors to cut open the bag? Sure. Then he asked very hesitantly if he could use our washroom. I directed him to go down the hall. He disappeared; then reappeared. Not only had he neglected to do up his fly, he had failed to tuck the alert bird back into its nest. He advanced, smiling.

"Rob!" I yelled. Robbie flew out of his office. Over six feet tall, athletic and compassionate, Robbie guided my new friend gently back down the front stairs, having ensured suitable dress, and out the door.

We parked our cars in the alley behind our office, and walked up the open staircase to the back door of our second-floor offices. In the early years, working late nights at the office often meant encountering a couple of the local inhabitants sheltering under the staircase, sharing a bottle in a brown bag. I would ask if they were behaving themselves; they would caution me to drive carefully.

Those friendly encounters ended a month or two after the needle exchange opened down our block. Our back alley and back porch became a shooting gallery. That staircase became totally enclosed and locked, razor wire abounded, the huge rhododendron bushes long gone, and the alley a prized film location for scary scenes, day or night.

I miss the guys under the stairs.

The feminist movement of the early sixties and seventies was well under way and brought some interesting conversations into my office. I had been giving many speeches on women's rights, so it was no surprise when women came to me as a lawyer.

On one occasion, a couple of young women had been

charged with disturbing the peace and assault, following a demonstration they had begun. They were pleading not guilty and I felt they had a good defence.

But when I gave them my usual advice-to-client to dress with respect for their court appearances, they stiffened. I explained the judges were all middle-aged, or older, conservative men who would likely be outraged at near-bare feet, breast feeding in court and the general hippie dress look of the day. Their dress did not matter to me personally; I wanted them to win their case.

It was their decision to make, not mine. I could only advise. Did they want to make a political statement, and risk having a judge convict because of prejudice, leaving them with a criminal record and all its ramifications, or win the case?

I was sounding like a sell-out. They went to another lawyer.

It was never a difficult decision for me — my politics or my profession. I was a lawyer. My clients did not need my politics, they needed my training. Although who I was as a person was undoubtedly shaped by my politics.

Other interesting discussions occurred when interviewing law students who were seeking to article with us. Did they like law school? Trick question. If they said they hated it and could not wait to get out, they weren't hired. If they were not enjoying studying law, the fascinating cases, the collegiality with their professors and colleagues, the combination of people, history, and language, I could not see them as litigation lawyers.

One other topic raised a dilemma for the future lawyer. More than one young female student looking for articles expressed great interest in litigation, particularly criminal law.

Then she would say, "Except I could never act for a man on a rape charge."

I understood well her politics. But felt she had to be clear about her desire to practice criminal law.

"Would you defend someone on a murder charge?"

"Oh, yes."

"Even if the accused had brutally murdered a woman? Or a child?"

"...uh...yes."

The cold reality of practising criminal law is eased by the certainty that our society demands the best prosecution and finest defence for those who commit the worst crimes. It is easy to defend the rich, the famous, the charming, those who commit lesser crimes. It is difficult to defend those who are despised, accused of terrible crimes, unappealing in every way.

A society without ethical, trained trial lawyers fosters lazy or absent prosecutors, gives police license to take shortcuts, or worse, and offers no justice for the truly innocent and victims, let alone the accused.

Most of those young lawyers stuck around, and they were great. They still are.

# CHAPTER 61

## *Farewell to Moira*

MY SISTER Moira continued to live in Calgary, loving the pace of the city, whose energy matched hers. She was barbecuing twelve months of the year, selling real estate, training her huge cat Sam to retrieve straws and fish olives out of your martini glass.

Our Dad had died in 1979, leaving us heartbroken. Mom continued to live in their home in Yorkton. Both Moira and I were back to Saskatchewan frequently, particularly in the summer to our cabin at Crystal Lake, Moira's favourite place. There was a darkness on the horizon none of us saw coming.

Moira did everything with enthusiasm, including smoking and drinking too much for her health. She'd had a cancer scare in the mid-seventies while in Toronto, had surgery and appeared to have made a complete recovery. But cancer reappeared, this time bladder cancer, in late 1981. Moira did not fold, not even for a minute; she survived several surgeries the last two years of her life.

She never lost her sense of humour, or her mother-bear instincts over her younger sister. She decided her doctor and I should be dating, wanting to make sure someone would be looking after me in her absence. I didn't seem to be doing well enough on my own. She told one of her best friends, "I know I am dying but I don't want to talk about it." And she didn't. Moira remained feisty, funny and brave, and the greatest of sisters.

I was with her in Calgary in the hospital when she died, late one night. Near the end, as Moira lay in a coma, one of her close friends, Margaret, and one of my closest friends, Sandra Lyons, were with me at Moira's side. We agreed there was only one way to see Moira out of this life, and on to the next: with a party.

Sandra went to buy wine, we rounded up glasses and invited the night staff to come in for a drink. Moira's favourite nurse stayed by her side, as did her doctor, and we toasted that vibrant loving soul out into the next world. Moira died April 27, 1983, in her forty-ninth year. That was when Jacquie, my lifelong friend, called to say, "I am your sister now."

After Moira died, Sandra and Hugh Lyons threw open their home for the wake. Their eleven-year-old son, Christopher, and his young friend David Mears were watching the trays of food being carried in by the caterers and asked why this food was being brought in.

Sandra explained to them that when someone dies, as Moira just had, her friends gather to celebrate her life and talk about how much we loved her, and will miss her. So Moira's friends were coming to their house to do that.

Eleven-year-old David announced, " Then I'll have to come. Moira was my friend." Sandra, a bit startled, agreed, if David's mother said it was all right. The darling child went home to check, and came back with his hair patted down, dressed in an immaculate white shirt and dark trousers.

After Dad had died in 1979, I offered to prepare a will for Moira. Moira gave me firm instructions that when she died I was to bury her ashes under the birch trees in front of our Crystal Lake cottage. "Oh God, Moira, what am I supposed to do? I'll be ninety-five, and I'm going to go and knock on the door of some total strangers who will have the place by then, and say, excuse me, but I have these ashes..."

That's as far as I got. Moira loved the lake, and proclaimed, "That place will always be in our family. It will never be sold to anyone else. That is where I want my ashes!" There are times when you do not argue with your older sister, and this was one of them. I figured I'd talk her out of the birch trees in the many years to come. There were no such years. Four years later, Moira was dead and I knew what she wanted.

Her wishes meant a second wake, this one in late June at the lake in Saskatchewan. Her ashes were buried under her birch trees, and another barn burner of a wake followed. Anything less would have been unacceptable.

*With Jacquie Sims (nee Vaughan) and Sandra Lyons*

For Moira's second wake, Jacquie flew in from Toronto, Bob O'Regan cruised in on his motorcycle from Victoria, and the three of us opened up the cottage, Bob even giving the Marine white glove treatment to the tops of the cabinets. We filled the cottage and deck with huge bouquets of lilacs and apples blossoms from Jacquie's Mom's yard, and invited all the usual suspects to come out on a perfect June day. Our next door neighbor, Keith Harper, had quietly bombed the woods and shrubs around — sorry Greenpeace — and there was not a bug in sight. Jacquie and I had cooked up a storm. We had a never-ending bar. It was a Moira day, we all agreed.

The only thing better than one first-class wake is two.

# CHAPTER 62

## *Abortion and Politics*

M ANY YEARS AGO, the irreverent American feminist Flo Kennedy opined, "If men could give birth, abortion would be a sacrament." First, this is about abortion in the late fifties and early sixties. It is an issue that has had a profound effect on my politics and feminism.

In the fifties, when I was in high school and university, abortion, illegal, was never discussed, but often performed. Performed in back alleys, almost literally at times, often by hacks with no medical training, using methods and instruments that rendered young women infertile, sometimes dead.

Good girls did not get pregnant before marriage. If you did, your family was devastated, you were sent away, alone. In the midst of this family and public condemnation, personal humiliation and terrible trauma, you had to decide — proceed with the pregnancy and put the baby out for adoption; keep the child and hope the father would stick around and help or marry you, or wonder how you could support yourself and a child; or try and find one of the many illegal abortionists, risking danger to your reproductive health, or your life.

One summer in the late fifties, there was a call from a hospital in another city. It was noon, Dad was home for lunch. The call was to say that Moira was bleeding dangerously from a botched abortion, in serious condition in the hospital. I have never seen my parents move with such speed. In ten minutes, they had packed some overnight necessities and were in the car driving to see their daughter. Moira survived.

This was years before the birth control pill and it was not legal for women to use contraception other than abstinence. Pharmaceutical methods were few, not widely used, hit and miss, frowned upon, maybe behind some druggist counter. The father was a married man. Having a child then was out of the question for her, so she fled to another city for an illegal abortion. She almost lost her life. None of us spoke of it. Decades later, Moira told me it had been twins. In today's world, her decision would have been different. But sixty-five years ago, it was a mean world.

Having a child out of wedlock in those days meant giving birth to a 'bastard', being cut off from what few career and marriage opportunities a young woman might have. It was public shaming at its best.

I never forgot that phone call or Moira's painful decision. I knew that I should never become pregnant before marriage. I believed it would kill my parents, whom I loved and admired. I knew that if that ever happened to me, I would have to kill myself. I even had the method picked out — the prairie way — close the car in the garage and keep the engine running. The least messy and painless way I could imagine.

I do not know if I would ever have elected to have an abortion. I was never put to the test. But I could never imagine the state or a controlling boyfriend or anyone else ordering a female to carry a fetus to birth against her will. Or a state that gives someone else a veto power over what a girl or woman can decide over her own body. To impose compulsory childbirth on any female is beyond my comprehension.

There will always be debate on abortion. It is the most difficult political and social issue, the most divisive. It is a paradox that many who believe in capital punishment, the deliberate killing by the state of a human being, believe abortion is a crime — the killing of a fetus. And many who believe capital punishment to be wrong are prepared to sanction abortion.

The rhetoric on both sides is inflammatory. "Abortion on demand" never described for me the distraught young girls and women desperately looking for help to end an unwanted pregnancy. "The right to life" and "the right of a woman to choose" are slogans that do injustice to the many facets involved in the abortion issue.

There are no easy answers to the young girl who has been raped, or who has been subjected to incest, some too young to look after themselves let alone go through childbirth. A woman trying to escape an abusive relationship, unwilling to carry a child to a second trimester. Should the law force her to give birth? Should the father of the fetus have a veto? Should the state?

Years ago I was one of the many lawyers and doctors across the country who campaigned to have abortion removed from *The Criminal Code of Canada* as a crime. The Criminal Law subsection of the Canadian Bar Association in British Columbia was particularly active on this issue, led by some dedicated male lawyers. In May 1969, the government of Pierre Trudeau passed legislation that made it legal for women to use contraception. And for the first time in Canada, a woman could legally obtain an abortion if she had medical evidence that indicated her health was at stake. That therapeutic abortion process was convoluted and difficult at best, and unavailable to women who did not have access to sympathetic doctors and a nearby willing hospital.

Before going on the Provincial Court bench in December 1972, I spoke to many groups on the issue, and took part in a number of debates. They were difficult debates.

For the nine years I sat as a Provincial Court judge, I never spoke publicly on abortion, or any other legal or political issues. I cut all political ties, as judges must.

In May 1981, after resigning from the Provincial Court bench and re-entering private law practice, I knew I would be free again to speak on political issues that were important to me, one of which was a woman's right to end an unwanted pregnancy. The United States was accelerating backward on the issue at that time, and I was concerned that Canada was in danger of losing what partial gains had been made so painstakingly in the previous decade.

Once off the bench, back on the public speaking circuit, I resolved: no matter what the topic or who the audience or where the speech, I would work abortion into my speech. It was easy to do, sometimes with only a passing comment. Meanwhile, Dr. Henry Morgenthaler and so many women's groups and concerned men and women across this country and others were dedicated to the issue of reproductive freedom and choice for all women.

When I ran for Parliament in 1984 in the Vancouver Kingsway riding, I knew my position on abortion was contentious with many voters, but felt it would be dishonest not to face the issue. So it was covered in my principal piece of campaign literature, along with the other issues of the day.

My wise campaign manager, David Ingram (a.k.a. The Sun King) would have preferred silence on the issue, but the brochure was written, printed and ready to be distributed.

Campaigning door-to-door is not for everyone. I welcomed it. One evening as I set out to knock on doors, new brochure in hand, David said, "Now Nancy, don't talk about abortion on the doorstep."

"David. Of course I won't. Give me credit."

Wendy Menghi, a friend, came with me that evening, her first time ever as a campaign volunteer. We came to a well-kept home where an attractive woman was gardening in her front yard.

"Hello, I'm Nancy Morrison, the federal Liberal candidate in this riding."

"I know who you are. And further, I know what you stand for." Her attractive face was not smiling.

There is only one issue that brings out that reaction.

"You mean my position on abortion."

"Yes, I do. I disagree with you totally."

"I understand. And I respect your position. Morally, and from a religious point of view, you are right. But in the practical world that I deal with, there are girls and women who cannot go through with an unwanted pregnancy, for many tough reasons, health wise, economic, emotional, rape, and so on. I know it is a very difficult issue."

"Well, I would never vote for someone who believes as you do."

"You might have a problem then. As it happens, all four candidates in this riding share the same position on abortion."

"Then I will not vote at all."

The candidate in me came to a full stop.

> Oh no! You mustn't do that. You must vote. You
> don't have to vote for me — but you must not
> give up your right to vote. People have died for
> the right to vote. And women around the world
> in so many countries are still denied the vote.
> You know, even in our lifetime, in Canada, not
> all women have had the right to vote, native
> women, women in Quebec in provincial elec-
> tions until 1947. You have to vote. It doesn't have
> to be for me.

Now I was feeling embarrassed at dumping a political science lecture on this nice woman who had simply been enjoying
an evening of gardening in her front yard. I lamely offered her
my latest brochure as I was leaving; she politely declined it.

I told her that her garden was lovely, and she finally smiled
and told me I was pretty.

The next morning I went into the campaign office, to be met
by David. "You have a message to call a Mrs. B__. She said you
might remember her. You spoke to her about abortion last evening on her front lawn."

His look said it all. I smiled, pretended not to notice the look,
and took the phone number.

The woman who answered said that perhaps I might not
remember her, that I had spoken to her last evening about abortion. I assured her that I certainly remembered her. She said,
"Well, as you know, I disagree completely with your stand on
abortion." I said that I clearly understood that, and reiterated
that I respected her position. She then said, "Well, I have been
thinking about things, and I just wanted to telephone you to tell
you that I do intend to vote, and I intend to vote for you."

Bruno had fun around the campaign. He cooked scrambled
eggs for a campaign office breakfast, popped down to the nearby
Legion with a couple of the volunteers after a long day, and generally cheered the troops. One day, he had driven to pick me up

*The campaign team, Vancouver Kingsway.*

after I was finishing canvassing door to door. As he waited at the end of the long avenue, he was watching my small team and I work the street.

It was around 4:30 on a Sunday. We were ready to head home. I thanked the young university students who were giving so much of their time, and went over to join Bruno.

He said, "I have been watching you canvassing down that street. You looked great."

"Thank you. That's nice," I blushed.

"You know, you'd make a hell of a Jehovah Witness."

I lost the election. I hated losing. Again. I had looked forward to being part of John Turner's government. John Turner was the reason I had agreed to run. I did not hesitate when he encouraged my candidacy.

Bruno eased the pain of this second political loss. He had said that if I were elected, he would come to Ottawa with me, and plant tulips, or whatever was required; but in the event that I lost, he would take me to Italy for a month.

After the election, the joke was that first prize was four weeks in Italy; second prize, four years in Ottawa.

# CHAPTER 63

# *Beachcombers*

I T WAS fascinating to be around an actor, a profession unfamiliar to me. The same probably applied to Bruno being around my profession, which intrigued him.

Not many women could say, "He does a better job of putting on his make-up than I do with mine." From early theatre days, Bruno always did his own make-up for theatre or filming.

I had seen Bruno on stage at Stratford. After we met, I saw Bruno on stage in Vancouver, in everything from a Pinter play to playing the Widow Twankey in *Aladdin*, the children's Christmas pantomime, his great legs showing as he sashayed down a long staircase in high heels, playing the traditional part of 'the dame' in the genre of the English pantomime.

In the seventies, for three years, when *Beachcombers* wasn't filming during the off season, Bruno hosted the television show, *Celebrity Cooks*. Many felt the highlight of the series was the episode when Dick Beddoes, famed *Globe and Mail* sportswriter, came on the show and told Bruno and Canada how to cook and eat beaver. When Bruno protested that the beaver was a treasured Canadian symbol, Beddoes growled it was just a buck-toothed, mean–tempered rodent. Most of the rest of Beddoes' dialogue would not pass censors today. Bruno's efforts to keep a straight face, filming live before an audience, were not helped by the camera guys and crew losing control.

Flora MacDonald appeared as a guest on *Celebrity Cooks*. Flora, known for being unable to boil water, later described Bruno and herself slipping around on grease which had escaped the hapless pair as she tried to cook her mother's cod cheeks recipe. In front of the live television audience, she had reduced Bruno to helpless laughter.

But it was *Beachcombers* that dominated most of our years together. It was a profitable CBC series that brought British Columbia and Canada into homes in fifty countries.

When we travelled, Bruno was often recognized, except in the United States where the show never ran. Although Americans who lived near the border and accessed CBC television would know him.

Some fans in Canada had a problem, usually needing to be solved by a bet. Bruno and I would be having a drink or dinner in a lounge or restaurant, and Bruno would laugh and say, "Here comes the bet."

Two men would arrive at our table, apologize for interrupting, then ask Bruno to settle their bet: "Peter says you're Greek, I say you are Italian." The confusion was easily understood; Bruno, the Italian, played Nick Adonidas, the Greek in the *Beachcomber* series.

Years ago Bruno and I were in San Francisco for a long weekend. We were in a leather shop, looking over some jackets. A little girl, about eight, was there with her parents. She kept staring at Bruno. She tugged gently at her dad's sleeve and he leaned down to listen to her. He then looked over at Bruno, who was unaware of this scrutiny as he tried on jackets. The dad looked back down at his daughter and shook his head, indicating no.

But the child kept staring. She tugged again at her dad, another quiet chat, and a second long look at Bruno by the dad. Again, no, he signalled to his daughter.

The little girl was crestfallen, but she kept looking back at Bruno.

I caught the girl's eye, gave her a big smile, and nodded a very emphatic yes. She was delighted, immediately grabbing her dad's hand. They came over and introduced themselves. They were from New Zealand, where *Beachcombers* was popular. There was no fooling that little girl. She knew.

Not all recognitions were that sweet. In August 1986 the cast and crew of *Beachcombers* travelled to Greece to film a special episode of the show. I went along for the ride.

After we landed at the Athens airport, a place bristling with armed militia and tanks, (common now but not then), Bruno and I were the last to receive our luggage. We followed the disappearing backs of our fellow travellers to exit the building, but before we got near the exit, a couple of big and serious men in plainclothes suddenly materialized and took Bruno off to one side. I was a half step ahead, and saw what was happening. Our fellow Canadians were out of sight by then, out of the building.

I felt panic rising. Bruno might need a lawyer, although what we could do in a strange country where we did not speak the language was an unsettling thought. I followed and stayed with them, refusing to be waived off. I stood by as Bruno produced his ID and quietly told them who he was and why he was in Athens. There was a discussion, but it ended and they let us proceed. *Beachcombers* was shown in Greece in those years.

We both thought – *trained police recognize a face – stop the person first – then ascertain – why is he familiar? Was this a guy on one of the wanted posters?* Bruno did have that don't-mess-with-me-look at times. He probably did then, after our long and awful flight on Olympic Airlines, featuring a lazy, partying, smoking crew, filthy bathrooms, inferior meals and questionable safety measures, crowned by collecting wet luggage

That beginning aside, our visit to Greece was amazing. The four lead actors were there, Bruno, Jackson Davies (Constable Constable), Robert Clothier (Relic) and Pat John (Jesse). Linda Davies accompanied Jackson, and Shirley Broderick, Robert Clothier's wife, was also with us. Linda, Shirley and I had our own adventures while the boys worked. One word, jewellery.

For a few dollars, we discovered we could swim at one of the private hotel beaches in Athens. Linda, Jackson and I were in heaven, waves lapping, escaping the heat of Athens in August while Bruno toiled. It was a topless beach, for most, and Jackson complained that as he strolled the beach it was not easy keeping his stomach sucked in.

One evening Linda and Jackson joined Bruno and me for dinner at a nearby hotel. The *maître d'* asked us where we were from. When we said Canada, he said, "I thought so. I recognize the little guy." That ruled out Jackson, who towered over Bruno.

Bruno and Jackson were fast friends. They laughed at the same things, and they laughed a lot. When filming in Gibsons, they ate dinner most nights at the Omega Restaurant, with Alex

Pappas, their noble and less mischievous pal. (Alex, an assistant director, the only member of the crew who spoke Greek, was not included on the trip to Greece!) They pranked one another, everything from mooning one another through the windows of Molly's Reach during filming to pies in the face in one episode.

On our last night in Athens, before moving on to Rhodes, most of the cast and crew were working late into the wee hours, so five of us went to dinner on our own in the Platka, the old part of the city. There was music and dancing. The older but very handsome piano and fiddle player decided I was the single one in the group. We blew kisses as we left. Linda threatened to tell Bruno all. I did, and he said he was going to put a note under Linda's door asking her to help him pack in the morning — as I had run off with a Greek piano player.

When we got to Rhodes, the Davies, Clothiers, Bruno and I ended up in a beautiful villa in Lindos, right next to Pink Floyd's villa. They were not in residence at the time. Our original accommodations in Rhodes had been at a mean, fly infested motel in the middle of a goat pasture, next to an actual cesspool. A full-blown mutiny happened; the entire company refused to take up residence, staying outside to eat and drink dinner, and rage at the organizers. A lot of drama. Bruno was the quiet one, surprisingly. The villas were found and the mutiny ended.

Our final night in Greece was at a small open-air rooftop restaurant in Athens, with the Acropolis literally across the street, bathed in the light of a full moon. Our hosts were the gracious husband and wife leading actors in Greece. It ended a magic three weeks.

*Beachcombers* produced twenty-six episodes a year for nineteen years. Some of the scripts were less than memorable, and drove Bruno around the bend, but so many episodes were good, whimsical, funny, family safe for kids of all ages, with little violence and no guns. There were strong roles for women and of course, the leading role for Pat John, the young aboriginal who played Jesse, Bruno's partner in the log salvaging business in the show. Pat and Bruno had a special relationship on and off screen.

Marc Strange and Jackson Davies wrote a book on the history of *Beachcombers,* called *Bruno and the Beach,* published by Harbour Publishing (2012). Their book details Pat John's entry into the world of acting as a nineteen-year-old, a dropout from a residential school. He was working at a sawmill when he was hired for the part of a native youth in *Beachcombers,* with no previous acting experience. Two or three years into the series, Pat was involved in a serious drinking and driving incident with the police and was immediately fired by CBC. Strange and Davies recount, in the book:

> P.J narrowly escaped death in a wild police chase amid gunfire that ended when he drove off a ferry slip in Earl's Cove into 10 metres of water. As soon as the Toronto office heard about it, P.J. was fired and plans were put in place to write him out of the series. When Bruno heard the news, there was no question whose side he was on.
>
> "If P.J. goes, I go!" He wasn't kidding. He threatened to reach out to the newspapers and blow the lid off The Corporation's callous exploitation and abandonment of a now twenty-one-year-old kid whom they'd shoved into a pressure cooker without ever bothering to check on his well-being, or provide him with any counsel or safety net.
>
> This was a crusade Bruno could really sink his teeth into. He liked Pat, ran lines with him, coached him and taught him how to handle himself when the camera was rolling. They were a team on-screen and friends off-screen, and he definitely wasn't going to let him be thrown to the wolves. Bruno never turned his back on a friend.

Pat remained on the series to the end.

Marc and Jackson's book also praises Bruno the director. In 1978 Bruno began directing some of the episodes:

> He quickly found out that not only did he like directing, he was very good at it, one of the best directors the series had. He was meticulous in his preparations and wonderful with actors.
>
> ...Bruno's years of stage experience had taught him how to stage physical comedy. His sense of timing and pacing, and his understanding of what his actors were capable of, was exceptional. And he loved working with Jackson.

While I seldom watched Bruno on the set, my week days being mainly in Vancouver in court, I knew of his passion for directing. On weekends we often drove the countryside on the Sunshine Coast scouting a particular setting, or Bruno would be sketching out scenes well in advance. One of my favourite episodes he directed involved a biker gang and Jackson as RCMP Constable Constable. There were hints of dark, sly humour and some dazzling road shots that Bruno had plotted in advance.

*Beachcombers* made a lot of money for CBC. In June 1989 when the suits in Toronto moved the series from Sunday evenings to Wednesday night, it was over the protest of many, especially Bruno. CBC brass assured him and the others that they would advertise the move well — the audience would all know and trot right over to Wednesday nights. The big numbers of Sunday night viewers were never realized in the new time slot. In April 1990, CBC brass announced the show would be axed; surprise, its numbers were down; the last episode aired December 12, 1990.

In more than one interview after the move to Wednesday nights, and then the cancellation, Bruno said, "It was like sending your kid to the store for milk and bread, and while he is gone, you move."

# *Darren*

M Y LAW PRACTICE now was varied. Half was as an independent labour arbitrator and mediator, the other half was general civil litigation. One day a call came late in the afternoon, a deep guttural male voice asking if I would take his family law case. I was tired and crabby. My clients and loved ones knew I was an early bird, and that late afternoon was sugar crash time for me, tired, brain on hold.

The call got worse. Was I prepared to see him at his home? He would not be able to attend my office. The annoyance grew. Oh damn, I breathed to myself, what now.

"I'm a quadriplegic," he explained. Eleven years previously, Darren had been a successful young businessman. He was helping his colleague secure a line while docking a boat when the line snapped, pitching Darren backwards down onto his boat from the dock high above. His neck smashed on to the boat railing. In that split second, this handsome athlete became a quadriplegic.

Darren had an amazing family and young wife. His parents and sister that I met bore the same good looks, humour and intelligence. He spoke of his wife with love and admiration, that she had stayed with him through such difficult years. There were no children. He had called me to help finalize the settlement he and his wife had agreed upon, to tie up the last loose ends, a separation agreement and the divorce. That would leave his wife free to continue on with her life. Meanwhile, he would stay in the home that had been built for his special needs.

I went to his home a few times as we did the necessary legal work. His ability to zip his wheelchair around, type at the computer with an aid held in his mouth, and generally function without assistance staggered me. He was still a handsome and virile young man. He must have been a killer before the accident. And he was funny, without an ounce of "poor me."Darren had learned my name from one of my other clients, also a quad. I acted for three other quadriplegics in my practice, all amazing and inspiring young people.

About two years after finishing Darren's divorce, I received a call from his sister. Could I go and see him in the hospital. He had a serious problem. My delight at seeing him again was devastated by his news. His upper body had been deteriorating for a long time, and finally his lungs had quit operating on their own; he would be able to live only by being hooked up to a large respirator 24/7. It was a life he was not willing to live. He wanted out. He wanted the respirator shut off and removed, and pain medication to assist his final hours. The limited freedoms he'd had in his own home, the remarkable adjustments he had made to function with such independence were gone.

Darren had the support of his family to end his life, and even his own doctor. He would be taken off the respirator, and the doctor had agreed to administer what pain and sedative requirements he would need to ease his death, which would come only hours after the disconnect. But then his doctor, as a precaution, had contacted the medical insurance lawyers in Ottawa, and ultimately told Darren that based on the advice of these lawyers, he could not assist him. He would need "a court order."

That is when I got the call.

This was many years ago, before Sue Rodriguez and her poignant story, before a Quebec Catholic hospital case that went to the SCC. There was little law and a lot of apprehension. What kind of "court order" were those cautious Ottawa lawyers suggesting? None I knew. Darren should have the right to be taken off the respirator, to refuse further treatment, and he should not have to face suffering without medication as he died.

I called Janice Dillon, a lawyer who had worked for the federal Law Reform Commission in Ottawa on medical/legal/ethical matters. She was also of the view that a patient had the right to refuse medical treatment, even in such a case where death would occur.

My visits to the hospital were frequent. For the first few days, I kept urging Darren to change his mind, reminding him how extraordinary he was, in every way, that he had dealt with a situation that would have crushed the rest of us. He smiled and listened. Smiled even more when I pointed out that he was getting an uncommon amount of enjoyment out of our battles with the hospital, the doctors and other powers that be. But he told me his mind was clear. It was time. Physically he could not pull the plug himself. He needed legal help to get the necessary medical help.

It took just over a week. The head of the hospital board was a senior doctor, empathetic but cautious. I told him, on instructions from my client, that not only would we be suing each of them individually in a civil action in Supreme Court for continuing treatment against his will, we would also be bringing criminal assault charges against everyone involved with Darren and his continuing medical treatment.

I swear there was a twinkle in his eye when the doctor said, "Now let me get this straight. You are telling me that you are going 'to sue the ass off me and everyone on the board, as well as the doctors and nurses' if we do not agree to assist your client by disconnecting the respirator and ensuring that he has the necessary medication to ensure no pain as he dies?"

"Yes. And don't forget about the criminal assault charges."

All of which was dutifully reported back to my client, as he watched yet another episode of *Jeopardy*, pinned to his hospital bed by the huge noisy breathing apparatus.

The hospital and its board were wary and conscientious. We papered their concerns with some 'legal documents'. A living will was signed by Darren with his aid in his mouth, now able only to sign an "X." Releases were drawn up to indemnify the hospital, the board, any doctors and nurses involved in Darren's care, affirming that the deponent of the release would never bring any action, civil or criminal, against them. There was a release for Darren to sign, and ones for his mother, father and sister. Even Darren's ex-wife signed a release. All were drawn with full disclosure and acknowledged agreement with Darren's failing condition, his current position and wishes, all duly notarized.

The hospital relented. Darren's own doctor was there to assist in alleviating the pain as he died. He died peacefully, surrounded by that loving and heartbroken family. It took twenty-three hours, his sister said, when she phoned me after Darren died. He was not in pain. It was what he wanted.

# CHAPTER 65

## *The Day Bruno Died*

I'M NOT QUITE SURE why I feel Bruno's last day should be documented, but he was an important person in many of our lives, and I have a sense this should be put down.

In March 1995, Bruno's carotid arteries were not in very good shape, one almost totally closed. So the talented Dr. Nick Marianatos opened up that artery, and Bruno was back in his hospital room yelling "fore" to an imaginary golf ball when I walked into his room supposedly to wait for him.

Nick, delighted with his patient, told us, "Bruno, you now have twenty-five years that you did not have before." When doing the angiogram prior to the surgery, they had also done an angioplasty on a blockage in Bruno's leg, with the result that he was walking pain-free for the first time in over twenty years.

Bruno seemed healthier and happier, and had finally had quit sneaking cigarettes when I was not looking. He had started smoking again in November 1994 when rehearsing for *Breaking Legs,* what was to be his final play. When I discovered that hated habit was back, I was so annoyed with him, with his lack of concern over his own health, I yelled a fake threat that he had to go to a hotel, that we were through. Bruno knew I went berserk, irrational, on the subject of smoking, blaming that wretched habit for the deaths of my sister, my mother and at least six dear friends. I was terrified it would claim him. He quit. No hotels. But I worried. They had diagnosed the carotid blockage when he began the play rehearsals that November, and Bruno had insisted on finishing the play before having the surgery done.

After the surgery in March, Bruno became more active, not as inclined to nap as much, and he had lost some weight without really trying. He was looking great. He was a whirling dynamo in September of that year when I broke my leg and got pneumonia at the same time. He was on 24/7 homecare, cooking, cleaning, caring, entertaining. He called himself "Flo," short for Florence Nightingale.

We planned our first cookbook, and resolved that in May of the following year, we would go to Italy again. First to see and stay with Umberto Menghi at his Villa Delia, delight in Italy again, and generally take more holidays. We also talked about selling our respective homes, and building three cottages on oceanfront property maybe somewhere north of Gibsons. A main cottage for our own living, a guest cottage, and a carving studio for Bruno. It was time to consolidate our living spaces, and build what suited us.

In late October 1995, Bruno had spent a couple of days at Gibsons, and returned late one afternoon in time to dress for the annual Jack Webster Dinner where Peter Newman was the guest speaker. He looked exhausted, and admitted being very tired. I could not persuade him to forgo the dinner. We went, but left immediately after Peter's speech.

That night was terrible. Bruno was having trouble lying down, and sleep was out of the question. He would not let me call Myron McDonald, his doctor. Bruno never bothered people after hours. He became agitated and adamant when I suggested I take him to the emergency ward at the hospital. He finally settled in one of the big chairs in the living room, saying he felt better sitting up, and was grumpy when he caught me sneaking upstairs throughout the night to check on him.

Looking back, it is hard to say who was more worried. He knew something was very wrong, but he was refusing to acknowledge it, even to himself. When morning came, I called Myron, with little resistance from Bruno. I drove him to the emergency on Myron's instructions. The doctors checked him over and told us he'd had a minor heart attack. I'm not so sure there is such a thing now.

They kept Bruno in the hospital in North Vancouver for several days. He attended the heart lecture series there, and readily went on to their heart program. On his release from the hospital, he could not drive a car for at least a month, and seemed relieved, really relieved, on looking back, to have me at home with him during that time. He did not want me to leave him alone. I didn't.

A nurse came by and started Bruno on his walking program, which he relished. His glow of health returned, and he was looking ten years younger. We were optimistic, having been told there was no real damage to his heart.

Then came November 21, 1995. Bruno had made me promise I would ensure he was up by 7:00 a.m. so he could have lots of time to shower and shave and have some breakfast, in order to leave an hour's time before 9:00 a.m., when his nurse was due for their heart walk. He woke up on his own, showered and washed that still glorious head of hair.

He was standing in his shorts, and did something that I had not seen him do for quite some time: he stopped in front of the mirror in the bedroom, looked briefly at himself, and put his right hand up to smooth an imaginary out-of-place hair on his head. It was the slightest of preen, and it signified to me that Bruno was once again feeling good about himself, his appearance, his health. I was drying my hair, and remember smiling to myself, happy to see that hint of well-being.

We went upstairs together with me telling him to go ahead, as I was still limping unsteadily on my broken leg. Our breakfasts since the heart attack had featured more hot oatmeal. I put the kettle on.

Ever the political junkies, Bruno and I had been following the morning news on television of Lucien Bouchard announcing that he was going to stay on to lead the Quebec separatists. Bruno swung the television around so we could watch Bouchard's announcement. As Bouchard was saying that his wife, Audrey, was in full support of his decision, the camera swung over to her rather grim visage, and Bruno and I started to laugh. I turned away for an instant to stir the oatmeal, when there was a loud and terrible crash. I turned around. Bruno was no longer sitting at the table. He and his chair were gone from sight.

I rushed around the small island of the kitchen; Bruno and his chair were lying in the corner. I grabbed for Bruno's Nitro, which he had never had to use. It was in his breast pocket, and I tried to give him some puffs. As I held his head up, it felt so heavy, and suddenly Bruno's voice said, very clearly, "What's happening here?" There was no fear or hurry or concern in his voice. It was simply a question. He was in another space, where I could not go. I knew the question was not directed at me. I knew Bruno was gone.

The operator on 911 instructed me on CPR which I was doing when the firemen arrived, about three or four minutes after I had called. They took over, and then came all the others, the police, the paramedics, more firemen. They all worked over Bruno, still in that corner. I had thrown the heavy chair out of the way, and it remained oddly out of place.

My first call was to Lyle Thurston, my friend, our doctor. They kept working on Bruno's body, and I knew it was only his body. A terrible thought occurred — what if they bring him back brain-damaged and nearly lifeless. Bruno of all people would be destroyed by such an outcome. I went over to the fire captain, who was watching his men and the paramedics still working on Bruno, at least twenty minutes having elapsed since their arrival.

"You must not let them bring him back brain-damaged, because if he can't kill you, then I will have to."

I know those were my exact words, and they may sound terrible now, but the Bruno I knew understood them. And so did the captain. He was a large, friendly man, and he put his big hand on my shoulder, saying, "We have to keep going until the medical officer arrives and tells us otherwise, but that is not going to happen." He knew as well, Bruno was gone.

I had to call Bruno's daughter Tina and son Rico immediately. Every fireman and paramedic, and there were many, who had come into the house, had recognized Bruno. They were mostly in their twenties and early thirties, and they would have grown up watching *Beachcombers*. The word would be out immediately, and I had to get to his children in Toronto first. I don't remember what I said to Tina. We were both in shock. I reached Patsy, Rico's wife, and remember suggesting that she and Rico get hold of the children in school, before they heard it from classmates.

The paramedics had stopped trying to revive Bruno around 8:30 a.m., and sure enough, there was a bulletin on the radio by nine o'clock. My attempts to reach Jackson Davies were unsuccessful. Jackson had been filming all day on a set, and only heard the news in mid-afternoon on the car radio as he drove home. He came straight to our house and walked in, dazed. Diana Filer, Bruno's brilliant and dear friend and producer from their radio days together, was another I could not reach. It turned out she was in Toronto.

As the paramedics and police left, I had gone and lain beside Bruno for a few minutes before phoning anyone, and wept about as much as I am now as I write this. But both Bruno and I were from the school that says you keep going. And I had a lot of calls to make. One of the last ones I made that morning was to Umberto. He loved Bruno; they were like brothers. I managed to reach him minutes before someone from the news media came to him for a comment.


The tributes to Bruno and the kindness of friends and strangers were overwhelming in the days to come. Our home looked like a florist shop. Bruno loved flowers; it seemed fitting. Rico, Patsy and Tina and the older grandchildren arrived from Toronto. Kenny Neal, who was fourteen at the time, a quiet and wonderful young man, walked into the living room, sat down on the couch and wordlessly began agonized crying.

The tribute to Bruno in the Queen Elizabeth Theatre in Vancouver that Saturday, organized by a heartbroken Alex Pappas and others, was so fine. Funny and moving, laughter and tears. Gino Gerussi, Bruno's nephew, sang his heart out, as did Bruno's son, Rico, and granddaughter, Syreeta Neal.

My best friends, Jacquie and David Sims, and Sandra and Hugh Lyons, flew in from Whitby, Ontario and Calgary, even though I had said not to bother. I was faking strength, and they knew it. They stayed and cooked and fed and threw the best wake at the house. They loved Bruno, and he them.

A couple of months later, there was a memorial in Toronto as well, where eastern friends had a chance to say goodbye. And another fine wake.

*With Bruno on the Island of Rhodes, near Lindos.*

Bruno's energy remains. As if it is fragmented in a million pieces around. In his children, grandchildren and great-grand-children. In the hundreds of memories we all have, those who knew him or saw him perform or heard him on the radio. So many times we say, wouldn't Bruno have loved that, or laughed at that. On and on, his ability to catch us and hold us.

Once in a while, I will be driving along, and a song, or a memory, will overcome me, and the tears will start. And I swear I hear Bruno saying, "Now don't carry on...." I tell that voice it is just for a moment, and no one is around anyway, and some-times, you just have to.

# CHAPTER 66

# *The Return to Judging*

WHILE BRUNO WAS ALIVE, I had no plans to return to the bench. My practice was busy and fun. Bruno and I had talked of having more free time. I had toyed with shutting down my practice and doing only arbitration work, which for fifteen years had been roughly half my practice. My hesitation in doing that was rooted in Paul Weiler's sage advice: "Always write an award as if it is your last." I wrote with that in mind, never keeping track of how many times one side won or lost, knowing that if the entire labour community decided not to hire me again, I had my law practice to earn my living.

There had been suggestions from Ottawa that I apply to be a judge on the Supreme Court of British Columbia. They were trolling for more female judges, but I was more content suggesting possible candidates other than myself. I even phoned a few to suggest they apply. Since resigning from the provincial Court in May 1981, I had been back in practice over fifteen years.

But my life changed with Bruno gone. The freedom of private practice was deceptive.

Joanne Senecal, a lawyer with the Ministry of Justice in Ottawa, travelled the country in search of judicial candidates. I'd had a few dinners with Joanne on her infrequent trips to Vancouver. She came again three months after Bruno's death. Joanne said it was time I went on the bench again. I agreed. I delayed making the application. I was writing the cookbook Bruno and I had planned before he died, and I also wanted to take to trial or settle a couple of cases for favourite clients.

My application finally went in, and I was appointed to the BC Supreme Court as a trial judge on August 7, 1996. The official swearing was set for September 3rd.

I tried to talk Chief Justice Bill Esson and Chief Justice Allan MacEachern out of an official public swearing-in ceremony. My excuse was that I did not want one of the unbalanced professional

*During R v. Kelly Ellard trial, by
courtroom artist Jane Wolsak.*

litigators to pop up and give the public her diatribe on how terrible a judge I would probably be. The two Chief Justices laughed and said they had both been the object of her attentions in the past, not to worry. The swearing in would go ahead.

What I really meant to tell them was that it was a ceremony that would recall my first time sworn in as a judge, in the Provincial Court in December 1972, when Mom and Dad, Moira and Bruno were all there.

For this second swearing in, twenty-four years later, the four most important people in my life were gone. I feared being overcome with sadness in public. I decided to get it over with and not tell anyone it was happening.

But Alison MacLennan assumed the interfering role of friendship and said, "You have to tell your friends. You have to have them present for such an occasion." " No, I don't." "Yes, you do." She threatened to let people know if I didn't.

Okay, I thought. I want my favourite broads there, as my family. The women who, from the early seventies, had been my friends, mentors and supporters, who thought as I did. We were now among the seniors of the women's movement of the early 1970s. Simma Holt, the fearless journalist; her wise sister, Hannah Smith; LaVerne Barnes, whose book *The Plastic Orgasm* had to be read with asbestos gloves; Rosemary Brown, a powerhouse like no other; Lisa Hobbs, a brilliant writer and leading feminist; and Lauris Talmey, whose humour, compassion and sagacity brought light to all things political.

They came to the swearing in ceremony, sitting in one row in that big courtroom, smiling broadly. They brought gifts, including a carved Haida talking stick. Part of my remarks would be for them. And for my fearless friend Alison, who not only lifts her head above the foxhole when real threats arise, but will leap out and do the chicken dance to draw fire.

It was a good occasion, and the famously eccentric lady never popped up.

This time there would be no whining on my part about wearing the robes. They were on. The first morning I stepped up onto the bench, something spooky occurred. Fifteen and a half years away from the bench evaporated. It was as if I had left the bench the previous afternoon. I felt back home. I also felt a couple of ghosts saying, *It's about time.* My Dad? Bruno?

It's a funny thing about our careers. Sometimes they find us, and others see it before we do.

# CHAPTER 67

## *Diamonds of the Sex Trade*

MARIA WAS a 'main girl'. She and her pimp were in court on two prostitution-related charges. On November 10, 1999, a Vancouver jury found both guilty of the charge that

> ... for the purpose of gain ... they did exercise control, direction or influence over the movements of a person, C, in such a manner as to show that they were aiding, abetting or compelling that person to engage in or carry on prostitution.

On the second charge of living off the avails of prostitution, only the pimp was found guilty.

The complainant, C, fifteen years old by the time of trial, had a background that was shocking, but not surprising in the sex trade. From age two to seven, she had been abused by her stepfather, and at eleven, she was sexually assaulted by another family member. Rejected by her mother, she was placed in foster care. She became a runaway, addicted to drugs. Supposedly in a foster home, she was not in school and was briefly turning tricks as a young teen. She then encountered Maria and her pimp; the pimp was also Maria's boyfriend.

As her pimp's main girl, Maria, twenty-one, was trusted to help recruit other girls into his stable, and groom them to perform well and make money for him. Her duties included telling C how to dress, behave and charge the johns. C was instructed how much she was to earn each night. Maria would take the money earned by C and hand it over to her pimp.

C was also obliged to have sex with both accused, and was threatened she could be sold to another family. C was fearful, but compliant.

Maria's background was similar to C's. Maria and her young mother had been abandoned by Maria's father at her birth. She had been sexually abused from four to ten years of age by a stepfather, whom she thought was her real father. She suffered from drug and alcohol abuse at an early age, and was placed in group homes. At sixteen she had been on the streets as a prostitute and was now a main girl. Eventually, as an adult, she had a criminal record of two assaults and one charge related to prostitution.

Maria, a victim of abuse and the street, had become an abuser. In the realm of family violence, we know not to be surprised when abused and battered children often become abusive and battering adults. I sentenced Maria to nine months in jail, plus two years of probation.

Maria and C are typical examples of what I call the "diamonds of the sex trade."

Prostitution is a social issue I have tracked for over fifty years. First, in 1958, as a naive social welfare worker in Prince Albert, Saskatchewan, when I learned of two aboriginal sisters, raped by their father when they were six and eight years old. Their sexual abuse continued, and by the time their file came across my desk, they were active child prostitutes at twelve and fourteen, on the streets of Prince Albert.

During my articles in 1961, there were so few women in the Toronto courts, it was assumed you were in the building because of your prostitution charge. When travelling alone to New York and later Halifax in 1966, the hotels where I had registered presumed I was a prostitute. "Do you have any luggage?" with a smirk, and my phone calls were monitored.

As one of only two female prosecutors in British Columbia in 1970, my rite of passage was to be assigned most of the cases involving sex charges. That meant I was prosecuting a lot of prostitutes, but never a charge against any of the customers, the johns. Pimps were seldom caught or prosecuted. Their girls, young and old, would be terrified to testify against them.

The police would show me before and after pictures of the prostitute who was before the court. "This is what she looked like when we first picked her up, and this is her now." A lovely young girl in the first picture and a ravaged, unbelievably aged young woman in the second picture, with only a few years separating. Many had substance abuse issues.

On one occasion, a beautiful young blonde woman appeared in Vancouver Provincial court on a prostitution charge. The investigating officer informed me she was not a female, but wished to be addressed as "she", not "he." Both the judge and I addressed her only as a female.

The women seldom went to jail on their first conviction. Beginning with the second and subsequent convictions, they faced jail terms from one month to a year, depending on the circumstances.

In December 1970, I opened my own law firm and found myself acting for dozens of prostitutes. Legal Aid had sent them initially, as few other lawyers wanted to act for them. These clients were often addicts, and, almost without exception, came from shocking childhood backgrounds of sexual and physical abuse and neglect. Almost all had begun as teenage prostitutes, some as young as thirteen and fourteen. They were adults by the time they were appearing in our courts.

For almost two years, my clients and I fought every charge, to the surprise of the vice squad. The press, particularly the indomitable Simma Holt, began reporting on our cases.

It was then I met Barbara Frum. Her radio show, *As It Happens,* telephoned. I had seen Barbara on television, a bright and skillful interviewer, but I was concerned that the issue of prostitution would be treated with the usual smirk, the view of so many — 'prostitution is the second-oldest profession in the world, chuckle, chuckle' — so I declined to be interviewed. The producers asked me why and I told them. They assured me Barbara would not take that attitude, and arranged for her to call me at home that evening.

Barbara reassured me that her view of prostitution was the same as mine, that it would be a serious discussion. Barbara was true to her word in the interview that followed.

In 1983 or 1984, after I had resigned from the Provincial Court bench and was back in practice, I made a submission to the Fraser Commission on prostitution. My views on prostitution were evolving, but I was still concentrating on the inequality of the treatment of the prostitute versus the john.

I have never encountered a case where incest was charged, or a john has been charged, although I am aware that there have been some cases. *The Criminal Code* provides tough penalties for those who purchase sex from teen prostitutes, but these cases are seldom discovered, let alone prosecuted. Even Maria and her pimp were not charged under the *Criminal Code* section that makes it an indictable offence to have sex with a prostitute under the age of eighteen years.

There is silence when it comes to trafficking children for sex. The demand for young girls and boys for prostitution in Canada and the rest of the world is great; it is an open secret. These children and teens are the diamonds of the sex industry, more valuable than adults, eagerly sought by predisposed customers willing to pay extra. These young teens are hidden away, cached in luxury high-end hotels and apartments, groomed and sold for sex in secret.

Who would know about them? Many. Their pimps, their customers, and other, older prostitutes. What about the managers of the fancy rental apartments that are being used, the hotel staff of high and low-end hotels where the young girls, and boys, are installed? Or the beauty parlours where pimps have them polished. To say nothing of the massage parlours which are in fact brothels where young girls are trafficked, often from abroad.

In Maria's trial, defence counsel argued the teenage C was acting freely, of her own choice. To suggest this is a life or career that these young girls or boys choose to live is nonsense. Freedom of choice requires at the very least being of the age of reason, old enough and educated to have an informed mind, to know all the alternatives, and to have the freedom and ability to decide which career or life path one will choose, absent threats, violence, poverty, drugs, addiction, lack of education, false promises. Neither Maria or C had such choices or freedom as child prostitutes.

In 2013, the Supreme Court of Canada decided in *R. v. Bedford* that it was no longer illegal to be a pimp, or to operate a brothel for the purpose of prostitution, or to communicate with anyone for engaging in prostitution.

In response to that decision, the federal government has passed a law which makes it illegal to purchase sex, but not illegal to sell sex, unless that is done near a school or day care where children might be present. Those new provisions of the *Criminal Code* were given Royal Assent in November 2014.

There is universal concern for the safety of prostitutes who are presently in the sex trade. The Nordic model, upon which the new federal legislation is partially modeled, seeks to limit and reduce the sex industry, decriminalize and assist the prostitutes, and deal with areas which were not before the Supreme Court of Canada in the Bedford case, namely: child prostitution, sex trafficking for prostitution, sex tourism, the role of organized crime in prostitution, and how to prevent the children of today from becoming prostitutes of tomorrow.

A 2014 human trafficking case in the Supreme Court of British Columbia, *R. v. Moazami,* presented the face of prostitution that is almost never portrayed by the media or those who clamour for the full legalization of prostitution.

On September 15, 2014, Justice Cathy Bruce rendered a decision in this trial where eleven young prostitutes testified against their pimp, Moazami, evidence that revealed their brutal initiation into prostitution. Ten of the eleven young girls began working as prostitutes as early as twelve, thirteen, fourteen to seventeen years of age.

These were children who were manipulated by threats, physical assaults and drugs. They were purchased by men to perform every sexual act demanded, individually or as duos, including anal rape. One traded sex for drugs; one was introduced to prostitution by an older prostitute; one was a recent young immigrant from Afghanistan; three were children in foster care at the time. The accused tried to sell one sixteen-year-old to another pimp. They were trafficked to different cities across Canada. Calgary was a big sell during the famous Calgary Stampede.

An investigation into an assault brought one of these young girls to the attention of the police. Moazami was known to them. What followed was a careful police investigation and skillful prosecution to bring this rare case to trial. "Rare" because almost all these young victims are so unknown to authorities, so hidden, and then so fearful of cooperating or testifying. Fearful for their lives.

The graphic testimony in this trial by these young girls was deemed by some editors in the press as too raw and graphic for the media to report in full. Protecting the public from such knowledge? Really? Such editing by the media is not protecting the young witnesses, known only by their initials, who had the courage to tell the court and the public what they had endured.

Sex trafficking for the purposes of prostitution is the fastest-growing and second most profitable criminal industry in the world, second only to trafficking in cocaine. In 2012, profits from human trafficking for the purpose of prostitution were estimated at $58 billion a year. By 2014, the figure was $99 billion a year.

Like Mr. Moazami, organized crime finds sex trafficking more profitable than dealing drugs, with less likelihood of being detected and much lower penalties if caught. The unbelievable preference and appetite for child prostitutes is worldwide. In Iraq, girls of thirteen and fourteen are called "rosebuds" and sell for $300 to $400 a night; as opposed to older prostitutes, from 20 to 30 years of age, who sell for only $80 to $160, according to an article in the October 5, 2015 issue of *The New Yorker* by Rania Abouzeid, titled "Letter From Baghdad." The author went on to write that virgins were particularly prized and one teenage girl was sold to a pimp for $4,200. Sex tourists know where to go. Thailand and Costa Rica are favourites for many North Americans.

I agree with those who regard prostitution as sexual violence against women and children, that it is akin to slavery; it preys on vulnerable women and children worldwide. The true face of prostitution is not a college graduate earning extra money for tuition or a comfortable lifestyle. It is the diamonds, the incredibly abused, exploited and trafficked boys and girls, young women and those made vulnerable through wars, substance abuse, cycles of family violence.

Sweden has taken the lead worldwide in dealing with the problems of prostitution. In 1999, Sweden passed the *Sex Purchase Act* which criminalizes pimps and the customers who buy sex. Prostitutes are subject to no criminalization, and are given assistance in leaving the sex trade. The law's aims are gender equality, safety for women and youth from violence, an attempt to curb human trafficking as well as prostitution, and a change in their culture, so that prostitution is no longer accepted as appropriate, that it is violence against women and children, and is contrary to gender equality.

Prostitution still exists in Sweden, but the culture is changing. Organized crime involved in the trade has been disrupted, and sex trafficking from foreign jurisdictions has decreased, along with the incidence of prostitution. A 2015 Swedish government report revealed street prostitution had been cut in half, and an estimate of the number of prostitutes decreased from three thousand to six hundred.

Sweden helps people exit the sex trade, providing safety, housing, help with drug and other addictions, treatments, counselling, education, career counselling and financial assistance.

In contrast, Germany decriminalized prostitution that same year, 1999. The sex trade mushroomed. By 2013, sex trafficking had seen an explosive increase. Many of the trafficked victims are from Romania, Bulgaria and poor former-Soviet countries. In May 2013, one German ad promoting a brothel read, "Sex with all women as long as you want, as often as you want and the way you want. Sex. Anal sex. Oral sex without a condom." German police reported that the first weekend after the ad appeared there were 1700 customers at the brothel. Included on the "menu" of another German brothel — sex with a pregnant woman.

Brothels are illegal in Canada under the 2014 amendments. But they are still operating under different guises. In the Bedford case, an affidavit from a senior Toronto police officer urged the Court not to legalize brothels. Brothels are among the few places where police can investigate and find human sex trafficking, under-age prostitutes, refugees or immigrants who have been preyed upon, and foster girls.

In Canada, the greatest gift to sex traffickers here and internationally would be to legalize prostitution, offering up Canada's most vulnerable girls, making Canada a destination for the criminals and their victims in the sex trade.

# CHAPTER 68

# *Death By Binder*

IT HAS BEEN fascinating to watch the innovations of computers and the internet and their impact on our justice system. An aficionado of toys, I love the laptops and iPhones. But when lawyers began bringing their laptops into the courtroom, I observed too many glued to their screens, missing the theatre and nuances of the action in the courtroom.

They were unaware of the judge putting down his or her pen (usually not a good sign), jurors straining forward, unable to hear, or looking puzzled, a witness with a stark look of terror when a certain person entered the courtroom, or a witness smirking while giving an answer. Instead, the lawyer was reading the questions typed into his or her laptop ahead of time and then automatically typing in the answer. Head down, eyes on the screen.

The notable courtroom lawyers I've observed are skilled advocates, quick on their feet, missing nothing, preparation in their heads, or readily indexed at hand. They do not have every question written out in advance. They are quick to abandon one line of questioning and follow a new and unexpected avenue that just opens up. For any judge, it is sheer pleasure to watch the great professionals in action.

Technology has helped and hindered our justice system. It has resulted in better organization and administration, but longer preparation is now required with longer trials burdened with mountains of evidence flowing from emails, texting, Facebook, wire tapping, cellphone transcripts, often requiring multiple language interpreters.

In civil cases, ask any lawyer or judge about "Death by Binder." The health care system was not set up with cat scans, MRIs and the incredible advances of technology in mind. The same applies to the justice system. Police, prosecutors, defence counsel, civil litigators and administrators are buried under the sheer weight of evidence available today, unheard of yesterday.

To long for the short trials of yesterday is to ignore the impact of technology today.

# CHAPTER 69

# *Leaving the Supreme Court of BC*

I WAS GETTING READY to resign from the Supreme Court of BC. At seventy-four, I knew I would no longer be able to serve as a federally appointed judge once I hit the statutory limit of seventy-five.

So nine months before that, I resigned — on my own time, not when some statute decreed. The profession had been a bit harsh to me at the beginning of my career, so it seemed right to leave on my own time, a final note of independence. I had other things to do, like write this book.

Before I left the court, I had the opportunity to address young lawyers at a call to the bar ceremony. Judges are asked to volunteer for such an occasion, and we all like doing it. So I volunteered for one last time, and tried to put into words how important our profession and the law are, not just to me, but to our entire society, our government and way of life.

Who else to consult but Shakespeare.

It was time to talk about Henry VI.

## Henry VI

On March 3, 1592, a new play was performed at the Rose Playhouse in London. The play centred around the early 1400s when England and France were perpetually at war. Henry V had died, and his mild and bookish heir, Henry VI, went on to become ruler of England. The play was Shakespeare's *Henry VI*, in which Shakespeare was doing what he did so well — chronicling English history through the mastery of his play — with some poetic license.

In Part II of the play, he wrote of the civil wars in England between the House of York and the House of Lancaster. Into this mix he recorded the role of Jack Cade, a rebel leader who, in 1450, saw his mission in life to lead a revolution, kill the King, Henry VI, and install himself as ruler of England. According to

Shakespeare's account, Cade feared neither sword nor fire. But Cade knew that for a revolution to be successful, all the lawyers would have to be killed.

One of Cade's lieutenants, Dick the Butcher, uttered the now famous line, "The first thing we do, let's kill all the lawyers."

Cade was way ahead of him. In addition to the plan to kill all the lawyers, Cade decreed that all those who could write would also have to be killed. The records of the realm would be burned, and youth would no longer be corrupted by schooling. Then they added that those who spoke a foreign language like French or Latin would be killed, as traitors. In short, the killings would be, "All scholars, lawyers, courtiers, gentlemen."

After taking London Bridge, Cade and his mob headed for the Inns of Court, to tear them down. History tells us Cade did not succeed. But attacks on lawyers and judges and the rule of law continue to this day, in countries around the world. Our profession has always been called upon to defend against the despotism of an individual ruler or the tyranny of a mob majority over the rights of individuals.

In 1974, Leon Jaworski, one of the Watergate prosecutors, wrote in the *Dallas Times Herald*

> When dictators and tyrants seek to destroy the freedoms of men, their first target is the legal profession and through it — *The Rule of Law.*

An education and training in the law equips one to serve society well, and many lawyers enter public service at the provincial, federal or international level. For those who choose to practice law in a city or smaller centre, there is the sense of community that goes with a profession that helps people with problems in a myriad of situations.

Lawyers are called upon to represent people from all walks of life, where every new day or week can seem like another novel starting. There is never a dull day, especially in a courtroom. It is easy to act for nice people, who pay their bills, and treat their families and you and others with respect; those who may be famous, or attractive, or wealthy, or fun to be around. But we judge a society and a country not on how well we treat the brightest and the best, but rather, how we treat the most difficult in our world. Those whose actions are mean, criminal, vicious even. Those who suffer from debilitating illnesses, mental, emotional, or physical. Those whose problems seem unsolvable, overwhelming. Those who have no voice, a cruel past and a seemingly hopeless future. Those who have no lobby, and often, no funds.

That is where lawyers serve, every day — across this country in big firms and small. They often act for no fee. The public seldom knows, but we in the profession know. We also know that without the law profession, and an independent judiciary, there is no democracy, no rule of law.


I may have entered my profession casually, not sure that is where I wanted to be. Some Scottish mysticism now tells me this was maybe where I belonged. Of those Scots, the Morrisons hailed from Scotland's Isle of Lewis, which, up until 1600 or so, was known as the independent Kingdom of Lewis. In those early times, the Morrison Clan were the hereditary brieves of Lewis, the judges. Their oath on assuming office was "to administer justice between man and man as evenly as the backbone of the herring lies between the two sides of the fish."

Doubtful my ancient kin ever envisaged a modern brieve being a woman.

# Acknowledgments

THIS IS really the most important part of any book; we do nothing on our own. It's embarrassing to have to admit how many friends have been pressed into service in reading the various drafts, fact checking, editing and critiquing parts or all of this manuscript. My friends have been my archives. But one person is a professional researcher, Judy Thompson, who can find the most hidden fact and gem better than a Paris jewel thief. Wally Oppal suggested I get her to help with my research and manuscript, and that was my lucky day.

Stevie Cameron kept encouraging me to write this book; Gary Dunford would pick moments over the years to ask when I was going to write it; John Skinner who not only went over early drafts but came up with the title *Benched*, was a skilled editor; Daphne Bramham with early reading had good advice; Bruce McLean, a discerning cousin encouraged me; and cousins Jim Grant and Bob Christopherson added their family lore to the ancestry chapter.

There were those whose early editing and suggestions were sobering and inspiring: John Banks, Amanda Lewis, Bill Deverell, and Tom Berger.

Others who read early drafts of some or all chapters and made valuable suggestions were: Linda McKnight, Anne Rowles, Alison MacLennan, Pamela McColl,

Pam Walker, Barbara Jo McIntosh, Bob Foulkes,
Jacquie and David Sims, Sandra and Hugh Lyons,
LaVerne Barnes, Dawna Armstrong, Pat LeSage, Burke
Doran, Terri Lefevre Prince, Vicki Gabereau, Garry
and Marion Fletcher, Michael and Carol Yaholnitsky,
Cheryl Denesowych, Joan and Norman Gish, Gerald
Thurston, Chuck Rosart, and Myron MacDonald.

This is a time to thank some extraordinary
paralegals who helped me in three provinces: Lois
Booth, Verna Robbins, Mary Domshy, Cheryl Friskie,
Val Chapman, Lorraine Kehler, Ada Jansen, Joanne
Ivans. I hope I am not the only one who thought we
had fun in the office.

Last and never least, I thank Lorene Shyba, my
amazing publisher at Durvile who made it a joy to
work again on the manuscript. She was a wizard with
this book, an artist with the cover and with all my
favourite photos.

# Index

ABOUT THE AUTHOR

Nancy Morrison practised law and adjudicated in
Ontario, Saskatchewan, British Columbia, Yukon and
the Northwest Territories. As a judge, she served nine
years on the British Columbia Provincial Criminal
Court, 1972 to 1981, and later, fifteen years on the
Supreme Court of British Columbia. Raised in Yorkton,
Saskatchewan, she now lives in Vancouver, B.C.